FAR FROM MY HOME
NEVER TO RETURN
A Polish Child's WWII Memoir

To Ellie, my good friend at Woodland Heights, with my best wishes

Nadia Seluga

Nadia Seluga

Feb. 26-2017

Martin Sisters Publishing

D1364045

Published by
Martin Sisters Books, a division of Martin Sisters Publishing, LLC
www.martinsisterspublishing.com

Copyright (C) 2001, 2012 Nadia Bogdaniec-Seluga
FIRST EDITION ("Winds of Change") 2001
SECOND EDITION ("Far From My Home, Never to Return:
A Polish Child's WWII Memoir") 2012
All rights reserved

ISBN: 978-1-937273-33-0

Memoir
Edited by Tiffany Nichols

Printed in the United States of America
Martin Sisters Publishing, LLC

DEDICATION

I dedicate this book first and foremost to my parents for their continuous and arduous efforts to ensure the survival of our entire family. Secondly, I dedicate this book to all of my siblings for their similar efforts and our enduring perseverance to survive. Without our combined group efforts, none of us would have made it out of the frozen tundra of Siberia.

This book is also dedicated to all Poles, living and deceased, who suffered experiences similar to those of my family and myself at the hands of the Soviets. May those still living be blessed and the deceased never forgotten.

ACKNOWLEDGMENTS

I wish to thank my daughter Susan Spanos for insisting that I write my experiences during the Second World War, and to Dr. Richard Robbins Jr., Professor of History, New Mexico University, for encouragement.

Also, I thank my sister Maria Polkowska for organizing and typesetting my manuscript, arranging its printing in England, and my brother-in-law, the late Zdzisław (Bob) Polkowski for financing the first edition titled "Winds of Change." Their encouragement, support and interest made this book possible.

A special "thank you" to my grandson, Jacob Seluga, for his continuous effort to get my book properly edited and professionally published. With his help, my book was finally brought to the awareness of publishers.

~ *Nadia Bogdaniec-Seluga*

Nonfiction, Memoir
an imprint of Martin Sisters Publishing, LLC

CONTENTS

General Władysław Anders
(reprinted from a commemorative publication [in Polish] issued by Polish House John Paul II in Rome, Italy, May 1984. No ISBN number was available in the publication nor copyright information.)

MAP OF POLAND

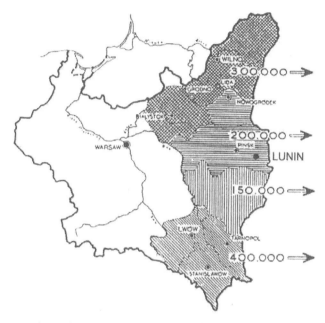

Deportation of Polish Citizens from the Polish Territory occupied
by the Soviet Union.
From 1939-1941 over one million (ie 7% - 8% of the total
inhabitants of this area) were deported.
*(Taken from Ain-Karem: Osradek Polskich Dziewczat Palestyna,
1942-47 (Polish Edition) Z. Alexander ISBN 0951402005
Ain-Karem Association 1988)*

PREFACE

For many years after the Second World War, a lot of people in our contemporary world knew very little about the Soviet invasion and occupation of Eastern Poland in 1939. They knew nothing about the Polish people who were deported at gunpoint and forced to live and work in the Soviet prisons and labor camps in regions such as Archangel, Kolyma, Urals, and Kazakhstan.

However, the Western World knows about the Soviet prisons from Solzhenitsyn's works, but in reality, how many people from the West have actually ever seen these prisons or labor camps, or the camp called "Listvinnitsa 22," where we spent two years of our lives, and where I lost the two best years of my childhood?

Perhaps our ordeals and suffering were not as shocking as those of the German concentration camps, but they were equal in their devastation. It is true that what Hitler had done surpassed human reason and imagination. Hitler's crimes against humanity shocked and outraged the Western World, and the people were asking: "How could it have happened in a civilized country like Germany?" But camps like Auschwitz, Majdanek, Dachau, and Buchenwald are solid witnesses to this fact, where six million Jews, Poles and other nationalities perished in gas chambers in the German concentration camps. Our only witnesses were the British, who were in Iran at the time of our evacuation from the Soviet Union. They saw what horror we lived through by just looking at us. In two short years we were reduced to living skeletons, dressed in rags, sick and dying.

After the evacuation from the Soviet Union, a British officer, Col. A. Ross, described the state of health of the refugees in the following statement: "The physical and mental state of the refugees on arrival in Teheran was generally very bad. The most prevalent diseases were dysentery, diarrhea, deficiency diseases due to prolonged malnutrition, many malaria's imported from Russia, and typhoid: 40% of the refugees were malaria cases. A visit to any of the hospitals at the beginning of the first or second phases of the evacuation was sufficient to create on the mind an indelible impression of unmerited hardships and physical suffering." (Taken from *An Army in Exile* by General Władysław Anders, Macmillan Co., 1st edition 1949)

Because of a policy of appeasement in dealings with Stalin, the British and the United States Governments did not protest nor publicize our plight. This, in turn, explains why many people often asked me: How come we never heard about the deportations and your life in the Soviet Union? We only know what Hitler had done to the Jews.

"Because," I often replied, "at the time of our liberation the world was at war, and Stalin was the ally of the British and Americans. They could not point a finger at him and say: 'You are a criminal,' especially when they needed his help to conquer the common enemy – Hitler."

It is common knowledge that after the war Stalin closed his borders to keep his people in and foreign intruders out. The rumor was that at one time Stalin allegedly remarked: "My only regret is that I let the Polish people out." I can only surmise that Stalin was perfectly aware that the Polish people knew firsthand what it was like to live in the Soviet Union and suffer untold tortures under his regime.

*

This is a true story as seen through the eyes of a child. Children often see things as they are, having no understanding of the underlying causes why this or that is so, and they accept everything around them as truths.

Because my notes were lost (they were like a diary) in a shuffle from one place to another, I have written my story from memory. Today, I would be interested myself to know what I had written in those notes many years ago. I only remember the first line about the deportation: On February 10, 1940, the Bolsheviks came while we were still asleep...

CHAPTER 1
Life Before the Soviets

Before the Second World War, the village Łunin (pronounced "WOO-nyin") was in a remote part of Polesie (pronounced "poh-LEH-sheh"), a part of Poland that is beautiful, untamed, and untouched by modern axe or saw. The village lay in the midst of fields of grain, potatoes and flax, surrounded by deep forests and treacherous quagmires, swamps, and marshes, where legendary giants grew such as ancient oaks, pines and spruces. Here Nature reigned supreme, unchallenged by man and progress and all life seemed to live by Her laws.

In his memoirs, "Happy Odyssey" (Pan Books Ltd: London, 1950/1955), Sir Adrian Carton de Viart writes most eloquently about this part of the country, who as a second in command, was attached to the British Military Mission in 1919, and lived there for 20 years. He described Polesie in these words:

The country had a wild flat beauty all its own, with limitless forests, lakes and rivers stretching into the distance. It was home of every variety of wildfowl, and obviously a sportsman's idea of paradise, and I fell in love with it at once (p. 97). The country is absolutely flat, consisting of forests, meadows and marshes, but with a certain amount of arable land to give the peasant enough to live on – but no more (p. 105). How far the Prypet Marshes stretch

I do not know, for though I was surrounded by them, I never reached their limit during the many years I spent there (p. 104).

Polesie was not well known outside Poland like Warsaw or Krakow, and hardly anyone ever heard of the village Łunin.

In Łunin there were neither factories nor industry, only a railroad that ran from the Polish-Russian border to Pinsk, Brest-Litovsk, and Warsaw. It had no strategic military value, yet it was deliberately bombed.

Łunin was home to my ancestors. Polesie was their country; it belonged to them, and they belonged to Polesie. That's where they were born, lived, and grew old. When they died, their children buried them under the tall, whispering pines in the cemetery that was as old as the village itself. How old was the village? Nobody knew. Mother and Father had hoped to live their days out in this quiet village and be buried in the familiar earth and among their own. Then World War II came and forced us all out of our homeland to suffer many hardships in the cold regions of the Soviet Union. However, we never lost hope of seeing our beloved Łunin again. Then, after World War II, we heard that Łunin no longer belonged to Poland. Disappointed and broken-hearted, we had no place to go but England. There my parents died and were buried in a foreign soil – among strangers.

Although I was only a child, I remember clearly the day our village was bombed. It was Sunday, a warm and peaceful day in early autumn. It began like any other day.

In the morning, Father watered the horses and turned them out to pasture. Mother milked the cows, and my eldest sister Janina (Janka, pronounced "YAWN-kuh") lit the fire in the stove. My other sister Aleksandra (Olesia, pronounced "oh-LESH-uh") drew buckets of water from the well, and my brother Antoni (Antek, pronounced "ON-tek") brought an armful of firewood into the kitchen. My task was to feed the chickens. The only one in our family who had no chores to do was my baby sister Maria (Marysia, pronounced "muh-REE-shuh").

Just as we were finishing our breakfast, the church bells began to ring from both churches. The bells from the Orthodox Church went "boing-boing," and the bells from the Catholic Church went "ding-a-ling, ding-a-ling." Mother told us to hurry and get ready for church.

Sunday was my favorite day. I liked to look at the people dressed in their Sunday-best clothes. I admired women's beautifully embroidered white aprons and their colorful scarves. Men wore embroidered shirts, riding pants, and black, shining boots, polished with soot. Many times I watched my Father polish his boots with soot until they glistened.

After attending the Service in the Orthodox Church with Mother, I joined my friends. They were discussing what to do next. Someone suggested we go to the railroad station, which was just across the fields. A train was due to arrive shortly, and we didn't want to miss the only excitement of the day.

Whether because it was Sunday, or because it was so warm, no one was in sight as we ran through the softly undulating wheat fields. When we reached the station, nobody was there except for an old attendant with a big, drooping moustache, standing on the platform and holding two bags. A few minutes later, the train arrived. To our disappointment, no one got off.

When we were about to leave the station, a freckled boy, Misha, pulled a coin out of his pocket and said, "Let's see what happens to this coin after the train runs over it," and carefully placed it on a rail. We waited. Soon the train moved, tooted at us, and sped away. I wished I was on it as the caboose passed me by, if only to see what would be beyond the bend and still beyond. At that time I did not know that my wish to see the world would come true in a few months and that it would come under the most adverse of circumstances.

I was so preoccupied with my thoughts of seeing exotic places that I did not hear my friends call me until Ania touched my shoulder. Ania informed me that they had decided to go to her place to play "hide-and-seek," and that I was to be "It." As we ran to Ania's house, I realized that since my family had just moved from the Ranger's station back to the village, I had to be the first "It" if I wanted to play with them. It was obvious the children considered me an outsider and pushed their rules to the limit. Life seemed so unfair, I thought.

As soon as we came to Ania's house and had a drink of water, we heard the most unusual explosions, something we had never heard before. With each loud explosion, the earth shook, windows rattled, then the old shed collapsed. We were terrified.

"It must be the end of the world," said Lydia, the tallest girl of the group. Ania's mother came out and urged us to come into the house, but I thought – if this is the end of the world, I want to be with my own mother. Without saying a word, I ran home as fast as I could.

Our home was several houses away, ten at the most, but to me it seemed like ten miles. When I finally reached home, I found Mother sitting on a bed by my baby sister, who was asleep. I was glad Mother was home. It was quiet in the house. Mother motioned to me, indicating a place beside her. By then, the explosions seemed to be closer and louder. I looked questioningly at Mother. She understood and said, "It is war." After a while, the explosions stopped. It was quiet again, but Mother and I just sat there as though expecting something else to happen.

"Mama, what is war?" I asked. Mother looked at me, and sadness covered her face. I thought Mother was pretty, dressed in her Sunday clothes. She was short, about five feet, two inches, round but not fat. She had black hair that was always braided and neatly pinned at the back of her head. And Mother had the bluest eyes, almost the color of a cornflower.

In her own words, Mother tried to explain the meaning of war. "Child," Mother began, "I had hoped that you would never know about war. It is the most terrible evil man has ever invented against his own kind. It is killing, burning, destroying not only homes like ours, but whole villages, cities, and even nations." Suddenly Mother stopped talking. She realized that I could not comprehend what she was saying. Then, still looking at me, she added, "The worst part of war is what some people can do to others; they can betray you, or desert you." Mother, of course, was speaking from her own experiences during the First World War.

Mother told me that when the First World War broke out, she was only fifteen years old. A Russian commander of a detachment, stationed in the village, issued an order that the village had to supply a certain number of people and wagons to take huge quantities of barbed wire to the front lines. That meant one person per household. Her stepfather, who was the village judge and administrator of Mother's estate after her mother died, called all his children together and said that one of them had to go. At this point Mother told me that her stepfather had had six wives. Her mother was the fourth, who died soon after giving birth to a baby girl, Mother's half-sister. He also had many children from his previous wives.

When all the children were gathered together, the stepfather pointed his finger at her and said decidedly, "You will go." Mother began to cry and protest. She reminded him that she was only a girl, that he had sons who were older than she and asked to send one of them., "Why me?" The stepfather looked straight into her eyes and explained that she was an orphan, and if anything should happen to her, no one would miss her, or shed tears over her, and her half-sister was too young; even she wouldn't remember her. Having said that, he dismissed all his children, except Mother. When they left, he instructed her that at dawn she should take the old and dispirited horse, the dilapidated wagon, and go with the rest of the people where she was told. Mother knew the horse her stepfather was talking about. The horse was old and set in his ways. Nothing could change his pace, "even if you set fire under him." Mother begged the stepfather for a better horse. She cried and pleaded, but he dismissed her, as though he did not hear a word she had said.

At dawn, Mother took the old haggard horse, harnessed him to the specified wagon, and drove off to meet the rest of the people. When she met them on the outskirts of the village, she was the only girl and had the oldest horse.

As they approached their destination, they saw a German detachment of cavalry heading straight for them. The men, afraid of being captured by the Germans, cut their horses loose from the wagons, mounted them, and fled. Mother was also frightened and called to the men as they passed by for someone to stop and let her ride double. Her cries were completely ignored. Everyone was for himself. They forgot about her.

Mother managed to turn the horse around, and she coaxed him, pleaded with him, and even took the whip to him to make him run faster. She even told him their lives depended on his speed, but the horse just kept walking at his usual pace, nodding his head with each step he took. By then, she heard the Germans galloping hard behind her. She was terrified. Then a miracle happened. The

Father Józef Bogdaniec

Father with dogs
Rex, Hermes and Bella

Mrs. Sultanowa and the wild boar
shot by her

Mrs. Sultanowa and ducks

Gajówka - Kpt. Nowak-Surveyor.
Mother's hand-made tablecloth

On the River Lachowiec

GAJÓWKA Ranger's Station 1937
and our faithful friend Bosko

Father Jozef Bogdaniec and
colleague convalescing after being wounded
in the World War I

Germans, probably seeing only a girl and not worth pursuing, aborted their chase and went in a different direction. This Mother said with a sigh of relief, and continued. As night fell, Mother could see a fire in the distance. She steered her horse towards it. As she came closer, Mother recognized the men from her village. They also recognized her and were very surprised to see her as they had given her up for dead. Mother was very angry. Her eyes were swollen from crying, and in a hoarse voice she asked, "Why did you leave me? You had good horses, and I could have ridden with any one of you!" They did not answer; they just hung their heads in shame.

When Mother finished her story, I looked up at her and saw tears roll down her cheeks and fall onto her apron, leaving two wet spots where they fell.

Suddenly Mother asked, "Do you know where Olesia and Antek are? I hope they are not at the station, because it is the most likely place to be bombed first." As she said this, my heart, I think, skipped a beat. "Other children and I were there only a few minutes ago, but we did not see anybody," I replied. Soon Antek and Olesia came in. "Did you hear what happened today?" Antek asked, full of excitement. "There were German airplanes, and they tried to destroy our railroad. They were flying so low I could see the pilots from my hiding place."

"Where were you?" Mother interrupted. "I was worried sick about the two of you."

"We were in the forest," Olesia explained, "looking for nuts and mushrooms. When the bombing started, other girls and I hid under an old oak tree. I was so frightened that I lost sight of Antek."

"When the bombing began, I ran until I found a hole under a bush and lay down," Antek said with assurance as though he knew what to do in such an emergency. "One of the bombs must have exploded close to us, because it got so hot that I thought the whole forest would catch on fire and that I would burn to a crisp. Cousin Jacob was with me and wet his pants.," Antek said this with a silly grin on his face, and finished his story by telling us that when the bombing had stopped, he ran straight home.

At that moment Marysia woke up and began to cry. Mother picked her up, and talking to her in a soothing voice, walked to a window. "The weather is changing," Mother remarked. "It is going to rain soon." She continued to look out of the window. I went to the window and saw the abysmal black mass of clouds as the last rays of the sun fell upon the village. The bright day was coming to a close, fast.

Janka brought the cows in from a pasture. Mother helped with the milking, and soon they brought two buckets of milk. Mother let Janka take care of the milk, while she lit a fire in the stove and began to prepare supper. I realized that I'd had nothing to eat since breakfast and wished that Father would come home soon so we could eat. I did not have to wait long. Father came in just as the first drops of rain hit the window panes, saying, "I beat the rain!"

I can still see my father as he stood by the door, taking his hat off and hanging it on a peg. Father was a tall man with wavy, blond hair, green eyes, and was always clean-shaven. There was a certain air about him that made him different from other men in our village; the way he carried himself, walked and talked. By the village standards, Father was an educated man. He could read and write in both the Polish and Russian languages. People used to come to the house and ask him to read their letters to them because they were illiterate themselves.

During the First World War, when Poland did not exist as an independent state, Father served in the Russian Imperial Army, fought against the Germans, and was wounded.

For the past six years Father had been a forest ranger, and we lived at the ranger's station gajówka (pronounced "ghye-YOOV-kah") near the River Prypeć (pronounced "PREE-petch") on the estate of Prince Drucki-Lubecki. A few months before the Second World War broke out, we moved back to the village to our own home. Father, grandfather, and uncles built our house on Mother's land. Actually, Mother had inherited two plots of land from her father. One was in a village called Wolka, where she was born, and the other one in Łunin.

At home, Father's word was law, and we, the children, did not dare to disobey him. Despite his autocratic rule at home, Father was kind, caring, and fair. He listened to our problems, often changed our tears into laughter and settled our disputes without showing favoritism. As far as I can remember, Father never spanked or shouted at us. He instilled in us respect for our Mother and older people in general. As children, we could never address Mother as "Ty" (You), second singular, but only as "Mama." This principle was so deeply instilled in me that I could not bring myself to address Mother as "You" even after I was married and had children of my own.

When I was growing up, I knew nothing about Father's or Mother's family backgrounds. I only knew that Father came from a large family. There were five boys and three girls. Father was the youngest. The grandfather and uncles lived close by, and I often visited them. They were all tall and strong men, though grandmother, Wiktoria, was small and slim.

It was many years later, when I lived in Germany, that I found the family crest in the German heraldic books. I had a copy made and thought that it would be interesting to show it to Father and ask him about it. When I visited him in England, I showed him the crest with the "Bogdaniec" name on it. Father smiled and said, "When I was still a young boy, my brothers, other boys, and I decided to pick some pears from the neighbor's orchard, just for fun, although we had all kinds of fruit trees of our own. This neighbor, a good friend of the family, complained to my grandfather. Well, grandfather Jacob called his grandchildren together, and with a serious look on his face, said, 'Remember, boys, that you come from a long line of the Polish gentry (szlachta), and always remember to conduct yourself as gentlemen,' and with a wave of his hand dismissed us." It was the only time Father said anything about his background, although I heard people call Father and his family "Lachy," meaning that they came from Lechistan, Poland. According to Mother, Father's family had no land to speak of. The land they did have when Father's ancestors came to Polesie with the prince was lost in one way or another. "Women," Mother summed it up in one word. Years later, in England, when Mother talked about their life in Łunin, she often said with a twinkle in her eyes that Father married her for her land.

Before Father could talk to Mother, we were all around him, telling him what had happened that day and how terrified we were by the bombing. Father sat down at the table, and Mother served supper. Father listened patiently to our stories. After a while he raised his hand to silence us and waited for Mother to speak.

"Józef," Mother began, "what does it mean? Are we at war with Germany?" "I don't know yet," Father replied. "On the way home I talked to others, including the priest and soltys (the village official). No one seems to know anything. Tomorrow we should know something. If it is war, then I might be called into the army."

"And what am I supposed to do, alone with the children, while you go to war?" Mother interrupted with tears in her eyes as she began to clear the table. Janka and Olesia helped her with the dishes, while I played with Marysia. Antek was unusually quiet as he sat by the window and watched the raging storm outside. Father lit a kerosene lamp (we had no electricity) and went into the front room. Mother joined him shortly, taking baby Marysia with her. The four of us, Janka, Olesia, Antek, and I remained in the kitchen. Janka added more wood to the fire and put a big pot of water for washing before we went to bed.

The door to the front room was wide open, and I could hear Father say that it was too early to worry about something that may never happen. Then Father used words which I had never heard before and did not understand, such as allies... treaties.... Francja and Anglia (France and England) will help.

As I lay in bed, I wondered who were Francja and Anglia (in Polish, they fall into the feminine category). I imagined that they were two old ladies, who would help Mother while Father went to war. I also wondered where they would sleep. While pondering on such important matters, the last thing I remember was the rain steadily beating against the windowpanes.

The next morning the sky was cloudy, and it was drizzling. Antek handed me my jacket and said, "Come on, I want to show you something."

We went out through the back gate and ran across the same fields as I had done the previous day with my friends. Only this time the wheat was bent, heavy with rain. We passed the railroad station and climbed onto the track. I saw huge holes in the ground on each side of the railroad. "These holes were made by the bombs yesterday," Antek informed me. "Are the bombs still there?" I asked him. "No, silly," he replied. "When a bomb hits the ground, it explodes, making a loud noise and a big hole in the ground." I went down to have a closer look at the hole. I was awed by its size and how perfectly round it was. I bent over to look inside, but I

25

couldn't tell how deep it was because the bottom was covered with water from the last night's rain. When a group of boys showed up to inspect the site, Antek, with an imperious gesture, told me to go home.

On the way home, I realized I did not know my own village, the place where I was born. When we moved here a few months ago, there were aunts and uncles to meet and visit, cousins to get acquainted with, and most important to me, to learn how to play with other children my own age. Before, at the Ranger's station, I only played with Olesia and Antek. Now there was no time to go exploring the village. I only knew where my aunts and uncles lived and, of course, my new friends.

As I recall, there were three streets. Two ran parallel to each other with fields between them, through which we ran to the station. The third street cut across those two and was partially paved. On the unpaved part, my uncle Stas lived. To get to his house, one had to walk ankle-deep in mud, and for me it was almost knee-deep. For that reason, he was not a popular uncle to visit. Uncle Janek, on the other hand, lived on the paved part of the street in the old family house, where I often played with his children – my cousins.

The street, where the railroad station was situated was called Lachowska, paved with flagstones, nice and smooth to walk or ride on. Walking away from the station towards the west there was a park on the right hand side. Inside the park, there was a manor house that belonged to Prince Drucki-Lubecki. In that manor house lived "Babunia," (granny). One day, I had the privilege of meeting her. It was late in the afternoon when Olesia took me with her to the "nice street," pointing out different landmarks and buildings.

As we approached the park, I noticed an old lady, elegantly dressed in black, crossing the street. The old lady recognized Olesia and struck up a conversation with her. She seemed to know our family, asking about Father and Mother, Janka and Antek, occasionally glancing at me. Olesia then introduced me to Babunia. Out of politeness, I kissed Babunia's hand, as was the custom there. She gently stroked my head and said, "So this is Katrinka's other girl?" After that, Babunia bid us "Good day," and insisted that we give her regards to our mother and father, and that we should come and see her soon.

"Who is this nice lady?" I asked Olesia when we were alone. Olesia explained that Babunia, an affectionate term for "Granny," was our relative on Father's side. When she was younger, she was a nanny to the children of Prince Edward Drucki-Lubecki. The princes Franek, Bogdan, and princess Zofia called her "Babunia," and thus the whole village came to call her by this name. When the princes grew up and moved away, they let Babunia live at the manor house for the rest of her life. Several times I wanted to visit Babunia, but Olesia always seemed to be busy, doing things with her friends, and I did not dare to go there by myself.

I don't know where each street began and where it ended. I know that there were two churches. One was the old Eastern Orthodox Church, and the other, Roman Catholic, small and white, with a high steeple. There were also a school, and police, and fire stations. On the west side of the village, there was a cemetery, where my ancestors and oldest brother were buried. Whenever Mother or Father went there, I went with them. I liked the old cemetery. It was peaceful and quiet there, a perfect resting place under tall, majestic pines.

The street we lived on was paved in a rough cobblestone. Whenever a horse-driven cart went over it, it made so much noise that I used to hide behind the stove with fingers in my ears. On each side of the street there were ditches, lined with sod to keep the earth from eroding when it rained.

One day I found out, purely by accident, what kept the sod from sliding to the bottom of the ditch. Mother was visiting a neighbor a few houses down the street, and I decided to join her at the time when shepherds were bringing in the sheep. The street was jam-packed with them, but the ewes and lambs made room for me and let me pass. Then I met a ram with huge, curly horns. I was not much taller than the ram, and he blocked my way and would not let me pass. To my surprise, the ram butted me in the stomach. I fell and rolled over the wooden pegs that held the sod to the bottom of the ditch. Thinking that the ram was gone, I climbed out of the ditch. To my surprise, the ram belligerently waited for me. As soon as I got to my feet, he butted me again. Again I rolled down over the wooden pegs to the bottom of the ditch. I looked up, and the ram was still there, looking down at me. Out of frustration and anger, tears began to well up in my eyes. I couldn't find anything, a stick or a rock to hit him and make him go away. I did not despair long, for a shepherd came to my rescue. He barely touched the ram with his rod, and the beast walked away. I did not turn back, but continued on my way. From then on, I had a healthy respect for rams with big horns!

Most of the houses in the village were built of wood, mostly logs, except one – a two-story brick house. It seemed out of place and did not fit in with the rest of them on our street. There were also a variety of roofs. Some were made of straw, some of shingles, and others of tin.

Many years later, in Africa, I enjoyed listening to Mother's stories about the village Łunin. About ninety percent of the village population were peasants and farmers. They tilled and lived off the land just like their fathers before them. They planted enough crops to feed themselves and their families, and what was left over, if anything, they sold to pay taxes. They were poor — so poor that they split matches in half, sometimes into quarters when times were really hard. Matches they couldn't make themselves. Most of them wore homespun clothes, were illiterate and superstitious, believing in all sorts of things. For instance, when they saw for the first time a man riding a bicycle, they thought that only a devil himself could ride on two wheels. They closed their doors, shut the windows, and hid their children so the "devil" wouldn't see them. Or, when Father bought a threshing machine and showed them how quick and efficient the machine was, they swore that the next year Father's fields would be barren because he violated the old ways and tradition of the forefathers of threshing wheat.

It seemed that this was a place where time stood still and progress was slow in coming. Even in the late thirties, these people still lit their homes with kerosene lamps, burned wood for cooking and heating, and drew water with buckets from wells. Sanitation was non-existent. The means of transportation were horses and carts or sleds, depending on the seasons. The majority of peasants were Byelorussians and Orthodox. But if you asked them what they were, they probably would have answered that they were "Poleszuki" (pronounced po-leh-SHUH-kee, meaning 'from Polesie').

The second largest group were ethnic Catholic Poles. Jews were the minority. I don't know what the Jews did in our village. I only remember one Jew walking along with his cart, crying loudly, "Give me your rags, your old, dirty rags." I never asked why he wanted those old and dirty rags. Another Jew owned a shop. I recall being there when Antek told me to take a couple of eggs and give them to the Jewish lady. I did as Antek told me, and the old lady gave me two pieces of stale candy, telling me to bring more eggs. I did not like the candy and never went back to the shop.

The other five percent were priests, teachers, administrators, and other shopkeepers. These were Poles. Once they gave me a little bag of candy for reciting a poem. It was the day when Olesia took me on a tour of our village. The shop owners and other people were sitting on a porch of a fashionable white house, and Olesia asked them if they wanted to hear a poem, recited by her little sister. The people nodded their heads "yes" and listened. Afterwards, I had this wonderful feeling that Olesia was proud of me.

Harvest was probably the busiest time of the year. The women cut the wheat with a sickle. It took them days to cut one field, whereas a man could have done it with a scythe in a day or two. But that was unheard of. It would have violated the old tradition and brought bad luck. The women also dug the potatoes with a hoe, and men brought them in. Towards the evening the street was full of carts with wheat, potatoes and other vegetables, making a lot of noise over the cobblestones.

Mother and Father stored our potatoes, beets, turnips, and parsnips in the underground cellar. Wheat, rye, oats, and millet they put into the barn where Father ran them through a threshing machine. Others did it in the old way – with heavy chains. Afterwards they took the grain to a miller and brought back sacks of flour.

I still see my Father shredding the cabbage, and Mother salting and packing it into a big barrel with a dash of carrots for color for sauerkraut. I see Janka braiding the yellow onions and white garlic and hanging them up in the large pantry adjacent to the kitchen. In the pantry, Mother kept all her herbs, flour, salt pork, dried eels, sauerkraut, and all sorts of other things.

I don't know exactly how flax was processed, but I remember how Mother and Janka combed it over the steel brushes until it looked and felt like hair. From this flax, Mother and Janka and all the women spun thread during long winter evenings. Teenage girls, Janka's friends, liked to come to our house with their "pocies" – two boards joined together in an "L" shape with "kudziela", the combed flax, tied to the vertical board. The horizontal board was for sitting on. It was a light and portable gadget, and it did not take up much room. Spinning the yarn with a spindle was an art in itself. Although Mother tried to teach me how to spin, I was still too young to master this art.

The girls came as soon as it got dark, and they sang songs or told stories as they spun. A few hours later, the young men came with an accordion and drums. For a while they sang together, accompanied by the accordionist and drummer. After a few songs, the accordionist would stand up and play dancing music. The girls would stop their spinning and dance with the boys. The whole house shook when the boys stamped their feet, dancing the polka.

In the springtime the women began to weave the linen on homemade looms. All bedcovers, tablecloths, towels, and many other things were hand-woven. Many years later, I gave my daughter, Susan, my Mother's hand-woven and hand-embroidered tablecloth which Mother made from scratch.

Despite the hard life and toils from sunrise to sunset, the people found time to worship, sing a song together, or listen to a storyteller, especially on Sundays.

A wonderful storyteller lived in our village, who loved to tell stories. Whenever women and children gathered in front of someone's house and saw him passing by, they would ask him to tell a story. After clearing his throat with a shot or two of vodka, he would begin: "A long, long time ago, there was a kingdom…" The audience was spellbound, and for a moment they lived in a world of make-believe, a world of wonder and beauty to which only their souls could escape.

For the next two weeks after the bombing of the village, nothing extraordinary happened that I can recall. Now and then I heard words like "Germans" and "war," but they meant nothing to me at that time. I continued to watch other children play strange games. Sometimes they let me join them on the condition that I would be "It" on my first go.

CHAPTER 2
The Soviets

One morning Antek burst into the kitchen and said to me, "Come on, you have to see this for yourself!" We went by the back gate and ran through the fields, as we had done before, to the main street. As we came closer, I could see a few children and old people standing by the roadside, watching something moving on the street.

"Look," Antek said, pointing to a "thing," rolling down the street. "That's a tank with guns, a Russian tank, to be precise. We had better hide under the bridge so they won't shoot at us." Before I could take a better look at it, Antek grabbed my hand and pulled me under the bridge, all the way to the center. It was a wooden construction over a little creek that ran through the west part of the village, forming a pond near our street, where we swam in the summer and skated in the winter.

As we stood there, I did not know what to expect until a tank started to roll over the bridge. For a moment I thought that the bridge and tank were going to fall on us. I wanted to run, but Antek held my hand and would not let go, laughing all the time.

"You nincompoop!" I began hitting and kicking him as hard as I could. "All you wanted to do was frighten me. The Bolsheviks won't shoot me. I will show you!" I managed to get away from him and ran up the street. Soon, Antek joined me and apologized, begging me not to tell Father for scaring me the way he had.

At that time a Russian soldier climbed on top of the tank and began to shout, "We came to liberate you!" From that day on, the Russian tanks kept rolling and rolling, and soldiers were repeating the same slogan, "We came to liberate you!" over and over again. It took only a couple of days for me and my friends to see and hear the same thing, so we decided what is enough is enough! "Let's go and play." I cannot say when the tanks stopped coming because we stopped watching.

Soon after the invasion, I heard that there were fights in the streets. Antek and I were under strict orders from Father not to play on our street because, "it is too dangerous," as he put it.

Then one day, towards the evening, I came home and overheard Mother telling Father that They (the Russians) took our soltys into the fields and beat him unconscious. His family had to bring him home in a blanket.

"I hope he gets well soon," Father replied, "because I don't want to be a soltys in these troubled times. There is no one else to take his place. I am the logical choice, but I won't last long. I am too outspoken, and for that reason, they will probably shoot me."

Although my parents did not think I was listening to their conversation, I heard them just the same. At first I was shocked, then frightened, as I did not know who were They, who would do such a terrible thing to my Father as to shoot him. I tried to figure things out for myself. In this case, I concluded that the beating up of our administrator and the possible shooting of my Father had something to do with the coming of the Russians. Before the Russians came, it was peaceful and quiet in our village. The people were friendly and nice towards each other. But now, they stayed most of the time in their homes, hardly speaking to one another.

Before I went to sleep, I wondered why our soltys was beaten up. I knew him. He was always kind to me and other children whenever we came to his house to play with his son Vasili. Sometimes he would give us a piece of candy, or a roll of white bread, the kind you would buy in the town's bakery.

The next day Janka went to town, Łuniniec, about 13 kilometers from our village, to buy a few things for Mother. Janka came back at supper time and told us startling news. First, she said that she could not buy most of the things Mother wanted, because the shops were nearly empty. The Bolsheviks bought everything in sight, and many shops were closed. On the way home, she went by the river Prypeć and heard a lot of shooting, then saw terrible fighting that left about 40 people dead and three big river boats sunk. One man was on fire, and he jumped into the river. Then the water began to burn all around him. The man probably perished. Janka did not see him come out.

Janka's stories terrified me. For a long time I pondered over the burning water. I reasoned that water usually put the fire out. Many times I have seen fishermen pour water on their fires to put them out. I even had done it myself, when we cooked in the woods. "How can water burn?" It was a mystery to me then.

On a Saturday afternoon I went to see the lame girl, Hannochka, who lived three houses away from us. She was the kindest of all the children I played with, especially to me. While I waited for Hannochka to bring out her toys, her parents were talking about some people who were arrested, and no one knew what happened to them afterwards, as though they had vanished into thin air. I wondered if this was the reason why my Father was hiding in the marshes with other men, but I did not say anything about it to anyone, not even to my best friend, Hannochka, as we played.

As a young schoolgirl, I knew nothing about the developing military and political situation which would culminate into the nightmare of violence and change for so many people. But of course, I was aware of an indefinable threat. Overheard remarks by my parents amplified this unease. I used to lie in bed thinking about it, limited by my ignorance of detail. Little did I know how near to an answer we were.

Several weeks had passed since the Soviet invasion. It became obvious that the Red Army did not come to liberate Poland from the Nazis, as everyone expected, but that they meant to stay in the occupied territory and "sovietize" the Polish people. One aspect of the sovietization that affected me personally was the fact that we found Russian teachers in our school one morning. From that day on, we had to learn a new alphabet and speak standard Russian.

One day, our teacher took the whole class to see three small Soviet airplanes, emphasizing the might and power of the Soviet

Union. I was not as impressed with these airplanes as I was with the tanks.

Another week or so had gone by, and our teacher announced that the next day there would be no school, but we must come anyway to march in a parade, wearing our best clothes. Since I didn't think that I had any "best clothes," I decided to borrow one of Janka's silk skirts. Janka had many pretty "Mongolian" silk skirts and blouses, which she bought with the money she earned working on the construction of a highway.

The morning of the parade, I chose a light blue skirt. The way it was woven, the skirt shimmered and sparkled in a bleak light coming from a window. I put the skirt on. It reached the floor. Naturally, Janka's clothes were too big for me. She was seven years older. I solved this problem of the length by tying a rope around my waist and pulling the skirt up. The excess I covered with my jacket and went to school, thinking that I would be the best dressed girl in the parade.

It had rained the night before, and there were many puddles on the streets. Sometime during the march, the rope somehow untied itself and the skirt was dragging over the mud. We came to the village hall known as Remiza. All other classes were in front of us, and I could not see the speakers. I only heard a voice, saying, "Today we celebrate the anniversary of the October Revolution." Suddenly, Hannochka, who was behind me, touched my shoulder and said in a low voice, "Look, Nadia, your skirt is all muddy in the back." I did not hear the rest of the speech, because my only thought was to get home before Janka did and hide the skirt. The longer the voice kept on talking, and it seemed for a whole eternity, the more I thought about Janka's wrath and punishment with her fists. Janka never found out. It was in Uganda that I told her about the skirt. Smiling, she shook her fist at me!

Whether because it was so cold, or because I stayed home and did not play with other children, I did not hear any terrifying stories about arrests, or shooting, or fighting. Then one day, before our lessons began, the teacher said that it was the Russian soldiers who brought peace and order to our village. We looked at each other and remained silent.

For a while the people were lulled into a false peace. Father and other men came home from their hiding places, and life seemed normal again, at least for me. The winter settled in, and the entire village was wrapped in a thick blanket of white snow. Then came Christmas.

On Christmas Eve, Father put his sheepskin coat on, harnessed a horse to the big sled, told Antek and me to dress warmly and come with him. We settled on fresh hay on the sled, and Father wrapped extra blankets around us.

"We are going to the forest to find us the prettiest Christmas tree," he said after we took off.

All snuggled and warm, we rode through the village and fields, far into the forest. When the horse stopped, we climbed out from the sled and began to look for the perfect tree. Each time we thought we found one, Father would look up and down at it and say, "It's not the one." Then we found one. It was tall and full. Its branches were evenly spaced with a little snow still on them, glistening in the morning sun, just like in a book I once saw. Father cut the tree down, tied it to the sled, and we drove back home.

Father stopped in front of the house to let us off, and he drove away to put the horse back in a stable. As soon as we walked in - oh, the aroma of cinnamon, cloves and other spices filled the kitchen. Mother was baking all sorts of sweet breads. Bulki (rolls) and pierniki (honeycakes) covered the kitchen table. Some were with raisins and nuts, and some were plain. Some were round, others oblong and twisted, sprinkled with poppy seeds and orange rind.

In making these treats, Mother used white flour, something special that she used at big holidays, like Christmas or Easter. Otherwise we ate rye bread. Needless to say, all bread-rolls and honeycakes looked delicious and made our mouths water just by looking at them.

"I saved some dough in case you wanted to make something to hang on the Christmas tree," Mother said.

We were delighted at the prospect of playing with dough. We made circles like the letter "O,", figure "8", snowmen, and something that looked like a lot of twisted dough, and, of course, some of it, we ate. Everything we made Mother baked.

In the meantime, Father made a stand, and brought the tree in. He put it in the front room by the window, and its tip touched the ceiling.

"Start decorating the tree," he said with a smile and showed us a bag of chocolate candy. Each piece was individually wrapped in beautiful colors of aluminum foil. We hung the candy and our own creations along with some red apples which Antek brought from the attic. Mother showed us how to make stars from strips of paper, and we hung them on the tree. On the very top, Father put a silver star.

By the time we finished decorating the tree, the sun went down. The murky light drifted into the room. Father lit a fire, and we watched how the light danced on the colorful wrappers of chocolate candy. To us, it was the most beautiful Christmas tree in the whole world.

In the kitchen, Mother was preparing the Christmas Eve dinner, the most important meal of this holiday season. Before the table was set, Father brought a handful of hay. Janka and Olesia spread it on the table and covered it with Mother's handmade embroidered tablecloth. The hay was symbolic of Jesus, who was put on the hay after He was born. As Janka and Olesia were setting the table, Mother reminded them to set an extra place. This was also symbolic. It meant that we were prepared to welcome any stranger who may come knocking at our door. The people in the village considered it to be a real blessing if a stranger, whether he or she were a beggar or handicapped, were to come and share their special supper with them.

At last the table was set, the candles lit, and we all sat down. Father stood up, said a prayer, and made a speech. Taking the holy Host, "Opłatek" (pronounced oh-PWAH-tek), which he had brought from the church, he broke it into several pieces and shared it first with Mother, wishing the best of everything, and many years of happiness. Mother in turn, broke off a little piece, ate it, and passed the rest to Janka, who was the oldest, wishing her lots of happiness. Janka passed it on to Olesia, she to Antek, who gave it to me and to baby Marysia. After this was done, Father wished us all a Merry Christmas. At such special occasions, we could not start until Father sat down.

Mother prepared a traditional meal. There were borsch with uszka (something that looks like tortellini stuffed with wild mushrooms), baked fish, potatoes, and other vegetables with mushroom sauce, bread, and butter. For dessert, we had cooked, dried fruit. When supper was over, Mother took all the leftovers to the cattle, since they, too, were part of Jesus' birth. This was the tradition, passed from generation to generation, which Mother kept and observed.

For a while we sat at the table and sang Christmas carols. Father began with his favorite: *Yesterday Evening, good tidings came to us from the Heavenly Host. A virgin brings forth a Son...*

Then carolers came, singing, "Good evening, to our magnificent host." Father let them in. When the carolers entered, one man was dressed as a goat with a wooden mouth in front of his face and a large sack attached to the mouth. Another man was dressed as a bear in a real bearskin. The "bear" and the "goat" danced and sang with all of us. Afterwards, the "goat" opened his wooden mouth and Mother put into it a ring of sausage, and the "bear" gave us a piece of candy. They wished us a Merry Christmas and left.

On Christmas morning, we opened our gifts. I got a pair of long stockings, and I was delighted, thinking how they would keep my legs warm on the way to school. Antek received a pair of brand new, shining skates. Olesia showed us her colorful headscarf, and Janka was thinking out loud what she was going to make out of a shimmering new piece of material. I was so busy looking at the presents my sisters and brother got that I do not remember if Mother and Father received anything. At that time, I could not have known that this was to be my last Christmas in our home, our village, and our country. Since then, there has been none like it.

*

~ *1940*

One Sunday in January, as I was playing with other girls, Krystyna suggested that we go skating on the pond by the bridge on our street. All girls agreed that it was a good idea and went home to fetch their skates. I had none, but then I remembered Antek's new pair, the ones he got for Christmas. When I found them, I hesitated for a moment, thinking: "Will I get into trouble by taking them without his permission?" I compensated by taking only one skate, hoping that Antek would not be too angry with me if I took only one.

It was a beautiful afternoon. The snow and ice shimmered and sparkled with tiny diamonds in the sun. There were other children with only one skate, so I did not feel out of place skating on one leg. Then I saw Antek with the other skate in his hand, standing on the edge of the pond looking at me. Although my brother never hit me and we hardly ever argued, except calling each other names sometimes, I don't know why I thought that he might do it this time. I took the skate off, threw it at his feet, and ran home.

I stopped running and began to walk at a normal pace. I was surprised to see how different the village looked in winter. The ugly cobblestones were covered by snow and so were the ditches, yards, and roofs. The white smoke was rising high from the chimneys over each house, and I wondered why I did not notice this before. I came to our house. Only one wall with two windows faced the street. The yard, like all the others, was closed off by two gates. A small one was for pedestrians, and the big one for vehicles and livestock. Behind the front yard, there was a fenced off orchard, Mother's vegetable garden, and Janka's flowerbeds. Behind the orchard were stables, sty, barn, and a shed. The back yard was closed off with a wooden fence.

Although I was cold and hungry, I did not go into the house right away. I stood in the yard and took a long look at my home that Mother and Father built on Mother's land which she inherited from her father. Many years later, I learned of Mother's fascinating family background. Her grandfather, Bohatyrewicz, as a young man of this ancient noble family, came from the north to the village called Wolka. At the vicarage he begged for some bread. The priest asked him his name, and hearing who he was, persuaded him to stay at the vicarage. Years later, he married a beautiful but poor girl. They had four daughters. He died when Mother was a little girl, but she remembered his visits and his unbelievable stories about the scientific future. He even prophesied that she would see the first man on the moon, and she did when living in London in 1969. Mother's grandmother on the other hand, died when Mother had two children of her own and had the opportunity of hearing the bygone customs and traditions.

I looked at the whitewashed exterior walls, glowing windows, and smoke rising straight up in the stillness of the evening. The kitchen window glowed from within, from a burning fire in the stove. I knew that Mother was busy cooking something tasty to eat. I could smell it. Suddenly I was overcome by the warm feeling and love for my Mother just because she was always there. I intended to tell her how much I loved her and how glad I was to have her for my Mother. But I was a quiet child, as Mother often said, and wouldn't express my feelings as openly as, for example, Janka would. Janka could swear, shout, and throw things, despite many reprimands by Mother and Father. Perhaps the reason why I was so quiet and silent was because I spent a lot of time by myself when I was growing up at the ranger's station gajówka, and often had no one to talk to or ask questions. My only playmates and companions then were Olesia and Antek, but sometimes they ran away from me and went off somewhere by themselves.

Despite what our teacher told us about the Soviets being in charge of law and order, we were robbed several times. They did nothing about it. They did not catch the thieves.

One evening after supper, Mother took baby Marysia and went to see my godmother, who lived across the street. Antek and I were alone in the house. We sat on the blankets by the fire, and Antek was telling me a story. Then we heard someone come into the kitchen and rummage through the cupboards. At first we thought it was our sister Olesia, as it was her custom to look for something to eat whenever she came in. Then we heard a heavy thump against the door that opened into the kitchen. Antek tried to open it but couldn't. He then put a finger to his lips and whispered, "hide someplace while I go and get Mother." He opened a window and, barefooted, ran across the street. In a few minutes, Mother and some neighbors came running with lanterns. They found that a huge log was propped up against the door that led to the room we were in. Mother looked around and discovered that the thief had stolen the money which she kept in a hidden drawer in the chest. One of the neighbors ran to notify the police. Instead of a familiar policeman, the NKVD came. They asked a few questions and then left. Nothing else was done about it.

January gave way to February as I watched Father turn a page on his desk calendar. The weather changed, more snow fell, and the temperature dropped 40 degrees Celsius below zero. I stayed home most of the time doing my homework, or playing with Marysia.

On a Friday, as we were coming home from school, Hannochka invited me to a doll party. "Don't forget to bring your doll," she reminded me before we parted.

I had never been to a doll party, and I wanted to find out what it was all about. I looked for my doll with a porcelain face that Father bought me a long time ago. I looked everywhere — under the bed, behind the stove, in the treasure box — but could not find it. I did not despair long. I found some rags and stuffed them into my white sock. I tied a string for a neck, a rag for a waist, and drew eyes, nose, and mouth with a pencil. I tied another rag around its head for a scarf, and not to be late for the party, I ran to Hannochka's house.

When I came in, other girls were already there. Their dolls were sitting at the "table," a long board covered with a beautifully embroidered towel. Hannochka took my doll, looked at it, and put it at the far end of the table. Other girls also looked at my doll, then at me, but did not say anything. I knew they thought that it was the ugliest doll they had ever seen. But I thought, "If only I could have found my real doll, she would have been the prettiest of them all." I was not ashamed of my doll; she looked cute with a kerchief tied around her head.

I enjoyed myself, singing and dancing with the rest of them. Then Hannochka served some refreshments, supposedly for the dolls, which we ate and drank for them. We did not realize how late it was until my friend's mother came and told us it was suppertime and that we should go home.

When we were getting ready to go, Hannochka suggested that we leave our dolls where they were and come tomorrow to pick them up and perhaps play some more. We all agreed. And that was the last time I saw Hannochka, my doll, and my friends.

CHAPTER 3
Deportation

It was Saturday, February 10, 1940. Before dawn, loud voices coming from outside woke me up. I opened my eyes. It was still dark; only a murky light outlined the windows. I wondered who it could it be so early in the morning, and I was not even dressed. A moment later, I heard Father's voice,. "It's the Russians and someone from the village." Then silence. Evidently Father was listening to what they were saying, because when he spoke again, he spoke louder with a note of alarm in his voice. "We are betrayed by our own."

"Russians." I turned this word over several times in my mind. Then I remembered. They were the ones who came last autumn. Antek and I had watched them as they drove through our village, shouting, "We came to liberate you!" Since their arrival, we had called them Bolsheviks or Soviets. Only now and then we used the term Russians. My thoughts were interrupted by the screeching hinges of the opening gate, then quick footsteps, and the impatient knocking.

Father opened the door, and I heard a man's voice say, "Hands up." Father, in turn, demanded an explanation for this intrusion. Instead of an explanation, I heard only obscenities directed at Father. I was terrified; I had never heard anyone speak like that to my father. I peeked through a crack in the door that was slightly ajar, and saw Father standing against the wall with his hands up. Three soldiers in long coats with red stars on their hats were pointing their guns at Father. I only saw their backs. Two had rifles, and the third one had a handgun. One had his rifle so close that it seemed to touch Father's chest; the other one was a step away, and the third one, with the hand gun, demanded that Father surrender all his guns he'd had during the service as a forester.

"I have no weapons," Father replied, "I turned them in when I quit the job." The Russian did not believe Father and ordered, "Revizia!" (search the house). When I heard these words, I ran to my bed and hid under the covers.

One of the soldiers ordered all of us to go to the kitchen. We sat down at the kitchen table, while he stood guard at the door, and the other two searched the house.

Being awakened from her sleep, baby Marysia began to cry. Mother got up, put her shawl over her shoulders, took a milking bucket, and walked to the door. The guard pointed his rifle at Mother and asked "Kuda?" (where to?). Mother told him that she was going to milk a cow, so she could feed her children. "If you wish, you can come along and hold your gun over me while I am milking," Mother said sarcastically, and then added, "I will not run away." The guard, however, did not let Mother go and told her to sit down. The other two soldiers came in and ordered us to go into the front room, so they could search the kitchen.

When we walked in, the room was a mess. Everything was thrown onto the floor, including photographs and pictures from the walls. With tears in her eyes, Mother picked up the photographs and the icons and put them on a table. The rest of us were too stupefied to do or say anything.

Soon the search was over, and the soldiers called us back into the kitchen. Mother, seeing what they had done, began to scream at them, mainly for pouring the bread dough onto the floor. Mother always baked bread on Saturdays.

"Where you are going, you won't bake bread anymore," said the guard with the handgun. "Now get dressed, and hurry. And you," he said, pointing the gun at Father, "go and hitch your horse to the sled and bring it to the front door of the house."

"How dare you come into my house and order me around!" Father said angrily. "And what is the meaning of all this?" Father demanded. The soldier, who was giving orders, was younger than Father. He was clean-shaven, wore a long overcoat, boots, and a fur hat with a red star. At the belt, there was a holster for the gun which he kept pointing at Father. The other two soldiers obeyed his commands without a question.

When Father was dressed, he put his sheepskin coat on and his hat and went out with a guard behind him. When he drove up to the house, the soldier told Mother to take only as much as we could carry. Mother took blankets and pillows off the beds and handed these to the other soldier and told him to put them on the sled. Janka and Olesia were grabbing their clothes. Antek could not make up his mind whether or not to take his skates, and I was looking for my shoes among the stuff that was thrown in the middle of the floor.

As we were walking out, Mother turned back, walked to the stove and took a little black pot with a handle. From a chest, she grabbed a handful of linens, also photographs, hiding them in her apron pocket. "No documents, papers, or photos are allowed to be taken," bellowed the soldier. We then climbed onto the sled, and together with the Russians we left our home.

As we passed the gate, I looked at our home. The shutters over the windows were still closed, as though the house did not want to see us go. Mother also looked back at the house and murmured something. It was years later in England when we were remembering this tragic moment that Mother told us of the heartrending thoughts then. Very strongly she wished that no one, except the family members, would live in this house. And so, many years later, when our cousin came to visit my family in England, he told Mother that Soviet officials occupied the house but never for long. In the end my godfather's family moved in. At this, Mother sighed and said that orphans' wishes always come true. Mother was an orphan.

The Russians told Father to drive to the police station, which was not far. Within minutes we were there. When we arrived, there were a lot of people from other villages. Recognizing most of them, Father remarked, "So the beheading of the villages has begun," which did not make any sense to me at that time.

As the day wore on, more and more people were brought in. It became very crowded inside the station. Some had to wait outside in the sub-zero temperature. As we waited, I began to think of the "whys." Why did They bring us here so early? Why didn't They let us have breakfast - the pancakes Mother always cooked before she baked the bread? Why were there guards at each door of the station, and where does one go to the toilet here? Suddenly I wanted to go home. We could put it back in order and live the way we did before They came.

It was already late afternoon when I heard the order, "To your sleds." When we were near our sled, we squatted down to relieve ourselves, the necessity They denied us when They came.

As we took our seats on the sled, Mother found two loaves of bread, hidden in the hay. Mother looked at the bread and said that one loaf was from her half-sister, and the other from Father's sister. My aunts knew that we had no bread, and it was their way of showing that they were thinking about us and that it was the only way they could help.

Finally, we left the station. A long procession of sleds was slowly moving to another village, escorted by the Soviet soldiers on each side of us. Women were crying; some openly cursed the Soviets, while others prayed. Men, too, I noticed, occasionally were wiping their eyes with a sleeve of their coats.

Thus we rode, helpless exiles, expelled from our homes and villages, while the pale sun hung in the western sky. Its cold rays could not warm us in the −40 degrees Celsius weather.

When we approached our destination, I saw a long train waiting on the outskirts of a village. It was our train. The soldiers told us to get in. Inside, there were two bunk-like shelves on each side of the door. We took the upper bunk by the window. When our boxcar was full, the soldiers closed and locked the door.

It was already dark when we arrived at the Polish-Russian border. Our train stopped parallel to another one that looked exactly like ours. A soldier opened the door and ordered us to get into the one that was opposite our car. We gathered our belongings, climbed into the boxcar, and settled on the upper bunk by the window. Again the door was closed and locked. After a while the train moved.

As the train sped faster and faster into the dark night, I became drowsy. Just as I was about to fall asleep, I sat up with a start. I forgot to pick up my doll from Hannochka. Also, I forgot to take my treasure box with a gold metallic ribbon, two shiny buttons, and a brand new grosh, a coin Father gave me. But I was too tired to think about it all for long. I lay down and listened to the rhythm of the train and fell asleep.

The following day most people were already awake by the time I got up. The first thing I was aware of was of the train speeding on, faster and faster, away from home. A few women were crying, "Boze, moj Boze, co z nami bedzie?" (God, my God, what will happen to us?).

Mother was combing and braiding her hair, Father and other men were standing by the stove, talking about something. I told Mother that I had to go to the toilet. Father helped me down, pushed a board away, and showed me a hole in the floor. "In front of everybody?" I asked, embarrassed. "Under the circumstances, do not be embarrassed," Father replied.

As Father was showing me how to get up and come down by myself, I told him that I wanted to go home. "So do I," Father whispered. I crawled back to my place by the window. Mother gave each one of us a slice of bread, the bread my dear aunts had left on our sled the previous day. As I ate, I kept looking out of the window. There was not much to see—a few houses here and there, and snow, long stretches of snow.

After a while, the people, especially children, began to complain of thirst. It had been a long time since we'd had something to drink. Someone suggested getting some snow, if we only had a cup. A family with four children below us produced an enamel-coated cup. Someone else came up with a long string and Mother, of course, had a small black pot. Father opened the little window and filled the pot with snow. When the snow melted, the children were the first to get a drink. This procedure was repeated several times, until everyone had a drink.

As we continued on our journey into the unknown, I saw onion domes, glistening in the sun. I told Father that we were approaching a large city. Father looked and said, "It has to be Moscow. I recognize the domes."

Our train pulled into the station. The soldiers unlocked the door and informed us that we would have something to eat – our first meal since we left home. There were other trains full of people like us. Through the little windows the people asked each other where they were from. The names of Wołyń, Baranowicze, Wilno, and many others resounded throughout the station. Then to our utter surprise, the soldiers came and put bars on our window.

Svoloch (the scum), Father summed them up in one word. This action of the Soviet soldiers caused a long discussion among the people in our boxcar. The main question was how did the soldiers know about us getting the snow through the window? In the end, the people concluded that there is donoschik (an informer) on our train. He had to inform them about our activities when men went to get the soup at the station. As far as I know, the people never found out who the informer was.

After we had eaten the vegetable soup, the people, mostly men in our car, were discussing what they had learned at the station, and how interesting it was that there were no trains from beyond the River Bug, only from the Eastern Provinces. At this moment I turned to Antek and asked him which way was east. He explained that east was where the sun rises, and the west where the sun sets. He also informed me that so far we had been going east, "and that's why we are in Moscow now."

"And where will we end up if we keep going east?" I asked. "Eventually, we will run out of land and come to a sea," Antek explained. "Then we will have to get on a ship to cross the sea."

"How big is a ship?" I interrupted him.

"A ship is so big that our whole village could fit into it," was his reply. I thought he was exaggerating a bit. Nothing could be as big as our village. I imagined a ship as long as our street, even though I did not know where it ended. I recalled this conversation when I actually saw real ships, and how right I was for doubting Antek's word.

Our conversation was interrupted by the whistles and clamor in the station. Soon the trains began to pull out. I could see the soldiers checking the locks on each car on a train next to ours. Then there was a sudden jerk, clashing of metal against metal, and our train started to move. I cannot recall anything in particular about Moscow except the shining domes and trains full of people like us.

It was dark and many hours after we left Moscow that Father, wanting to get the bearings of our direction, looked at the stars through the window. "The stars and the drop in temperature tell me that we are going north, perhaps to Siberia," Father said to Mother, but loud enough for everyone to hear. This remark caused a great commotion, especially among women. They began to cry that they had no warm clothing, neither for themselves nor for their children, to withstand the Siberian cold. Only men, including my Father, had sheepskin coats, which they had been wearing on the day of our deportation.

On our journey northwards I noticed that our train was getting shorter and shorter after each stop. Soon I couldn't see the caboose when the tracks bent.

Again the train stopped in the middle of nowhere. It was dark, and I was unable to see anything, except the snow and forest. From the other side, the people said they could see flickering lights by the train. The door opened wide, and the soldier said that this was the end of our journey.

We gathered our belongings and came out. There were a lot of sleds with lanterns, the only lights in the vicinity. A Russian woman walked up and greeted us with a big smile and told us to follow her.

As we walked to her sled, Father asked how long the winters lasted there. She replied that winters did not last long. "Only nine months, and the rest is summer, and summer, glorious summer." Having no concept of time, I did not know how long was a week, a month, or a winter. But since she repeated "summer" three times, I thought that it would soon be summer.

As soon as we settled in the sled, Father asked the woman if Russian men were so lazy that they allow women to do their jobs, like driving horses in the dark. The woman replied, "Our men are at the Front. The commandant ordered us to meet you and bring you to the camp Listvinnitsa 22."

On the way to the camp Father asked her many questions, but I did not hear any of them. I was too preoccupied with the wonderful summer, which was going to last a long time. Although I was thinking of a long, hot summer, in reality I was shivering from cold. It was so cold that it seemed as if I had icicles inside my nose.

The Russian woman drove the horses at a slow pace, telling Father something about the camp. The sky was cloudy, but in semi-darkness I could see the forest on both sides of the road. The camp, or settlement as the Russians called it, was not far from the railroad, and we arrived there in no time. The woman stopped in front of a big building and told us to go inside. "They" were expecting us. Then she drove off to return the horse back to the kolhoz, a collective farm.

CHAPTER 4
Siberia

We walked in. The large hall was lit by kerosene lamps, and a fire was burning in a round stove. To the right, I saw long tables. Several men, dressed in uniforms, were sitting at a separate table. When the rest of the people arrived, one of the men told us to sit down. He waited until everyone was seated, then made a long speech. I do not remember anything about what he had to say, except one sentence, "If you do not work, you do not eat." I thought about it and wondered what I could do so I could eat, and that I was very hungry.

For supper they gave each family a small piece of bread and kipyatok (hot boiling water). In the months to come, we were able to make a distinction between plain hot water and "kipyatok." Kipyatok could be anything you wanted it to be—tea, coffee, soup—depending what you put into it. You could even drink it plain as a warming remedy on a cold day.

Realizing that the piece of bread was much too small to divide among the seven of us, Mother brought out her black pot, cut the bread into small pieces, poured kipyatok over them, and adding a little salt and pepper, made a bread soup. Mother's resourcefulness still amazes me.

I can only surmise that the man in the uniform said in his speech that this building would be our temporary quarters for only a few days, because after we had eaten, Mother and other women began to claim spaces by spreading their blankets on the floor. Warmed by the "soup," I immediately fell asleep.

The first phase of deportation was carried out quickly and efficiently, at least in our case. From the time of our arrest, it took the Soviets only four days to bring us to the camp Listvinnitsa 22, about two hundred kilometers south of Archangielsk, Archangel, a port on the White Sea in the Arctic.

When I woke up in the morning, the people were standing in a line to register for work, Olesia told me. Soon Father came over and said, "Janka, Olesia, and I are going to work in the sovhoz (state farm), and Mother to work in the kolhoz come spring. Since Antek and Nadia are too young to work, they will have to go to school." Mother asked about Olesia, saying that she was also too young for work, and that she should be going to school. Father said that he, too, argued that point, but they told him that Olesia was going to be thirteen in March and was old enough to work. And thus they decided the division of labor for us. Marysia's name didn't even come up at all since she was only two and a half years old.

Olesia, Antek, and I went outside to explore our new environment. Looking around, we discovered a latrine and took turns using it. Afterwards we saw many wooden houses scattered here and there, not like in our village where houses lined both sides of the street. It was very cold, and we did not venture far. The freezing cold forced us back inside.

As we sat, huddled together, with a blanket around us, I asked if I had missed breakfast. They told me that there was no breakfast, not even a kipyatok. We waited for lunch, but there was no lunch either. Having nothing to do and no place to go, we fell asleep.

When we woke up, Father received a ration card for bread, and coupons for hot meals at the stolovaya (cafeteria). For dinner we had a small piece of bread and soup which resembled kipyatok with one exception: it had a few noodles floating in it.

The next day, the guards escorted the people to their workplaces. Father, Janka, Olesia, and many others went to work in the forest, cutting and loading logs on trains, while others, mostly women, went to the kolhoz.

We lived in the hall for a couple of weeks, dirty, unbathed, and our clothes unwashed. Then one day, I discovered I had lice, not only in my hair but also in my clothes. I was horrified. The big question was how to get rid of them. I went outside and brushed them off my dress onto the snow. Then I found a piece of a newspaper and a comb and started to comb them out of my hair. It must have been Sunday afternoon because Olesia came and took the comb away from me, saying that I should not be doing this in front of all these people. "What will they think?"

"But these lice must come from them," I argued. Olesia did not argue with me. She took the newspaper and threw it into a stove and watched it burn, lice and all. From that time on, I combed out the lice in a latrine.

One evening, the commandant of the camp came and said that we would no longer be sleeping on the floor, but in regular beds, now that we had joined the ranks of the working people. Two NKVD men handed out addresses to the heads of each family.

When Father got our address, we packed up our belongings and went to look for our new home. It was in a big building, not far from the hall. The superintendent showed us a room which was small and narrow with one window. There were only two single beds, a small table, and one chair. Seeing the two beds, I asked Mother if I could have one. It was a long time since I had slept in a real bed. Mother agreed. "What luxury," I thought as I lay stretched out. Mother and Marysia claimed the other one. The rest had to sleep on the floor. So much for the Soviet promises.

Before we went to sleep, Father sat down at the table and began to write a few letters home. (Upon issuing separate quarters, the NKVD men told Father we were permitted to write letters to relatives in Poland, but under no circumstances could we meet in anyone else's quarters.) Then Father read them to Mother. I remember the beginning of one: "It is late, but the night is so bright that I don't need a lamp to write this letter," Father wrote to Mother's sister. Having finished the last letter, Father took some blankets and put them down by the door. Janka, Olesia and Antek occupied the rest of the floor.

I awoke during the night, and in this strange light I saw the wall covered with bedbugs. I looked at my bed, and to my horror they were there also. My arms and legs had red blotches where they had bitten me. I tried to brush them off my bed, but they kept coming back.

The next night I told Janka that since she was working, it was only right and proper that she should have the bed. Janka was surprised at my generosity and even thanked me for it.

After a few days of living in such close quarters, someone in the family caught the mange, or the itch, a very contagious skin disease which begins between the fingers, then spreads to the rest of the body. I knew it could not have been me, because I was the last one to get it. The next day, Father brought a big jar of black ointment and told us to smear it all over our bodies before we went to sleep. The ointment smelled awful, and soon the room had the same odor. Mother had to open the window to let some fresh air in despite the sub-zero temperature outside.

Just as we settled for the night, there was a knock on the door. We immediately became frightened. A knock on a door, especially at night, meant trouble—most often, an arrest.

Father couldn't open the door right away. He had to pick up his blankets, tell Antek, who slept next to him, to move, and only then he was able to open the door. While this was going on, the knocking continued. When Father finally opened the door, it was the commandant himself, demanding the explanation for the delay.

"Look for yourself," Father replied, and began to explain the whole process. Looking at us lying on the floor, the commandant did not say why he came. He only told Father to come and see him the next day, and left. After Father saw him, we moved to another apartment with two spacious rooms and a stove. There were two double beds and a cot, also a table with four chairs. We could actually move around here. Unfortunately, there were bedbugs here also – the plague of the Soviet Union, lice and bedbugs!

Soon we were allowed to burn wood in the stove for one hour each morning and evening. Immediately, Mother started a fire and began to heat water in borrowed pots for our baths. We had almost forgotten what it felt like to be clean.

After we had our baths, Mother soaked the lice-infested clothes so she could wash them the next day. Then Mother rummaged through her linens, looking for something to trade for soap. She chose a towel and went across the hall to the apartments where the Russians lived.

Our neighbors were a young woman with a baby, whose husband was at the Front, and an older tall woman and her hunchback husband, who knew a lot about everything, even America. One day when we were terribly hungry, he told us that in America, people don't eat bread, because they have plenty of other things to eat. I could not imagine such a country where people ate so little bread when all I wanted was bread, so much of it until I could eat no more. Then the hunchback man said that someday we, the Russians, would have everything that America has.

We lived in this apartment for more than a year, and our life fell into the following routine: as a rule, Mother was the first to get up and start a fire in the stove, not to cook breakfast, which was forbidden, but to take the chill off and warm some water for washing. After Father had washed and shaved, he would go to the "stolovaya" or mess hall, to buy tea. To break the monotony of the same food for breakfast, we made a game of it. One day we had tea with bread, and the next day bread with tea. After breakfast, Father, Janka, and Olesia went to work, while Antek and I went to school, leaving Mother and Marysia at home.

Our school was in another Camp, called 24, about three kilometers from our Listvinnitsa 22. Between these two camps, there was a patch of woods. Beyond it was an open field, covered with snow during winter, all the way up to my chest. All the children used to gather in front of the camp's office before going to school, just in case the commandant had to send someone with a sled to the Camp 24, and give us a ride, or mark the way after new snow fell. Most of the time we walked to school, falling into the snow and pulling each other out.

One day the temperature dropped to 45 degrees Celsius below zero! Antek and I decided not to go to school that day. We virtually froze in our thin clothes before we even came to the office. We walked into the office on a pretext to ask about the time, but that was not the real reason. In fact, it was to warm up for that one minute. Since no sled was going to the Camp 24, instead of going to school, Antek and I and a few other children went home. It was simply just too cold to walk the three kilometers in a thin cotton dress and a jacket stuffed with newspapers. That evening, when Father went to buy bread, two portions were cut off.

"Two people don't eat today," Father said when he brought the bread. "Tell me what happened." We told him that it was too cold. Father agreed with us. Antek and I were broken-hearted, and I bitterly cried over the piece of bread. We lived for that piece of bread from the moment we got up, stood long hours in a line, and were most obedient for it. From then on, no matter what the weather was like, whether it was a blizzard or a sunny day, we went to school so the rest of the family would not have to share their meager portions with us.

The next day at school, Antek and me and the children who hadn't gone to school the day before were talking about what it was like back home in Poland, and the food we had, when our teacher, Maria Petrovna, came in and listened to our conversation.

"Forget about Poland," Maria Petrovna began, "you will never return there. The only time you will see your country again is when the hair begins to grow on the palm of your hand," she added, pointing to the palm of her hand.

"With God's help, we will return," said a girl from the second grade. At the mentioning of God's name, Maria Petrovna became very sarcastic, saying that all the prayers in the world wouldn't put food on the table, but if we were willing to pray to bat'ko (father) Stalin, we would see what would happen. It was an old trick, and none of us challenged her. We knew that if anyone said a word entreating Stalin, she would produce a roll of white bread. We felt insulted, as we discussed this matter after school.

When I came home, I asked Mother if hair ever grew on a palm of a hand. Mother thought it was an odd question, and said, "Of course not. Why do you ask?" I told her what had happened at school. "Just believe that soon we will return home, no matter what anybody says," Mother said with a conviction. "For the time being, learn all you can, so you won't be 'blind' like me."

As a child, Mother was wealthy, but becoming an orphan at a very early age, neither her aunts nor her stepfather, who was the administrator of her estate after her mother died, took any interest in her education as was fitting for the granddaughter of Bohatyrewicz. She remained illiterate, but her inborn intelligence and knowledge always amazed me.

"And when you get older, you will sort out in your head what is right and what is wrong," Mother added. After this conversation with Mother, I did my homework and went to take a place in a line for bread, so Father would not have to stand a long time when he came from work. It seems that we spent most of our time in lines for bread and soup. Bread and soup were not free. We had to buy them.

As the time went on, the hunger became so intense that we thought we would perish from it. Then one day, being fully aware that there was no food in the house, we asked Mother to give us something to eat. Tears of helplessness welled up in Mother's eyes, and she quickly turned her back on us and said in an even voice, "It is written that if God gives us this day, He will also provide for us."

After Mother had made this quote, an episode of long ago, concerning God, came to my mind. I was about six years old. Olesia, Antek and I were lying on the green bank of the Lachowiec, a river that began and emptied into the mighty River Prypeć. It was a warm and lazy afternoon in summer, and we were looking at the cloud formations in the sky. I said that I saw an eagle which was changing into a lion, and pointed my finger at it because they could not find it. To my complete surprise, Olesia and Antek slapped my hand. I didn't know how to take their assault on me. As a rule, we seldom fought between ourselves.

"Why did you hit me?" I asked, terribly hurt.

"Because the sky is where God lives, and you do not point a finger at God," they quickly replied. For my punishment they told me to bite my finger as hard as I could. I bit my finger until it hurt. Olesia and Antek inspected it and said that I was forgiven.

As I lay back on the lush green grass, I thought about this God who lives in the sky. All I wanted was to look into this god's eyes to see if he were still angry with me for having pointed my finger at him. Suddenly, I found myself somewhere "above," in a large room. I knew I was lying in the grass and yet I was at the same moment "above." Where I stood, it was murky and dark behind me. There was a space between this God and myself. He was sitting in a chair with a very high back which was carved all the way to the top. I had never seen such a chair. He wore a dark brown robe. He didn't say anything to me nor I to him. My main objective was to look into his eyes. Somehow I knew that eyes told the truth. I don't know how it had happened that I had been looking into his eyes without having made a step in his direction. His eyes were very kind, so kind that I felt that I could run up to him and sit on his lap. I knew that he was not angry at me. On this note, I found myself back on the riverbank next to Olesia and Antek. However, I did not tell them what I had just seen and I don't know why I didn't tell them.

The image of this kind God remained with me always. So when Mother said, "God will provide for us," I immediately thought of my God and that I had nothing to fear because He was looking after me. In my older years, I understood that the image I had of this kind God must have been Jesus, because I now realize that God is a spirit that cannot be seen.

It is true that Mother was a religious person, but she seldom quoted the Bible and never preached hell and brimstone. She said this only once, but it lasted me a lifetime.

To supplement our diet of bread and soup, Mother traded her linens for whatever she could get. On one occasion, Mother traded a brand new towel for a cup of flour, on another, a tablecloth for a small bucket of potatoes. Even Janka's pretty skirts were not spared. One Russian woman made two skirts out of Janka's one, and came to show them to us through the window.

We tried to survive the best way we could, but soon the hunger was taking its toll. It was a great shock to me when Krysia, my friend and schoolmate, suddenly died. Mother thought I should go and pay my condolences to the family. It was the first time that I saw a dead person. Krysia lay in a wooden box, made by her father. She was so still and white, and there was peace on her little, young face. If only they didn't put the coins on her eyes, which made her look sightless and strange, I would have thought that she was asleep. We buried her by the patch of wood that lay between the two camps.

As I was walking home from school one day, I decided to take a shortcut through these woods and look at Krysia's grave. To my astonishment, I saw food on her grave. Evidently her family shared their meager portions of food with her. The food looked fresh as though someone had just left it there, but I didn't touch it, despite my uncontrollable hunger. It was for the dead, I told myself. When I came home, I told Mother about it. Mother explained that this was an old pagan custom which some people still kept, "but we don't believe in it and don't practice it," Mother assured me.

After a long and harsh winter, suddenly there was spring. The snow began to melt, and I knew the summer, that "glorious summer," was on its way. The white northern nights had ended, and the forest burst into a green flame.

At the first sign of spring, Father and other Polish men approached the commandant and asked him for some land, so they could plant potatoes to carry us through the next winter; otherwise we would certainly perish. The commandant, being of Polish descent, allotted them some land where the forest was cut down, dividing it into small plots. These allotments were full of tree stumps.

After working hard all day, Father, Mother, and the rest of us went to clear our plot. With an axe borrowed from the Russians, Father cut and chopped at the roots of the stumps. Then he tied a rope around the stump and pulled with all his might, while we cut and shoved until the stump was out. Even little Marysia helped by picking small twigs and branches. We worked until midnight for several nights until the land was cleared. The commandant then gave each man some seed potatoes, and we planted them. About a month later, we had a new commandant.

It was already May, and the dirty, ugly snow was still on the ground in the camp, melting fast under the warm sun. I went outside to enjoy the sunshine, and I saw an old Russian woman coming down the wooden sidewalk. I stepped into the mud to let her pass. She stopped, and with a thin, wrinkled hand gently patted my head, and said, "Bless you my child, who still respects the old. Nowadays, the young demand that the old step aside for them." Then she pointed to a young man, who was talking to a group of boys, and whispered, "Tell your parents to watch what they say and do in front of him, because he is a 'red dog.' He is responsible for the disappearance of the old commandant." I didn't ask what she meant by the "red dog," but I knew that this man was an informer.

The spring was in full swing, and the world looked fresh and beautiful. The ground was covered with a carpet of green grass, dotted with a multitude of colorful wildflowers. One warm and sunny day we were on our way home from school, approaching the patch of wood. Antek bet me that I wouldn't find him and ran ahead. It was the first time that we had really played since we'd arrived there. I didn't have to look for him very long. I saw his bookbag sticking out from behind a tree, where he was hiding. I quietly walked up to him and said that it was my turn to hide.

As I ran off deeper into the forest, I discovered wild mushrooms, lots of them. Some were as big as a plate. I called out to Antek to come quickly. Seeing the mushrooms, he suggested that we pick some and surprise Mother. We collected a variety of sizes, mostly the large ones. We practically ran all the way home, our bags bouncing on our backs. Mother came home earlier than usual to take care of sick Marysia.

"Wait and see what we have found," we proudly told her and began to empty our bags. To our great disappointment, most of the mushrooms were crushed. Mother looked them over, picking out the smallest ones. She said that we shouldn't pick the biggest nor the smallest ones, but pick those in between, then carry them as we would carry eggs. Mother also asked if we still remembered which were the poisonous ones. Oh, yes, we remembered.

From the time we were old enough to walk, Mother used to take us with her whenever she went to pick mushrooms or berries in the forest near our village. She taught us well, always showing and reminding us which were poisonous ones, so we wouldn't forget.

The next morning, Mother gave us a small bag for the mushrooms. After school, we filled the bag and took care how we carried them. In the evening, when we could have fire in the stove, Mother cooked all of them so everyone could have as much as they wanted. We ate mushrooms as long as the season lasted.

Then Mother told us to look for the raspberry and blackberry bushes, if we still remembered what they looked like. We found them, but the berries were still green. When the berries were ripe, first we ate as much as we could, and started picking them, filling a basket and a pot. Mother sold or traded the berries for other food.

We, the children, had the most freedom of movement since we had to go to school in another camp; only adults never had the time to go into the forest to pick mushrooms, berries or nuts. With the help of Mother Nature, we survived the shortest seasons of spring, summer, and autumn.

During the warm months, we also managed to explore our camp. It was not like a concentration camp with barbed wire or towers. No, it was more like a settlement, yet not quite like a village. There were two water wells. One was at the top of the camp from which we drew water was at the top of the camp, and the other one was further down near the kolhoz, where a donkey walked around and around all day long, drawing water for the livestock and the people who lived close to it. On the east side there was a big building, where meetings were held. It was more or less a cultural center and a movie theater. Whenever there was a movie, I remember hiding under the seats because I didn't have the money to pay for a ticket. The Russian women even helped me by covering me or claiming me as their own child.

Most of the population were Russian pereseltsy, or people forcefully relocated due to some crimes they had committed, and more than a hundred of us (30 families), the Polish people who had committed no crime against Stalin or the Soviet Union, except that we lived in a capitalist country and were the enemies of the Revolution. And for that, Father and his family, like so many other Polish people, were sentenced to five years of hard labor. That is how long Stalin thought it would take to exterminate the Poles by starvation. Thus, my Father summarized Stalin's reasons for our deportation and annihilation.

To the north of the camp, there was a deep, dense forest where the people worked, cutting down trees and loading them on a train. Women did the debarking of the softer wood, such as birch or aspen. To the south, there were fields which belonged to the kolhoz, then open space, and beyond that, dense forests.

To the east lay a railroad to a town called Plisieck. In the middle of the camp, there was kholodnik, or a cooler, used to punish "criminals." The "criminal" received only bread and water once in 24 hours. Once, out of curiosity, Antek and I went to check this cooler out. It was just a hole in the ground and a guard standing nearby. We wanted to see what it was like inside, but the guard would not let us enter and chased us away. We heard from the Russians that whoever spent a day in the cooler was never the same when he came out.

One Sunday afternoon in summer, Father went to get some water from the well. He was gone a long time. My brother and I decided to investigate. The line was moving very slowly, and Father's patience was running out. He asked those in front of him why it was taking so long to get a bucket of water. The women told him that the well was getting dry, and that it took a long time for the water to accumulate to fill a bucket. Father told them to go and get their men, bring a flashlight and a pickaxe, if possible. When the men came, Father told them to lower him down into the well. Seeing him being lowered into the well, I was terribly afraid for him. Then I heard him digging. After a while he told the men up above to pull and empty the bucket which was full of rocks. This went on for about an hour or so.

In the meantime, the women stirred such a commotion that the commandant came and inquired what was going on. After a few more buckets of rocks, I heard Father say, "When I pull on a chain, lift me up." When they pulled him up, Father's boots and pants were wet. Otherwise, to my relief, he was alright.

Then the commandant walked up to Father and asked who authorized him to do what he had just done. Father replied that it was conscience and common decency to help these women, Polish and Russian alike, by digging a little deeper. "That's what authorized me," Father said with finality. The women began to thank Father for his good deed. Without a comment, the commandant wrote something on a piece of paper and handed it to Father. The note said: "For the humanitarian services I authorize you to buy a liter of milk and a pound of margarine."

As soon as we came home, Father went to the kolhoz to redeem the promissory note. It had been a long time since we'd tasted milk. The last time we had it was back home, in Poland. As for the margarine, its taste could not compare with our butter, which we made ourselves from fresh cream.

We then began to remember all the little things that made us happy back home: a taste of a carrot pulled fresh from the ground, or a tomato picked from a vine, or the new potatoes smothered in fresh butter and sprinkled with dill. On this note, Mother interrupted and asked Antek how tall were the potatoes. Antek answered that they were so tall, indicating the height of them by raising his hand about eight inches from the table. Mother thought that it was time to tend to them. That following evening, we went down to our "field" of potatoes and piled a lot of soil around each plant. When we harvested them, we were amazed at the size of these potatoes. They were as big as the Idaho baking ones.

One day after school Antek and I went to see where Olesia worked. He led the way, and I followed. We walked through railroad tracks and then through a dense forest, until we came to a clearing. Here, the women were debarking young birch trees. When we found Olesia, she was crying. Antek asked if someone was mean to her. All she had to do was to tell who, and he was ready to go find that person and beat him or her up!

"I can't fulfill my norm," Olesia replied, sobbing. "That means I can't have my full ration of bread." We asked her if she had any spare debarking knives. After showing us where they were, we began helping her. Even with our help, we could see that she would not be able to do it. Then Antek came up with an idea. He watched a foreman marking off those women who already fulfilled their norms, and told them to take a short break. The women walked away from their place of work and sat down under a tree. In the meantime, Antek began stealing debarked trees from their piles. He didn't think he was cheating these women. After all, the foreman already marked them off. With our help and a little bit of cheating, Olesia made her norm.

"Alexandra Iosifovna," the foreman addressed her formally, "You have done it, at last!" Olesia didn't say anything; only a faint smile appeared on her tired face. She was barely thirteen years old!

Then the foreman told Olesia that the kolhoz was asking the sovhoz for some people. He thought of transferring her, and would she like working for the kolhoz? She thought anything would be better than this heavy work of debarking trees. The foreman told her to report to the superintendent of the kolhoz. On the way to the camp, Olesia wondered what her new job would be like. Before we reached the camp, she said, "Thanks for the help."

The next day, Antek and I came straight home from school. We saw Olesia banging on the door, imploring Marysia to let her in. We could hear Marysia answering her, "Mama told me not to let anyone in." Olesia was telling her, "I am your sister, and I live here, so let me in." Then Antek knocked on the door and said, "It is us coming home from school." Immediately Marysia unlocked the door and let us all in.

When Mother came home, Olesia told her that this little squirt wouldn't let her in. Mother said she was sorry, but she forgot to tell Marysia to let Olesia in before she left for work. Mother explained to Olesia that before she went to the fields, she reminded Marysia to lock the door and not to let anyone in, except us when we came home from school. Olesia shouldn't have been angry with her because she was only doing what she was told.

To change the subject, Mother asked Olesia about her new job. Olesia described it down to the smallest detail. She had to take care of piglets, keep their sty clean, and cook a special diet for them, using milk, "kasha," potatoes, and other vegetables. In the end, she said that the pigs ate better than we did, because the supervisor wanted to have the best and fattest pigs in the region. When we heard this, we couldn't believe it, especially Mother, who began to name all the things she had already traded for an egg, a cup of milk, or potatoes, "and they give them to the pigs!" Mother was beside herself when she thought about the kind of food we actually bought. Soup with noodles or rotten cabbage or old, dried fish. I recall that many times we got plain broth with exactly five noodles in it. Mother grumbled and cursed everybody, beginning with Stalin and ending with a person who dished out the soup, saying, "How do they expect us to do a day's work on plain water?" It came to the point that Marysia refused to eat these noodles because, as she put it, "they remind me of worms." It became obvious to Mother that "they" were purposely starving us to death.

I looked at Mother, and for the first time I realized how thin she had become. Father, too, was thin and gaunt, with sunken cheeks. "How my parents have changed in such a short time," I thought. Then a vivid picture of my friend Krysia, who died of starvation, appeared before my eyes, just the way she was laid out in a coffin with coins over her eyes. After all, Mother was right. They wanted to starve us to death.

Summer, that "wonderful summer," was drawing to a close, and my dreams of having fun and basking in the sun were never realized, certainly not in the Soviet Union. There was always something to do: to go to school, pick mushrooms or berries, gather wood for fire, fetch water, and stand forever in a line for one thing or another. Besides, we were becoming listless due to the lack of food and couldn't spare the energy for play. We never attempted to make any close ties with the Russian children, nor they with us. We didn't know what kind of games they played, if they ever played. By the time we left the Soviet Union, I think, I had forgotten how to play.

To be truthful, I do not know or remember what kind of relationships the grown-ups had with the Russians. I only know this, that we were on friendly terms with our immediate neighbors, especially with the hunchbacked man, and a Russian woman Mother befriended, who had a cow. Very often on the way home from work, Mother carried an armful of green grass, which she took to the woman with the cow, and returned with a cup of milk for Marysia. Because of restrictions imposed from the beginning by the NKVD, we never socialized with others. Only we, the children, had a free reign of the camp, and visited other children's homes and they ours. It seemed to me that it was a well regimented camp, because after supper no one was allowed to be outside his or her home, unless there was an official meeting or a movie.

The safest way to communicate and pass any news to one another was during the supper time while standing in a line. Usually, the people began lining up long before the mess hall opened, and they had plenty of time to talk. I didn't want the summer to end, but little signs from my personal observation from when we still lived in the woods by the River Prypeć indicated that the winter was not far off. Soon the leaves began to turn yellow, orange, gold, and red, until the forests all around our camp were blazing with color, just as suddenly as they had burst into a green flame in the spring.

It was harvest time. We were still out of school, and the "kolhozniki," asked us to help with the produce which they were shredding and storing in the underground silos. It was a winter feed for the cattle. Our task was to pack it tight by jumping around. At first, it seemed like a lot of fun, but as the day wore on, it became hard work for which we didn't get anything in return.

I climbed out of this huge silo on the built-in ladder. On the way home, I took a little head of cabbage, thinking that the cows would not mind if I took it. After all, I worked for it. To my dismay, a guard saw me and shouted, "Drop it!" I took off running, and a guard chased me with a long gun in his hands. I dropped the cabbage when I turned a corner and hid behind a house to see what was going to happen next. When the guard saw my cabbage, he picked it up, looked around, and hid it under his coat. I was very angry with myself for dropping the cabbage, and with the guard for taking it. It was such a little head of cabbage which no one, not even the cows, would have missed, if it hadn't been for the guard, who took it for himself.

The next day, the commandant gathered all the school children and asked for a volunteer to take the pigs to a pea field. I was the first to volunteer, because I knew where the field was. As long as the pigs ate the peas, so did I. In the meantime, I was thinking of a way to take some peas home. At that time, I was wearing a loose shirt without a jacket. I made a belt out of the cornflowers and tied it around my waist. I began to stuff the peas inside my dress, distributing evenly around my body so there wouldn't be any bulges. From the same flowers as my belt, I also made a necklace and garland for my head. Then I took the pigs back to the kolhoz. Olesia met me and took over, saying that she would put the pigs into their sty. I could hardly wait to show Mother my treasure. I ran all the way home for the fear that a guard or NKVD may stop me and ask why I had suddenly become so fat.

When I came home, Mother looked at me and asked, "Are you going to someone's wedding dressed like this?" meaning the flowers. I stood in the middle of the room and untied my belt, letting the peas fall to the floor. Mother was surprised and pleased and gave me a big hug.

Soon Olesia came and brought two potatoes, which she had concealed in her mittens. From these fresh, wonderful vegetables, Mother made the best soup ever, even though she was not supposed to cook in our quarters.

Before we went back to school, Mother told us to go into the forest and look for a special type of mushroom. Mother described it as orange-red in color. In Polish they are called rydze, known in English and Latin as saffron milkcap or lactarius deliciousus, respectively. They were suitable for pickling. Mother managed to borrow a small barrel for these mushrooms, but alas, we ate them before the winter set in. Mother's only regret was that she didn't have enough containers to pickle more of these delicious mushrooms to carry us through the winter.

Our second winter in the Arctic region was harder on us than the first. For one thing, it seemed much colder, or was it because our clothes had worn thin? There were never any warm clothes in the store. A few months ago, Father had ordered shoes for Antek as his were worn out. When he went to get them, the shoes turned out to be "valonki," or felt boots, which were far too small for my brother. Father had to buy them after a saleslady marked them as "delivered." The boots fit me, and I wore them only to school.

Janka was transferred to another camp to work on a railroad, checking for defects in rails or ties. It was there that she was authorized to buy a "kufajka," or a cotton-stuffed jacket and pants.

The meager supply of our potatoes was diminishing fast. If we thought that we had been hungry last winter, it was nothing compared to this one. There were times when Antek and I licked salt, first with a finger, then we spread the salt on a table and licked it with our tongues until it tasted bitter. "Now let's go to our friend's house and ask for water so they will think that we had such a good meal which made us so thirsty," Antek said afterwards.

In order to survive, nothing was sacred. We stole whatever we could, but not from our own people, not so much myself, as my brother. Sometimes, Antek and a distant cousin Viktor Zuk from Dziatlowicze would go to the "stolovaya" and stage a fight, creating such a disturbance that a woman, who took the coupons, would leave her post to break up the fight. While the woman was giving my brother a good talking-to, Viktor would steal a few coupons from the box. Then the boys would apologize, make friends, and go away to take their place in a line for soup, using stolen coupons. They ate one portion in the mess hall and the second at home.

Olesia managed to survive by "tasting" the special diet she cooked for the piglets, and continued to bring home two potatoes as usual in her mittens. The rest of us had to do with whatever Mother could get in a trade. There were many stories about our fight for survival against hunger, cold, lice, sickness, and death in the Soviet Union.

One day, I went to help my friend Zosia with arithmetic and heard a woman sobbing in the next apartment. To my inquiry, Zosia replied, "Her youngest had died." Before we attacked the problems of arithmetic, Zosia told me how the poor woman had nothing else to trade for food, and that's why her baby died. A week or so later, there was another woman sobbing, and the sobs could be heard all over the camp. This time, the woman had found two of her children dead.

From then on, each time I heard a sobbing, whether in the daytime or at night, I knew that someone had died. The saddest time was when the little children watched one or both of their parents die. They just sat by their dead bodies, trying to wake them up. When I heard of this case, I cried for several days, thinking of those poor children who were younger than I. The commandant put these children in the Russian "d'etdom," or orphanage.

Soon more people had died, first the young, then the old, and those in between. Women, who had lost someone, began to curse and hurl obscenities at Stalin each time they saw his picture, and there were many of them posted all over the camp. They disregarded what might happen to them for such a crime. After they used up every possible curse and name-calling, these women would plead with him (Stalin), saying, "What have our children done to you or your country to deserve and justify such treatment?" What these women were saying was absolutely true;, we had done nothing to offend Stalin himself or his country. Yet, we were punished with a policy of ruthless extermination through hard work, starvation, and lack of medical care, precisely because we were Poles.

At school, our teachers never for one moment stopped sovietizing us. They read aloud beautiful heroic stories about the Komsomol, or the Komunistischeskii Soyuz Molodezhy (Young Communist League), and that our goal in life should be to become a komsomoletz (a young builder of communism). But first, we must be Pioneers, then Oktiabrists (Octoberists), and then, and only then, we could become komsomoltsy (plural of komsomoletz), and how glorious it would be to become one under Stalin, the greatest leader in the world.

At the mention of the name Stalin, none of us believed a word she read or said. The name was so hated among us that when our teacher left half a class after school, we not only punched out Stalin's eyes in a huge portrait but also those of Lenin. The next day both portraits were replaced, and no Polish children participated in the parade or celebrations of the Anniversary of the October Revolution. The teacher meant to punish us by denying us the chance to take part in the festivities. We were not hurt. On the contrary, we were glad that we didn't have to walk that far for nothing.

Christmas came almost unnoticed, if it were not for the seven baked potatoes Mother made for supper. Can you imagine, one whole potato per person in addition to everyday soup and bread.? Unthinkable! Unless, of course, it was a very special occasion. It was Christmas! Father said a prayer, ending with words: "If God is willing, next year we will be back in Łunin." After supper we sang one or two carols, then went to sleep.

A few days before the New Year, 1941, Maria Petrovna, our teacher, taught us a couple of songs about the "yolka" – a Christmas tree. One of them I still remember. She told us to come to school on the New Year's Day to take part in a little program and to celebrate the "yolka." Only "yolka" brings gifts for the children on the New Year's Day. We came and found "yolka" decorated like a Christmas tree in front of our classroom. We sang the songs Maria Petrovna had taught us, and watched a few sketches performed by other children. Afterwards, she pulled out a big box from under the "yolka" and opened it. The box was full of white bread rolls. On the way out, she gave a roll to each one of us. Before we left the schoolyard, Antek ate his in a few bites, then asked if I would share mine with him. I told him that I was saving a piece for Marysia, so she could know what white bread tastes like. So far, she had eaten only the black bread which we bought in the store.

To help us celebrate the New Year, Father was allotted a double ration of bread and half a pound of sugar. Mother sprinkled some on slices of bread and gave them to us. Nothing tasted as good as this bread with sugar. It was quite a treat by the Russian standards in this remote area.

We continued to live day to day. Today was no different than yesterday, and tomorrow was still far away. Besides, hunger never allowed us to think about tomorrow. Once Mother told me, "It is most important that you live through today." On other occasions, she would tell me that soon, all this would be over and we would return to our country – Polesie, our home, fields, forests, and to that huge pear tree in our backyard. Remembering home, I would add that there were apple, plum, and other trees in our yard with a fence around them to keep the pigs and cows out. Mother always encouraged me to remember not only our home but also the people, especially close relatives, and where they lived.

Sometimes, Father would add something, or tell a story, like the one when his father went hunting in the forest and met a stranger. According to my Father, my grandfather was deep in the ancient forest when night overtook him. He built a fire, took a piece of salted pork and bread out of his pouch and began to cook it over the flames. Suddenly, out of nowhere, a stranger appeared and sat down by the fire. The stranger, too, had a piece of bread and pork, and like my grandfather, was cooking it over the fire. My grandfather thought that there was something unusual about this man. For one thing, he was not dressed like a hunter, nor had he asked permission to sit down. In the meantime, grandfather kept an eye on a thick, well-burning branch and on the stranger. Then, taking a pinch of incense from his pocket, which he always carried with him whenever he went hunting, he sprinkled it over the fire. While the incense was burning, grandfather noticed that instead of pork, the stranger had a frog on the end of his stick, and that he had a piece of dry bark for what grandfather thought to be bread. Neither the stranger nor his face appeared to be human, and that's when grandfather grabbed the burning branch and —"wham!"— hit him over the head. The stranger immediately disappeared, and only hair-raising laughter echoed through the woods. I do not know if it really happened, because every hunter carried a bottle of vodka with him. Besides, the story took my mind off the hunger. Mother and Father told us many stories as we sat by the fire on the cold winter nights, and I remember most of them.

Remembering or telling stories helped to pass the time away, but most importantly, it took our minds off the terrible hunger which blocked the awareness of other things which were going on around us, especially for me. At that time, the only thing on my mind was bread, to eat it until I was full!

There were many evenings when we were too tired to talk or tell stories, and we went to bed early. Before falling asleep I would think of something pleasant in order to forget the gnawing hunger, cold, and all the misery of life which we were forced to endure. I desperately wanted to go home.

Overcome by the intense tęsknota (longing) for home, I often thought about the ranger's station, gajówka, where I had spent the happiest years of my early childhood, and where my baby sister Marysia was born in 1937. The ranger's station was the place of my childhood and deeply impressed in my memory, indelible by distance or experiences. Gajówka belonged to the estate of Prince Drucki-Lubecki. There, Father worked as a forester. Besides his usual duties, Father issued permits to local people to mow the meadows for themselves and the estate. On the nearby meadows, Father mowed the grass for our livestock. When Mother raked the hay, I often heard her sing.

Those were the years of awe and wonder, magic and mystery, beauty and splendor that Mother Nature so gratuitously bestowed on the land. It was here that I became aware of my environment, like discovering the tree for the first time, which grew by the front door, wondering how it got there so fully grown. Or watching the buds burst open into leaves as if by magic. But the greatest mystery to me were flowers, especially the sweet-smelling ones. I used to take them apart petal by petal, looking for that tiny bottle of perfume, the kind Janka had, and never finding it. This place, in the words of the Polish poet Adam Mickiewicz,: "will always remain sacred and pure like the first love." Ggajówka was burned down by the Soviets in 1940, soon after our deportation. This is how I remember my beloved gajówka.

On a slight rise in the otherwise flat terrain stood the forest ranger's house on the left bank of the river Lachowiec. It was a big house, built of logs, with a thatched roof. The windows had white shutters and four white columns, which gave the house style and elegance. A wooden fence separated the house from the stables and other buildings. Along this fence, yellow acacia grew, sprinkling its golden dust onto the ground. Huge oaks shaded and cooled the house on the hot summer days. About fifty yards from the house, there was a huge hangar in which a big motorboat hung, suspended from the ceiling on heavy chains. In this boat, Olesia, Antek, and I took imaginary trips around the world, sailing along the rivers (we didn't know about the Seven Seas at that time). Not all our trips were imaginary. We explored the surrounding area on foot, within certain limits imposed by Father, who warned us about wild boars, wolves, and bears, and that we must never stray too far from home.

We were the intrepid travelers or hunters in the forest. On one particular day, Olesia, Antek, and I were not too far from home in an area with many thick bushes. Antek asked, "What would you do if a wild boar appeared?" Olesia immediately said, "I'd hide in the thickest bush." I said, "I'd climb the highest tree." Antek said, "I'd run home and get Father." As fate would have it, unbeknownst to us, Janka was walking nearby and overheard our conversation. Janka then decided to scare us. She put a black scarf over her head and rustled some bushes, making sure we'd see her black scarf. When we saw something black, we screamed. True to our words, Olesia hid herself in a thick bush. I was climbing a tree, and Antek started to run home yelling, "Tata! Tata!" (Father! Father!). Janka then quickly showed herself and said, "Don't be afraid; it is I!" She knew that Father was home at this time, and probably would come with his guns. So much for our undaunted courage.

Despite the fright Janka gave us, we continued to roam through the forest. We knew where the rivers Brobryk and Lachowiec emptied into the mighty Prypeć, and that beyond the Bobryk was another ranger's station called Domalka, where foresters Mr. Korzeniewski and Mr. Karol Mieljaniec lived with their families. The Korzeniewskis had a little girl who crawled into an open fire and burned her foot so badly that she was maimed for life. Karol's wife was Marysia's godmother. These families were also deported at the same time as we were.

In the opposite direction was a small village, Stachow, where Antek went to school. The rest were forests, laced with creeks and dotted with lakes. At these lakes, Father hunted for wild ducks with Commander Witold Zajączkowski or with Prince Drucki-Lubecki and his party.

One summer's day, we decided to go fishing. Antek pulled out a handful of hair from the horse's tail, Olesia cut three pliant rods from a willow tree, and I dug up worms. Since we couldn't find any hooks, we just tied the worm at the end of our "lines," and watched the fish eat it in the translucent waters of the Lachowiec. We fished like this for hours, until we became hungry and went to pick some berries. Oh, those were the good days, filled with laughter and happiness, and we seldom got ourselves into trouble.

And even if we did, it was unintentional, like tasting vodka for the first time.

Father always kept a bottle of vodka in the cupboard. In this particular bottle was very little vodka, maybe a shot, and we wanted to know what it tasted like. By the time we'd all had a sip, the bottle was empty. In the evening Father asked who had drunk the vodka.

"Father, we didn't drink the vodka. We only tasted it," I said. Mother quietly said to him, "You cannot punish the children for having tasted the stuff." Father then began to laugh and asked us if we liked it.

"No, we did not like it at all," all three of us replied in unison.

In winter, we built snowmen and skated on the frozen river Lachowiec. When the snow and ice began to melt in the spring, the river flooded the meadow and surrounding area up to the forest and even beyond. The water virtually came up to our doorstep, and Father kept a boat close to the house to get to the stables to feed the cattle and horses. As the water started to recede, the storks were the first to arrive, filling the air with their clacking. These storks were our meteorologists. In the evenings, when they were in their nest, we would ask, "Stork, stork, cast a lot, will tomorrow be rainy or hot?" If the storks were standing only on one leg, it meant good weather.

The world was wonderful when the waters receded. The riverbank became like a bright yellow carpet, covered by marsh marigolds, and thousands of little flowers looked towards the warm sun. The tall oaks unfurled their green leaves, and the forest glowed with a green flame, shimmering in the breeze. The air was fresh and clean, full of birds and clacking of returning storks. In the meadow the frogs croaked their serenades, and the busy swallows were building their nests under the eaves of the hangar where the motorboat hung.

In early autumn Prince Drucki-Lubecki came to hunt wild boars and ducks. I do not remember what he looked like, because I was a little girl. I do remember, however, that there were a lot of people milling around gajówka when the Prince was present.

At the ranger's station, the most frequent guest was Commander Witold Zajączkowski, the commanding officer of the Prypet River Flotilla. In these parts he was known as the "Prince of

Polesie." I remember him very well. Every time he arrived, he called me and taught me Polish and Russian poems. For reciting them, I was rewarded with a bag of candy wrapped in pretty, colorful wrappers. He told me that when he came again I should wait for him on the riverbank. And so I waited. One day he saw Antek and me bathing in the river naked, so the next time he brought us swimming trunks, similar to his own and taught us to swim.

The next time I heard the Commander's motorboat, I didn't want to see him, and I hid myself in a barrel which was by the fence. When the Commander arrived, he called. I didn't answer. As he was walking to the house, he saw me and asked what I was doing in the barrel. I said that I was mad at him. The Commander pulled me out, held me for a little while, and asked, "What have I done to make you so angry that you would hide from me?" I told him that three times in a row, he brought me candy wrapped in papers with only crab pictures on them. Then he asked what kind of candy I would like. I said that I would like for each piece to be wrapped in a different paper because I was collecting the candy papers and making skirts out of them for my paper dolls. Now he had a smile on his face as he put me down. True to his word, in the next bag each piece was wrapped in a different and beautiful paper.

Commander Zajączkowski had a great respect for Mother and in his own way helped to minimize Mother's problems and worries about us children. When Janka did not return home on time from town, he sent his motorboat to look for her. The sailors found Janka sitting on a bridge crying, because she was too tired to walk home. Also, he came when my sister Marysia was born. In his own professional manner, he walked into the house, took the baby from Mother, placed her on the table and looked at her tiny hands and feet, and all over. After the inspection he handed the baby to Mother and said that she had a lovely daughter. I eagerly watched his every action with wonder. Very often he discussed our education with Mother, saying that he would ensure that the girls would have the best education, mentioning towns like Pinsk, Wilno, and Warsaw. But this was the year 1937.

The last time I saw the Commander was in 1939. He arrived in his small airplane and landed on the meadow. It was the first time I had seen a plane, and I asked him to take me up and fly above the river Prypeć. He made all kinds of excuses, then, looking at me with his intense eyes, he said that one day soon we would fly over the marshlands. In the meantime he went to see Father, took some documents and flew away. After that, I never saw him again. Years later, in England, I learned that he had died in Canada, not knowing that his dreams for me had come true – I received my B.A. degree 40 years later in America.

Another frequent visitor at gajówka was Mrs. Sultanowa from Wilno. Whenever Mrs. Sultanowa came to hunt, there was much ado at the gajówka. Besides Father, other rangers showed up with information about the best places for hunting. I overheard some rangers saying that Mrs. Sultanowa was a good hunter, and never missed her target when shooting.

Once, during one of these hunting outings, Commander Zajączkowski was at gajówka with several sailors and his hunting dogs before Mrs. Sultanowa arrived. That morning, Father and Commander Zajączkowski went out to scout for the best place for hunting. While I was still in the house, I heard a shot. I ran out to see who was shooting and saw a sailor with a gun and a dead sparrow. I buried the sparrow, thinking what would happen to the babies if the sparrow was a mama sparrow. I wanted to say this to the sailor, when one of the Commander's dogs, Rex, started to bark. The sailor hit the dog with his gun, and the gun broke, and Rex howled in pain.

The next morning, the Commander had all the sailors standing in a row, at attention. The Commander was walking back and forth in front of them when I was passing by on my way to the river. I heard the Commander ask the sailors who had broken the gun. I walked up, tugged the Commander's sleeve, and pointed at the sailor, saying, "He hit Rex and the gun broke, and Rex cried." Having said this, I continued about my business, whatever it was. Several times the Commander came to gajówka with sailors, but I never saw that sailor who broke the gun again.

Another event that stands out in my memory from gajówka involves Janka and a bull. It was getting cold outside. Janka put on a warm jacket and a wide leather belt and went out. After a while, I wanted to check the weather myself. I looked towards a meadow where cattle were grazing, not far from the house. To my horror, I saw a bull running around the meadow with Janka on his horns. The tips of both huge horns were under Janka's belt on her backside. I screamed! Father came out and followed where I was looking. Father told me to go into the house, and then he ran towards the meadow to help Janka. Sitting in the house, I tried to imagine how frightened Janka must have been, and that brought tears to my eyes. Finally, Father and Janka came in. Both of them seemed physically fine, only Janka appeared to be too tired to talk and went straight to bed. I did not pay attention to Father as he sat at the table and began to write something. To this day, I still don't know how Janka got on the bull's horns or how Father saved Janka from the bull!

Now, my gajówka is far away. The War and deportation to Siberia separated me from it forever. But when I close my eyes, I see everything as if it were yesterday. I see my older sister Olesia returning from the forest, adorned with red kalina berries on her head, around the neck, and holding bunches high up above her shoulders, looking like a beautiful wood nymph.

Oh, to be there once again during spring, summer, autumn, and winter. Once again to hear the chirruping of birds, sleep on the fresh-smelling hay in the barn, pick wild flowers, or lie on the green grass and look at the river and the clouds in the sky.

But gajówka is no more. The Soviets burnt it down after our departure in 1940 – that's what our aunt wrote when we were in Siberia. Only my memories remain. Sometimes I wonder who walks in the woods where my Father walked, who sings in the fields where my Mother sang? Who gathers red berries and adorns herself as my sister Olesia did? These are only a few memories from the past which I summoned to mind to escape the harsh reality of privation. It is true that only a memory remains, but for me gajówka is just as unforgettable as are Commander Zajączkowski and Mrs. Sultanowa. This was a free, happy, and active world, and for me it still remains so.

*

The cold, long months of winter had passed, and the warm spring followed. Once again the Polish people approached the commandant and asked for permission to plant potatoes on the lots we had cleared the previous spring. Without explanation, the commandant categorically refused. Needless to say, his refusal was a hard blow to our morale and courage.

After a while, a sort of depression took hold of us, with an awful feeling of the world's indifference, not only to our plight, but to our very existence. It seemed that we were the forgotten people, without hope and no one to turn to.

That same day, Antek and other boys staged a protest against the commandant's decision about planting potatoes. They sat opposite his office and wrote witty but derogatory notes, shooting them in with slingshots through an open window. Evidently the commandant chose to ignore the boys and their notes, since neither he nor anyone else came out to talk to them. The boys sat there for a long time. When I came out to ask Antek what they were doing, he told me to get lost and not to interfere in their business, adding, "We are dealing with a serious matter, so scram!"

Later in the afternoon, the boys, disappointed and frustrated, climbed on the roof of the meeting hall and let all the shingles fall to the ground, on the side that could not be seen from the office. I must admit that the old building looked sort of strange without half of the roof when I saw it just as the boys were coming down. Antek made me swear not to tell Father that he was the one who had instigated the whole operation.

That evening after work, the commandant called in all the fathers of the boys who were involved in this "hooliganism." He told them to put the shingles back. They had to do it in their own time; otherwise, they would have to go to prison.

I could see that Antek was worried after Father told him what the commandant had said. But instead of punishing my brother, Father said, "I don't object to your protesting, only do it in such a way that it does not involve me." Antek let out a big sigh of relief and promised never to do it again. The next evening, the fathers put all the shingles back on the roof.

In the following months, nothing extraordinary happened in our struggle for survival. Occasionally, one of us would come down with a cold or the "flu." If we had something else, we attributed it to influenza because there was no doctor, only a "feldsher," a doctor's assistant, who came once a month to our camp. He was an old man with gray hair, softly spoken, and he gave me some castor oil to quieten down the growling in my stomach. For the rest of the day and late into the night, I spent most of my time in the latrine. The next morning Mother told me to stay in bed, but I insisted on going to school so I wouldn't be deprived of my slice of bread. Besides, the feldsher did not give me a written excuse because I had no fever. Only those who had a fever were excused from school or work.

It was almost the end of June, and I was sitting at the table writing the events of the day in my so-called "diary," when the hunchback, our neighbor from across the hall, came over to talk to Father. They were sitting by the warm stove, although the fire had gone out; only glowing embers remained. Nevertheless, they chose to sit there and talk about the war, something about Hitler attacking Russia. Being preoccupied with my own thoughts, I did not pay much attention to their conversation. When I stopped writing, I heard Father say, "Perhaps it is a way for us to get out of here... to be free again." As the man was leaving, he said to Father, "When you are free, and I hope you will be, remember us." I was thinking, "Why is it so important to him that we should remember them?" After locking the door behind our guest, Mother asked, "Is it really possible for us to be free again?" Father replied that anything was possible, "Only time will tell."

For the next few days, the people, standing in the lines for bread and soup, talked about nothing else but the German-Russian war. The main topics of their conversation were Stalin and Hitler, who in 1939 were partners in the partition of Poland, and now they were fighting! I had stood listening for nearly an hour when Antek came to relieve me. On the way home, I was troubled by what I had heard. All this time I thought that it was the Soviet soldiers who deported us, but now the whole blame fell on Stalin and Hitler for starting the war. I wished I could talk to my brother now. After all, he was in the third grade and knew much more than I did. I wanted to know why there was war to begin with, why we were deported from our homes, and why Hitler attacked Russia.

When I came home, Mother was still at work and only Marysia was home. Marysia wanted me to read something for her. I took a book which I had checked out at the school library and began to read a story about a goat and her two little kids. It was a sad story in which the mother goat was shot by a hunter, while the two kids were left waiting for their mother to return. In the end we both sat and cried, and I forgot the talk I had heard earlier and all of the "why's."

Sometime in September, a Russian woman came up to Mother and asked if she could buy some berries from her. Someone told her that we had picked some. Since Mother couldn't invite her in, she brought the berries out. The woman bought all we had left. Before leaving, she asked Mother if she knew of a young girl who would watch her two small children, while she and her husband dug up their potatoes. Mother called me over and asked the woman if I would do. She looked me over and said, "She will do fine."

At first I was puzzled and looked questioningly at Mother, who told me to go with this woman to look after her children. "But I don't know anything about the children," I said. "I will tell you what you need to know," the woman said with a smile. "While you get your things together and say goodbye to your mother, I will go to the commandant to tell him that you are going with me."

Mother put a few of my things into a sack, just a change of clothes and some underwear, and told me that looking after children wouldn't be so bad. Besides, the woman said, "You can eat all the food you want!"

I really did not want to go, but I knew that Mother meant well. We were barely surviving, and Mother didn't want to see me perish from hunger. As we were just about to leave, Mother kissed me and said that if I didn't like the woman, I could always come home.

The woman's name was Larisa Andreievna, and she lived about two kilometers east of our camp, not far from the railroad. As we came close to where she lived, I saw several buildings with tall chimneys. I asked Larisa if she lived in one of those buildings. Larisa smiled and said that she lived in a small house, just to the right. Then she told me that a few years back, coke had been made in those buildings. Since there was no longer need for the coke made from wood, the whole operation was abandoned. Now the buildings stood idle.

The sun was setting when we came to the place where she lived. I saw huge piles of coal in the yard, and the smoke rising straight up from the chimney of a small house. Larisa led the way, and I followed. She opened the door, and we entered into a small room lit by two windows. At one end, close to the kitchen, there was a table. At the other end, there was a crib with a baby in it, a cot, and a double bed. Larisa introduced me to her husband, Alexander Nikolaievich, whom she called Sasha. He was a pleasant-looking man with dark hair and blue eyes. Then she led me to the crib to say "hello" to a two-year-old Masha. At the first glance at Masha, I knew that there was something wrong with her. She didn't behave like a two-year-old should; she just lay in her crib without moving around. Larisa told me never to pick Masha up because she didn't crawl or walk yet. The four-year-old Nina was a quiet child; she sat on her cot and played with a doll. They were strange children. During the two weeks I stayed with them, they seldom cried.

After I became acquainted with the children, Sasha surprised Larisa by setting the table and serving supper. I don't exactly remember what we had, but there was so much food that it would have fed my family for a week. Besides the potatoes and meat, there was also a whole loaf of white bread and real butter! For the first time since we were brought to Russia, I went to bed without feeling hungry.

Larisa gave me two blankets and a pillow, and I slept on the dirt floor opposite the front door. After two nights, I developed a bladder infection, which caused a lot of embarrassment to me; I do not remember ever wetting my bed until then. Larisa noticed it too, and gave her husband a funny look. I felt terribly ashamed of myself, but there was nothing I could do about it then, but to take my blankets and hang them out to dry. That night, as I went to sleep, Larisa covered me with another blanket. After a while my problem disappeared.

While I stayed with Larisa and Sasha, my duties were simple. Before going to dig the potatoes, Larisa fed the children and prepared their lunch. She told me to feed them again at twelve noon. I didn't know how to tell the time and told her so. There was a clock on the wall, and Larisa explained, "When both hands are on number twelve, that's the time to feed the children." From then on, I thought that when both hands of the clock were on a certain number like ten, to me it meant exactly ten o'clock and so on.

At exactly twelve o'clock, I gave Nina her lunch at the table and spoon-fed little Masha, first propping her up with pillows since I was not allowed to take her out of the crib. After lunch, I put them down for a nap. Once they were asleep, I used to go outside to look around. First of all, I wanted to see the buildings with tall chimneys. They were nothing more than very long, very narrow ovens where the coke was made. I also noticed that they had chickens and a goat. The goat was very friendly, and I played with her while the children slept.

One afternoon while the children were sleeping I was outside, as usual. It was sunny and warm and very quiet. I was only within a few yards from the house when I saw a man coming from the direction of our camp. As he came closer, I recognized him as a friend of the family of long ago. I thought it was strange that he did not recognize me at first glance, and he greeted me as if he didn't know me. He walked around the place for a few minutes, as though looking for something, then he came up to me and asked for an axe and a saw. I told him that the people who lived in this house used neither axe nor saw to cut wood. "They use coal," I said pointing to the piles of coal in the yard. He looked at me and said, "I know who you are. You are Józef's daughter," and he went out into the forest without saying goodbye.

I was inside the house, checking on the girls, when I heard a fierce barking of dogs. I ran outside to see what was going on. The NKVD man and the guards with the bloodhounds were almost in the yard when they saw me. They asked if I had seen anyone in the last half hour or so.

"Only a man," I replied, "who wanted an axe and a saw."

"Did he harm you in any way?" they asked.

"No. He did not," I answered.

"Do you know which direction he went?" they asked again.

"Right through this clearing," I said, pointing in the direction of the forest where the man had disappeared. They took off running, following the bloodhounds in the direction I pointed. I stood and watched until they disappeared into the forest.

The next day, Sasha and Larisa came home earlier than usual. Sasha gave Larisa some papers and told her to deliver them to the commandant of the "Settlement 22," our camp. Larisa thought that it would be nice for me to visit with my family and took me along.

On the way to our Camp 22, I asked Larisa, "How come you have so much food, white bread, butter, milk and meat, while we have none of these things, except black bread and whatever they cook in the stolovaya? Larisa said that her husband was a member of the "Party," which gave him certain privileges. He could buy all they needed in a special store in a small town not far from there. I glanced at Larisa and caught a smile on her lips out of the corner of my eye. I seldom looked fully into Larisa's eyes. There was something about them that disturbed me, and I avoided looking at her as much as possible. Perhaps this explains why I cannot recall any of her facial features. I only remember her as a tall, big-boned woman, who always wore drab clothes. Larisa was kind to me, even if she didn't believe me when I told her that it was a cat that ate the cream, not I.

We walked on for a while in silence, then Larisa asked me to tell her something about our life in Poland. I told her all I knew, and how happy we were until the Red Army entered our village and deported us. Also, I told her how much I missed my home, and how I wished to go back. Larisa said only one word, "Privykniesh!" (You will get used to it!). I did not tell her that I thought it was impossible to get used to the constant hunger and cold. During our conversation, I didn't notice how quickly the time had gone by. We were near our house when Larisa said that she would go on to the commandant's office, while I visited with my family. She would knock on the window as a sign that it was time for us to return.

I was very happy to see Mother and Marysia, who were home at the time when I came in. After a warm greeting, which I received from both of them, Mother asked if I had enough food to eat as the woman promised. But by just looking at me, Mother knew that everything was all right with me. To Mother, the main thing was that I was well. She wanted to offer me something to eat, and was very apologetic because there was nothing she could give me. I told Mother I was not hungry and it was my turn to apologize. I should have asked Larisa if I could at least bring them some bread.

Afterwards, Mother began to tell the latest news. Our friend of long ago had gone insane, and the guards were still looking for him. I told Mother that only yesterday he had come by, asking if I would look into the attic and tell him what was up there. Of course I hadn't looked, as I could not find a ladder. I thought that they had found him by then. Mother instructed me to keep the door locked when I was alone.

"You never know what people like that might do."

About half an hour later, there was a knock on the window. I said goodbye to Mother and Marysia and left with Larisa.

On Sunday morning, Sasha took the wagon and drove off somewhere. Larisa heated a lot of water, bathed the girls, then told me to get in so she could wash my hair. There was no such thing as shampoo, and Larisa used plain soap, the kind she washed her laundry with. Washed and clean, Larisa, little Nina, and I went to look for eggs. By sheer accident, Larisa discovered that one of the hens had laid eggs at the end of the oven. She called me and asked if I would crawl in there and collect the eggs. Being a big woman, Larisa couldn't do it herself. The oven was too narrow, so I said I would try. Larisa went into the house and came out with an old dress and a scarf. I put on her dress, and she tied the scarf on my head, "so as not to dirty your beautiful blond hair." She gave me a basket and said, "Once you have collected all the eggs, don't try to turn around, just back out, or you might get stuck." I wished she hadn't said anything about getting stuck, because that's what I was thinking while crawling. For many years afterwards, I had dreams, always finding myself in dark and narrow places, struggling to get out. But at the end of my dreams, I always managed to come out into the bright light.

In the afternoon Sasha returned with a cart full of fresh, white bread. The weather was changing so Larisa and I helped Sasha bring the bread inside. He stacked it against one wall all the way to the ceiling. I wondered what they were going to do with so much bread.

On the next day, after we had eaten our supper, there was a lot of commotion going on in the yard. Sasha didn't seem to be surprised, as he said, "Ah, here they are."

We went outside, and I saw the Polish men from our camp and a few guards sitting on the wagons drawn by the horses. Sasha greeted them and explained why they were brought here. The men were to go the meadows in the forest and mow the grass for the fodder. For this work each man would receive a loaf of bread. To the hungry men, this was like a gift from heaven. Sasha motioned to the guards to come, and they began to load the bread on the wagons. In the meantime, Sasha brought out his own wagon and told us to get in. The children and I sat in the back, while Larisa sat beside Sasha, who led the way through the forest into the meadows.

At the first meadow, Sasha divided the men into two groups. To one group, he gave scythes and told them to start mowing, leaving one guard and a wagon with the bread. The second group he led to another meadow, which was bigger and grander than the first one.

Larisa spread a blanket on the edge of the forest and put the girls on it. I took a walk along the meadow, then came back and sat down by the girls and watched the men at work.

It was already dark when the men finished mowing. Sasha told the guards to give each man two loaves of bread. Just then, the full moon appeared in the sky and lit the way home. Before we left, Sasha told the men to come back the next week to gather the hay, and again they would be paid with bread.

The following Friday, Sasha and Larisa were late. The sun had gone down, and it was dark in the house. Since I was not allowed to touch or light the kerosene lamp by myself, I decided to light a fire in the stove. Once the fire was blazing, I put a lot of coke into the stove, not realizing the heating properties of coke. Soon the whole stove was red, and I thought I would burn the house down. I told Nina to sit on her bed and stay out of my way.

First, I opened the door wide, took a shovel and began to take the coke out. Very carefully I carried the red-hot coals across the room and dumped them into a mud puddle outside. I took most of the coke out, and the stove turned black again. Then I put the kettle on. The water was about to boil when Sasha and Larisa arrived, bringing with them the potatoes they had dug up during the two weeks I was with them. Larisa was pleased that there was hot water in the house, and immediately made some tea. She used the rest of the water to wash up, then she asked me to put on some more water for Sasha. When he came in, we were drinking tea. Larisa poured a cup for him. While we were still sitting at the table, Larisa told me that it was my last night with them. She said that I had done a good job taking care of the children.

The next morning, after breakfast, I put all my belongings into the sack Mother had given me and said goodbye to the children,

Sasha, and Larisa. As I was walking out of the door, Larisa gave me some bread for the road. I thanked her and left.

CHAPTER 5
Amnesty?

When I came home, everybody was at work. I gave Marysia the bread, and she, poor thing, devoured it in a minute she was so hungry. Soon Antek came in and shouted excitedly "We are free! Last night the commandant announced it at the meeting. There was a lot of rejoicing, and we sang Jeszcze Polska nie zginłea, the Polish national anthem."

"Does this mean we can go home?" I asked him.

"Oh, no! Not yet," Antek began to explain., "First Father has to get udostovierenia (documents), then we have to go south to meet the Polish army."

"After we meet the Army, then can we go home?" I asked again.

"That I cannot say. This is all I know," replied Antek.

"We are free! We are free!" cried the old and the young. The effect of the amnesty was tremendous. It not only boosted the morale of the people, but changed them from slaves to free human beings. The change was instantaneous; they no longer performed the work beyond their strength. Father and other men quit the backbreaking work in the forest. Women visited in each other's homes, which had been forbidden until then.

Mrs. Wolinska, with her goiter as big as a watermelon, and Mrs. Z., whose teeth were so loose that I thought they would fall out each time she opened her mouth, came to see Mother for the first time in almost two years. They looked over our two-room "apartment" and admired Mother's "wallpaper." Mother had had a good idea. With my paints from school, Mother painted colorful flowers on old newspapers and pasted them on the walls to hide the revolting remains of bedbugs left by the previous occupants. While they discussed Mother's ingenuity, Mother used a few of her precious tealeaves and offered them some tea.

I thought that any day now we would be going home, but nothing was happening, not even one word about going back. Finally, I asked Father, "When are we going home? You said many times that when we are free, we will go home."

"You can't go home just like that," Father replied, snapping his fingers. "First, we must have the necessary papers, some kind of identification, saying who we are. Then we have to wait for a special train which will take us south, and perhaps then we will go home."

Naturally, I was very disappointed. A week after the amnesty, nothing seemed to have changed. The hunger, the lines, and the scarcity of warm clothing and food were still the same.

When Father received our identification papers, we moved to the Camp 24. There he worked as a slaughter man. This was the same camp where Antek and I went to school. The house we lived in had two rooms and an attached bathroom with a hole in the floor and a drawer underneath. Inside the house, there were three beds, a table, and four chairs. Also, there was a typical Russian brick stove, only squared off, and one could lie on top of it. As soon as we moved in, Antek and I climbed up to the top of the stove, but decided never to sleep there because the cockroaches lived there.

The house stood on a hill, more or less fifty meters from the railroad. Downhill, there were the "stolovaya," mess hall, water well, and the slaughterhouse where Father worked. Below these establishments lived the Russian "peresieltsy" and Polish deportees. The rest was forest and more forest.

One day, out of the forest came heavily guarded prisoners, just from the other side of the railroad. Antek and I ran up to them to have a better look at these prisoners. At first, I noticed that the guards had long guns (rifles) in their hands. There were about six of them, one in front, one at the back, and two on each side of the column. In the middle were the prisoners, chained one to another. The prisoners wore long coats with patches all over them. One in the middle had no shoes, only rags were wrapped around his feet.

We shouted, "Where are you from and where are you going?" The one with no shoes looked at me. I shouted, "What is your name?" But before any of them could answer, one of the side guards pointed his gun at us and said, "I will shoot if you don't go away," swearing terribly under his breath, but loud enough so we could hear. As we watched from a distance, the lead guard with a different gun (machine gun) slung over his shoulder, led them along the railroad for a while, then turned right, and the whole column disappeared into the forest.

After the so-called "amnesty," the school was closed to all Polish children. There was never any time for us to be just plain, ordinary kids and play games with other children, like we used to back in Łunin. The never-ending need for water and firewood occupied most of our time. When my turn came to bring a bucket of water, I usually spilled most of it by the time I reached home, and had to make several trips down and up the hill. This is the reason why I remember so vividly where we lived in the Camp 24. The rest of the time we searched for firewood outside the camp.

Now that Father was a slaughter man, the opportunity presented itself to store some tallow and lard for the trip south, which was sure to come someday. First, Father brought two bladders, one from a steer, and the other from a hog. I remember Mother cleaning them with ashes until they were as thin as balloons. Then she blew the bladders up and hung them to dry. While skinning the slaughtered animals, Father would cut a small piece of fat, hide it inside his coat, and bring it home. Mother would melt it during the night, and pour the drippings into one of the bladders. After a while, it became impossible for Father to bring home any more fat because he was searched by a guard who watched him. Since he could no longer do it, Father would tell us in the morning what time to come by where he worked so he could give the fat to us. Father always skinned the animals outside. Antek and I used to make a game of it. Whenever we were close to Father, Antek would push me and tell me to fall down. Pretending to be hurt, I would run to Father, crying loudly that Antek pushed me. Father would stop whatever he was doing, give me a hug, brush the dirt off my jacket, and discreetly slip some fat into my pocket.

On other occasions, I would chase my brother with a stick. He would then run to Father for protection, pretending to be afraid of me. Father would take away the stick from my hand, make peace between us, and we would walk away with the fat.

One day I was very bored and asked Mother if could visit Larisa and the children. Mother went outside to check on the weather. It was beautiful, sunny and warm, a perfect day to go visiting. Mother agreed. I told her that if I did not return by nightfall, I would be spending the night with them, if they asked me.

As I was leaving, Mother wanted to know which way I would return. I told her I would follow the railroad there, and come back the way we used to go to school. The railroad ran through the forest, and I was in no hurry. I tried to name the trees, although the leaves had already fallen off. When I came to Larisa's, no one was there; they had moved.

To return the way I had told Mother, I had to go through our old camp. I walked by the house where we used to live, and noticed that someone else lived there now. I walked by the commandant's office and was about to turn to the road which would take me back to the Camp 24, when I heard Larisa's voice calling me. She greeted me warmly and said that they had moved there for the winter. We went to her house, and she invited me to stay for supper and to spend the night with them. During the supper, Larisa told me the latest gossip about us.

"Now that your Father is a butcher," Larisa began, "I heard that your mother makes sausages and you no longer buy your food at the stolovaya. At least you could have brought some for us."

"Eto nie pravda" (It is not true), I said. "Father is getting constantly watched during the work and searched before he goes home."

I didn't say anything about the fat we were stealing. While Larisa was talking, Sasha seemed deeply engrossed in his own thoughts. Then he looked at me and said, "Someone from your own people reported your Father to the NKVD." To soften the blow of his words, he started to tell me how grateful they were to me for taking such good care of their children when I was with them. Again he looked straight at me and said, "Someone will tell your Father when the NKVD will come to search your house."

I was shocked to hear that our own people would so unjustly betray my Father. I didn't know what to say, yet I felt I had to say something. "Alexander Nikolaevich," I addressed him respectfully, "My Father will be very grateful for the warning. Spasibo, thank you." He only smiled and told Larisa to prepare my bed because I must be tired after a long trip. Larisa got up from the table and made my bed, as usual, on the floor.

For a long time I couldn't sleep. I imagined the NKVD bursting into our home and arresting Father. Then I worried, if this should happen, God forbid, how would we get out of this country without him? When I finally fell asleep, I had a dreadful nightmare. I dreamt that we were looking everywhere for Father and could not find him. We banged on locked doors but no one was there to unlock them.

I woke up when I heard Larisa get up and start a fire in the stove. I gladly rose from my bed, got dressed, and folded the blankets. Larisa showed me where I could wash my face and hands. Sasha went outside to feed the goat and the horse. Probably they still had the chickens, because Larisa made scrambled eggs and bacon for breakfast.

After we had eaten, I said goodbye to them and the girls, promising to visit again these kind Russian people, who had done no harm to me nor I to them. It did not matter to me that he was a member of the Communist Party.

I walked the three kilometers at a brisk pace. This time I was in a hurry to get home and tell my parents what I had learned.

When I came home, Mrs. K. was sitting at the table, telling Mother something about how lucky some people were, while her little girl went hungry. Mother interrupted her conversation and asked if I'd had a nice visit and whether I was hungry.

"I had a very interesting visit," I answered, "and no, I am not hungry. We had bacon and eggs and lots of bread with butter." I was most anxious to tell Mother the news, but Mrs. K. stayed on and on. She was still there when Father brought soup from the mess hall. For a moment I feared that Mother would ask her to stay for lunch. Finally, the woman said "good day" and left.

Now alone with the family, I told them almost word for word what Larisa and Sasha had told me. Before going back to work, Father instructed us not to come near him until the whole matter was cleared up.

Two days later, Father came home very excited but nervous nevertheless. "Today I received the word," Father began. "Sometime tonight the NKVD will search the house."

The only thing we had which would incriminate Father was the fat in the half-filled bladders. The problem was where to hide it. We looked everywhere. In the bathroom Father found some loose floorboards. He lifted them up, and beneath them was a hole, a perfect place to hide our lard. Mother wrapped it in the newspapers and handed it over to Father, who put it in the hole and replaced the boards. However, thinking that the NKVD is not stupid, Father had second thoughts about it and decided to remove the fat when Antek came up with an unexpected solution to this problem.

"Leave everything where it is," he exclaimed., "I need to go to the toilet, and I will just defecate on this spot. They won't touch it, you will see."

We went to sleep at the usual time. The NKVD came after midnight. Olesia, Antek, and I slept in the kitchen and were the first to be awakened by the loud knocking on the door. We didn't get up but waited for Father to open it, as planned. Father took his time to open the door, despite the impatient banging and threats.

"As a free man, I demand an explanation for this disturbance in the middle of the night," Father said very convincingly.

"Hee, hee, who do you think you are, a tsar of Russia to demand an explanation for our entry into your home?" said one of them, pointing his revolver to Father's head. "Don't be a fool," said another voice. "Remember our orders. We are here to search this house. Nothing more."

In the complete darkness of the room, I could see Father's face illuminated by the flashlight, a hand, and a gun. I told myself that this was only an awful nightmare, and not a reality. Propped up on my elbow, I could see Father turn around, walk to the table where the lamp was, fumble with the matches, and light the lamp. In the lamplight, I saw only two young men, dressed in police uniforms, with red stars on their black caps. First, they told us to get up. Then they turned over our mattresses, and anything else they could find that could be turned over. They went to the bathroom, taking Father with them. Mother and the rest of us were only one step behind them. The guards looked and searched, being very careful as not to step into Antek's pile. They even looked into the hole in the floor.

As they were walking out, Mother apologized for a dirty toilet, that she did not know that one of her children would do such a thing, and that it must have happened when she was already asleep. Before they left, they took another look, checking the floorboards in the house.

After they had gone, Antek was beside himself, saying, "I told you they wouldn't touch my pile." While Antek was still raving about his ingenious idea to save the fat and Father from prison or worse, Mother, Janka, and Olesia straightened out our beds. To shut Antek up, Father told him that the NKVD might be listening outside the window. Father blew out the lamp, and we went back to sleep.

The next day, Father found out that it was Mrs. K. who reported him to the NKVD and spread the other gossip about us. Mother was very agitated and could hardly wait to confront this woman. As soon as Father left for work, Mrs. K. came. Mother, controlling herself, very calmly asked her, "Why?"

"Well, your frying pan always looks as if you fry meat in it," Mrs. K. confessed, turning red. Before anything else was said, Mother sent us out to find firewood. By the time we came back, Mrs. K. was long gone.

The cold, the snow, and the bitter wind came once again. The temperature dropped well below zero. I realized that I really disliked, no, hated winters over there. I could never keep warm. My jacket was too small and torn at the seams, although Mother had lengthened the sleeves, patched the holes, and sewn and re-sewn the seams. Mother even knitted a pair of socks for me out of old rags that were good for nothing else, not even patches. Nothing kept me warm when Antek and I went out to look for the firewood.

One day we brought a big load of wood and began to cut with a saw. It was close to suppertime, and the temperature dropped. I told my brother, "Let's stop. My fingers hurt from the cold." He insisted that we finish the last two pieces. By the time we had cut them, I had no feeling in my fingers. I came inside, and, before I could take my jacket off, my finger began to hurt so badly that I started to cry. At that moment Father came in and asked what had happened. I told him, and he immediately took both of my hands and put them in a bucket of water. "Keep them there until your fingers stop hurting," he told me., "Next time, don't let them get so cold, or you may lose them."

That night the temperature dropped to -40 degrees Celsius. (Someone had left a thermometer fastened to the frame of the door on the outside.) Father had to go somewhere to get the information about a train that would take us south. We were already in bed when he came home. He took his sheepskin coat off and covered us with it. Sometime in the middle of the night, Antek had to go to the toilet. He woke me first, then Olesia, begging us to come with him. We got up. Instead of going to the toilet where it was dark, we went outside, barefooted and wearing only our worn-out nightgowns. Antek was in his underwear.

The moon was full, clear and bright, with a huge circle around, suspended in space in the strange tranquility of the night. We stood there for only a minute, awed by this phenomenon, and our feet froze to the snow. We wriggled them very carefully so as to not tear the skin off our soles, and quickly ran into the house, then to bed. We huddled together for warmth. Olesia said, "We must ask Mother what this ring around the moon means."

First thing in the morning, we told Mother about the moon and the bright circle around it and asked her to interpret the meaning of the strange occurrence. Mother dismissed our wonder of wonders with a wave of her hand, saying, "It means that it was very cold last night." We felt disappointed; we expected to hear something else, like it was a mysterious omen, something awesome and foreboding, but not that. Of course, Mother was right. The circle was nothing more than frozen crystals, reflecting in the moonlight, but we learned that much later in life.

In the afternoon Antek and I were sitting by the window, just looking out, when we saw several people walking along the railroad. First there was one, then a man and a woman, then two men and a boy. This man and the woman sat down on a rail to rest. Antek said, "Let's go and ask them who they are and where they are going."

We grabbed our jackets and ran out. When we came closer, I saw that the woman's legs were swollen. She had no shoes, her feet were wrapped in rags, and she had a blanket over her jacket. The man was just as shabbily dressed as the woman, except he had shoes. Antek greeted them in Russian, then asked, "Where are you going?"

"To Plisieck," the man replied.

"You must be Polish," Antek said in Polish. Yes, they were Polish and were going to the station in Plisieck to wait for the train to take them south. There were twenty of them when they started out on this long journey, they told us. "Some turned back, some died along the way, and only a few of them are left besides us." Not waiting for the rest to catch up with them, the man and the woman picked up their small bundles, and with the sticks in their hands, they left.

"It is a long way to town," Antek shouted after them.

The man turned and shouted back, "We will make it." We stood on the railroad and watched until the man and the woman disappeared beyond the bend. I was very sad and felt sorry for those people, wondering where they slept during the night. They were so pathetic, yet so brave and determined to reach their goal.

Father brought the soup and some bread and put it on the table. Mother was carrying the bowls and spoons when someone knocked on the door. Father opened it and a young boy came in, asking for a drink of water. He was no older than fifteen, and by the way he was dressed, we knew he had to be Polish.

Instead of giving the boy just water, Father invited him to have lunch with us. Father evenly divided the soup and bread, and asked the boy where he was from. The boy mentioned a name of a camp, which I do not remember, about fifty kilometers from here. He said that his parents and brother had died, and that he was left all alone. To Father's next question—where was he going? He said he hoped to join the Polish Army, as soon as he could find it.

After we had eaten, the boy said, "It was my first meal in two days. Thank you." When he was about to leave, Father asked him if he had the papers with him. Yes, he did, and they both left. When Father returned, he told us that he was able to obtain some bread for the boy. We all hoped that the boy would find the Polish Army.

Occasionally, Father would tell us when something interesting happened at work. On this particular evening he told us something unusual.

In the morning, a woman, who took care of the pigs, discovered three dead piglets. Immediately the veterinarian office was notified, and three vets came. They told Father they needed vital organs for examination. When Father was taking them out he was also examining them. The organs were "clean." Neither Father nor the vets could determine the cause of death. Nevertheless, they told Father to bury them. A guard watched as he buried the piglets outside the camp. Before going to sleep, Father said that he would go around midnight to recover the piglets.

Sometime at night, the three of us woke up to a wonderful smell of cooked meat and low voices. We sat up and saw Father cutting the piglets into portions, and Mother wrapping them into clean linen. A blanket was carefully hung over the kitchen window. When all the meat was wrapped up, Father took it outside and buried it in the snow, the best freezer at 30 degrees below zero Celsius. Mother woke the rest of the family for a bite of meat. Afterwards, Mother and Janka cleaned the kitchen thoroughly. For the next two weeks, we had our best meals in the middle of the night. When all the meat was gone, Father quit his job. Soon we moved to the Camp 8.

I do not remember how far the Camp 8 was from the 24th. I only know that we left in mid-morning in the horse-driven cart and arrived there late in the evening. On the way, there was nothing to see, only naked trees and snow.

At this camp, we shared a one-room house with another family who had also arrived there at the same time as we did. After we brought our belongings into the house, including the two bladders of fat very carefully hidden from prying eyes, we made our beds on the floor and went to sleep.

In the morning, I went outside to see what I could see of our new location. It was no different from the others, with its wooden houses under a thick blanket of snow. Also, there was a railroad running alongside the camp. The food we bought was worse than in the previous camps. Sometimes the stolovaya was closed for the day because the cooks had nothing to cook. It was there that Antek and I licked plain salt until it tasted bitter. First, we spread the salt on the table and ate it by licking our fingers, then we licked it with our tongues just to see if it tasted any different.

Christmas went unnoticed. I think it was Christmas morning when we put everything we owned on the small sled—blankets and pillows, Mother's black pot, wooden bowls and spoons, two handmade and embroidered unused tablecloths, two towels with a crocheted lace on each end, and, of course, two not-so-full bladders of fat—and went along the railroad to Plisieck, a town which was about eight to nine kilometers away from the Camp 8.

We walked in the middle of the track, Father pulling the heavy sled, when a train appeared behind us. I only heard Father's shout, "Jump!" I jumped off the track and landed in the snow up to my armpits. As the train went speeding by, I tried to get out from my predicament, but could not. The train went by us as quickly as it had appeared, and everybody got back on the track except me. Stuck in the snow, I was screaming for help. Father found a long thick stick and told me to get a good hold on it. I held on for dear life, and Father pulled me out. We continued on our journey without further interruptions until we reached Plisieck.

What amazed me most about the station was that this one track, which had led us here, split into five or six or maybe more. I didn't count them. My thoughts were preoccupied with a man sitting on his bundle between these tracks. A guard came up and kicked him with his boot, and the man fell over. As we passed him, he still lay on the ground with his face in the snow. I think he was dead.

We came to the station, and so many people were already there that the waiting room was packed. Others stood or sat outside. As we stood there looking around for a place to sit down, two men carried the body of a woman out from the waiting room and put her on the side of the building with many others, piled one on top of another. Father found us an empty spot, not far from the "morgue" and told us to wait there while he went to get the information about the train. Soon he came back with good news. The train was due to arrive in about two hours.

We sat on the snow, huddled together, and waited. In the meantime, Father gathered together about fifteen families, collected money from them, and took it to the ticket office at the station.

At last the train arrived, and other families and ours piled into the box car. The inside of the box car looked very familiar. It was just like the one we had traveled in before, when "They" had brought us here. On each side of the car, there were two tiers of boards and a round stove in the middle. As before, we were on the upper tier by the little window.

When everybody was settled in, Father was about to shut the door when he saw a family of five still sitting in the snow. We knew them. They were from our camp. Father called all the men together in our car and said, "We can't leave them. They will surely die."

The men looked up and down for a space for them, but there was none. Father suggested they put a few boards across the space between the tiers, but the men objected to this idea because the boards would block the door on that side. Still trying to save this poor family from certain death, Father said, "So we will use only one door." Reluctantly they agreed.

Then Father called Mr. Woronski to come, but the man just sat there, oblivious to everything that was going on around him. Getting no response from the old man, Father called his sixteen-year old son, Jurek, and with another man they went to look for boards. Soon they came back and placed the three boards on the same level as the upper tiers. Jurek brought their belongings and spread blankets over the boards, then helped his father up, then his mother and two small sisters. We all settled down, but we were still shivering from the cold.

There was still some time left before the train was scheduled to leave, and Father said to the men who were standing near him, "Let's go and find some coal, wood, or anything that will burn and warm the car, because the people, especially the children, are freezing." They brought back a few sacks of coal and some wood. Someone started a fire in the round stove and in a short while it became warm, and we took our jackets off.

Suddenly the train gave a quick jerk, the wheels screeched beneath us. We were moving, at first very slowly, then faster and faster. With loud cheers and "hurrahs," we were leaving Plisieck and the camps behind us and going into the unknown.

When we woke up the next morning, the train was going at full speed. Those from the lower tiers were already up, boiling water on the hot stove. Then the women from the upper tiers took turns by the stove to cook breakfast. Most of them boiled only water, and gave it to their children to warm them up. After all the necessities were taken care of and everybody had settled down, the men gathered around the stove to choose a spokesman, or a leader among themselves. They went about it in a democratic way. Someone nominated Father, and they put his nomination to a vote. The vote was unanimous.

As a leader, chosen by his peers, Father organized them into groups. One group was responsible for the fuel, coal or wood, to keep the car warm, and another group for water and sanitation. It was their duty to clean around the hole in the floor and empty the buckets of human waste (smaller children were afraid of the hole and used the bucket). Father and three other men were responsible for food. Each time the train stopped at a station, Father would go out alone at first to inquire how long the train would stay, where to get fuel, water, and food. Then he would come back and tell the others about it. This system worked. We were warm, the car was clean, we had plenty of water to drink but not to bathe, and some food, which Father always divided fairly and evenly among the people.

At one station (I've forgotten its name), Father went out as usual by himself to get the necessary information. Before he returned, the train took off, leaving him behind. We were in despair. We cried and prayed for his return. Father was gone for three days. Each time the train stopped at a station, the men from our boxcar ran up and down the station calling: "Bogdaniec, Bogdaniec, we are here!" In the meantime they neglected their duties. There was no wood or coal to keep the fire going, no water for drinking and hardly any food.

On the second day someone managed to get some bread, but he did not divide it evenly. We and another family didn't get any. The people began to quarrel among themselves, and it became very frightening, at least to me.

By the third day, the car stank of human waste and of unwashed bodies. It was cold, and everyone put on their jackets. Everyone was hungry, especially our family. It had been three days now since we'd had any bread. To cheat our stomachs, we ate snow, pretending it was ice cream, a different flavor each time. Antek pulled up our little black pot through the window, which this time had no bars.

The third day, I woke up early. Everyone else was still asleep. Some were snoring, others talked in their sleep, and children whimpered. It was hunger that woke me up. Stomachs cannot be cheated for long, and sooner or later begin to demand food. But there was none and I knew it. Perhaps my stomach knew it, too, and allowed me to go back to sleep to dream a vivid dream.

I dreamt that I was sitting in a warm, sunny room, combing my blond hair. Only this time, there were no lice. The hair seemed so light, almost translucent. When I woke up, I told Mother about it and asked what it meant.

"You may expect a visitor," Mother replied.

I disregarded Mother's interpretation because it was unrealistic. How can one expect visitors when a train was running at full speed? To forget the nagging pangs of hunger, I propped my chin on my hands and looked out of the little window. The railroad ran through endless deciduous forest with dark clumps of tall spruces or pine here and there. The whole area was covered with snow, white and clean, unmarked by human footsteps. Sometimes I saw the roofs of the houses of small villages and the smoke rising high above them from barely visible chimneys. I often wondered if those people were as hungry as we were at this moment. But soon I dismissed this thought and began to wonder how the engine turned around to go in the opposite direction when the track seemed to be endless, constantly running south. But where was the promised south?

The train began to slow down, which meant that we were approaching a town. Perhaps we would get some food there. As soon as the train stopped, the men ran out and started to call, "Bogdaniec, Bogdaniec! We are here!" A few minutes later Father appeared in the doorway. Seeing him in his sheepskin coat, tired and unshaven, I felt secure and happy and knew that everything was going to be fine now that he was back.

"Here is your visitor," Mother said, referring to my dream. Father greeted us warmly and he, too, was happy to be back. Then he looked around and noticed that the fire was out, our "toilet" was filthy, and there was no water. He turned to all the men, who stood by the cold stove, and asked the meaning of this neglect. By the tone of his voice, I knew that Father was very angry. All at once he became like a military commander, reprimanding his troops. He reminded them of their duty to the women and children.

"Keep them warm and fed, whenever possible, and take care of the sanitation," Father said, looking at the mess around the hole. "The train will stay here for a while, so let's put this car in ship-shape condition." Then he walked out to look for food, and the rest followed. Before he came back, there was a fire burning brightly in the stove, spreading the long awaited warmth around us. The car was swept clean and buckets were full of water.

Father and the three men returned, carrying bread and some flour. As usual, he divided the bread according to the size of the family. He did the same with the flour. It wasn't much, but every family received some. Mother used the flour to make soup, adding some fat to it. We ate it with a great appetite, and wished we had more of it. She also gave us a very small piece of bread, saving the rest for the next day.

After Father had eaten, he stretched out on the edge of the tier, where Woronski's boards met, to rest and get some sleep after his ordeal of three days. Not wanting to disturb him, we sat very quietly, talking only in whispers between ourselves. Come to think of it, it was unusually quiet in the car while Father was resting.

When Father woke up, he told us how he managed to catch up with our train. Father spoke Russian fluently and the station officials gave him information about the schedules of trains. It was most helpful that Father knew the number of our train. "Always remember the number of the vehicle you're traveling on," Father stressed on us. The Russian officials told Father how he could find the several connecting trains in order to catch up with our train. It took him three days to catch up with us.

In the evening, the train moved and kept going on and on. It was still going when we went to sleep. Prior to sleeping, I lay on my "bed" with my thoughts racing through my mind, reviewing my strange new life. The priority was to stay alive and that meant securing food. We were starving, and I really mean starving. Much of the time in winter, we were bitterly cold, facing temperatures of -30 to -40 degrees Celsius. We were inadequately clothed, wearing patched, worn and torn garments. In addition to these threatening problems, we were constantly reminded of the proximity of death.

I recalled the incidents at Plisieck, our last stop, where I saw the pile of dead bodies by the station wall and where I witnessed the guard kick a man sitting on his bundle, who fell to the ground. He was dead! The impact of all such experiences on the mind of a young schoolgirl was incalculable, and whatever depth of impression was made, it was a permanent one.

When we woke up in the morning, the train was still on the run, then it stopped in the middle of the forest. It stayed there all day. We didn't get out for fear that it might leave at any minute.

The next time the train stopped like that, it stayed for two days. In the other cars, a few people had died and were buried in shallow graves by the railroad. Their graves were marked by the crosses made of two sticks tied together. We were lucky; no one died in our car.

One day, in the afternoon, our train stopped again in the forest. Thinking that it would stay there like the previous times, many people and children, including us, got out from the cars to stretch our legs. It was a nice, warm afternoon, and there was hardly any snow by the railroad. There were a lot of pine trees and the air was fresh and clean. Many who had suffered from diarrhea squatted down. Then the train, without any warning, began to move at fast speed. Father happened to be standing in the doorway when this happened.

He shouted, "Come on, run!" We ran for dear life, disregarding the toll taken by the constant plodding of our feet upon the gravel and wooden railroad tracks. I was the first one. Father and Mr. Konopacki grabbed my hands and pulled me up, then Olesia, then Antek, but Janka could not make it. By now the train was going very fast, and we saw Janka disappearing from our view. We were very distraught. I began to cry, because I was so concerned about my oldest sister. She had no jacket, and she must be very cold. I hoped that the train would stop soon, but it kept going faster and faster.

Father and Mr. Konopacki kept grabbing the children and pulling them in. Those they missed were saved by others in the cars behind us. When all the people and children were safely inside the cars, Father closed the door. Soon Mother asked him about Janka, and he replied that she was on the train. He saw her on the steps of the car behind us.

The curses flew at the engineer of the train from each side of the car. Father called him "Svoloch!" He used this word to describe base people, people without moral principles, and the engineer was one of them, who deliberately tried to condemn mostly children to a certain death in that wilderness.

Finally, late at night, the train pulled into a big town, Jaroslav (pronounced "yah-RO-slav"). Father immediately opened the door and called Janka. I saw Father helping her in, and then telling her to stand by the stove to warm up. She was shivering. As she stood by the warm stove, Janka told us how at the last moment she grabbed the handles of the steps that led to the little platform behind the car. During the journey she tried to keep warm by stamping her feet, blowing air into her hands, occasionally dozing off.

I remember it was Sunday when we arrived in Buzuluk, but which Sunday? I do not know. Even grown-ups had lost count of the days by now. Anyway, Buzuluk was the headquarters of the Polish Army in the Soviet Union organized by Gen. Władysław Anders. The Polish Russian Military Agreement was signed on August 14th, 1941, by Gen. Władysław Sikorski, Premier of the Polish government in exile. After this agreement, Stalin declared amnesty for all the Polish people who were in the Soviet Union.

In Buzuluk, the Polish soldiers shared their food and bread with us. Father brought with him a sack of bread, two men carried a huge cauldron of soup, and the third a pot of kasha (millet gruel). It was like a feast for us. The soup was thick, with potatoes, beans, peas, cabbage, and pieces of meat, not like the one we used to buy in the camps. While we were eating, Father announced that Mass was going to be said in about an hour, and not far from the depot.

"Those who wish to attend may do so. The train will wait." Most of the people from our car went, including Father and Janka. They returned a little different — a little happier, perhaps? Attending Mass in person seemed to lift their spirits; it renewed their hopes and gave them courage to endure. Janka talked about the all-military choir and the hymns they sang, about the thousands and thousands of people who were there, and about the encouraging words they heard. She talked about it as if it was a miracle. Perhaps it was. She also repeated other people's remarks, who were saying: "Imagine, the Mass is being celebrated so deep inside the Soviet Union in open fields for everyman to see and that the hymn 'Our Free Country give us back, O, Lord' would be sung by the people whom Stalin tried to annihilate."

We left Buzuluk and kept going south. After a few days journey, the forests and fields had ended and the steppes began. They were just as endless as the woodlands in the north. There was nothing on this softly undulating terrain to obstruct the view all the way to where the earth and the sky seemed to meet.

Remembering what Mother had said on several occasions about the Cossacks, I tried to understand why they loved their steppes so much and sang songs about them. One song in particular came to my mind: On the wings of a falcon or an eagle I will soar high over the steppes, so I can live in freedom. The steppes certainly afforded them the unobstructed freedom of movement in any direction.

It was late in the afternoon, and the sun was low when our train stopped in the middle of nowhere on the steppes. There was nothing around us for miles, not even a house. We only hoped that we would not stay there for days.

Father checked our water supply because there was no longer any snow on the ground. We resigned ourselves to wait for God knows how long. After a while the local women appeared on the incline on the east side of the train, carrying big loaves of bread, about a foot in diameter. I was looking out of the window when I saw them and told Father. He and other men went out, crawling under the train since the door on that side was blocked by the Woronskis.

I opened the window so I could hear what they had to say. After the greetings were over, Father asked them, "How much for the bread?" But the women said that they didn't want money, they wanted to trade their bread for something else. When Mother heard this she started to rummage through our belongings. The first thing she found were my shoes which were still in a pretty good condition. Mother pushed me aside from the window and said to the woman, "A loaf for these shoes." Evidently the woman agreed, because I heard Mother telling her to give the bread to "my husband." Antek's old valenki (felt boots) were not spared either. All in all, we ended up with two loaves of bread.

Mother, happy with her trade, moved from the window to hide the bread by her pillow. I continued to watch. One woman, a mother of six children, took off her wedding band and offered it to the woman with bread. Two loaves were offered, but she wanted three. The Russian woman said, "I have children too, they need shoes and clothes; they can't wear this ring." The Polish woman took the two loaves of bread with tears in her eyes, saying, "Sentiments won't feed my children."

The trade was over as the sun went down, and the train took off. During our journey south, we neither bathed nor washed our clothes. In the meantime, the lice multiplied by the millions and became unbearable. Everybody had them; they were so thick that we used to take handfuls and throw them out of the window. Seeing us do this, Father initiated a method of keeping the lice population down.

In the evening, he told us to strip and shake our clothes over the red-hot stove. The lice popped like popcorn. Then he told each man to do the same. From then on, every man was doing it, except Mr. Woronski, who refused to submit himself and his family to such indignity.

One morning, as Mother was straightening out our "beds," she called, "Father come quickly, you have to see it with your own eyes to believe it." Father came over and was aghast at what he saw. There was a line of lice, migrating from the Woronski's bed to ours. Father must have realized that he was the first recipient of the "immigrants," since he slept on the edge where the boards rested to support the Woronskis. Controlling his temper, Father asked if he would try and do what the rest were doing to control the lice. The man refused again. Then Father ordered Jurek to do it, beginning with his sisters. At first the boy was shy and waited to be the last one to strip his family then himself. After a while it became a routine, and we slept better for it.

I do not remember exactly when Antek and I started to go out to look for food each time the train stopped. At one station there were a lot of trains. One train had sacks stacked high on flatbeds that were covered with tarpaulin. Antek opened one with his pocketknife. It contained flour. He put a few handfuls into our little bag which we carried with us. Then we heard a rough voice shout, "Stop, stop!" We glanced back. It was a guard with a gun. We took off running and the guard ran after us, swearing profusely. We ran under and between the trains. Then a shot rang out behind me just as I got under a train. We continued to run until we lost him. Later we laughed about it and at the guard, how funny he looked under a train with his long coat getting in the way.

At another station there were no trains, only one off to the side – its flatbeds were full of rocks. Antek took one, turned it over several times in his hand, and put it back. Then he put his finger into his mouth and said, "These are no ordinary rocks; it's salt." He gave me one and took one himself, and we brought them to our car. Father opened the door for us and, seeing the rocks, told us to throw them away, but we insisted on keeping them. Father gave in to our pleas.

We left the steppes and arrived in Tashkient, Uzbekistan. Here, the Polish soldiers also shared their food with us. From Tashkient we went to Bukhara, then Kitab, the last place on the railway line. It took two months to get there, that is, from Plisieck to Kitab.

The railroad officials told us it was the end of our journey. We gathered everything we owned and got out. It was here that I found out how engines turned around to go in the opposite direction. Finally, the mystery of how trains turned around was solved.

As we were standing in front of the boxcar, an Uzbek, a local man, came up and told us to follow him. Besides carrying a small bundle, I also carried my rock and Antek carried his. The Uzbek led us to an ox-driven cart. When Father saw our rocks, he again told us to throw them away. Antek defended the rocks, saying that they had been with us for so long, and we didn't have to carry them as they could ride with us in a cart. Again Father gave in, and we took our rocks with us.

The Uzbek drove through the town and over a wooden bridge. The river was not very wide, but the water was red and running fast. When I saw it, it frightened me. I closed my eyes and kept them shut until we were on the other side. We rode in this cart for seven kilometers. Finally the Uzbek brought us to a small kolhoz and stopped his ox in front of a little kibitka (mud house). This was it, the end of our journey. We got out, took our bundles and rocks, and went inside. One little window did not shed much light, but I could see that there was only one bed and a small sideboard against the wall, nothing more. There was no floor, only hard packed dirt.

As soon as we put our belongings by the wall, and rocks in a corner behind the door, the kolhoz official came in. He informed us that tomorrow at sunrise everyone must go to work in the cotton fields. Father must to go to Kitab and work in the vineyards. By working in town, Father could buy bread there at the end of the week. Looking at Marysia and me, he said that we were too young to work and could stay at home. When he stopped talking, Mother asked him where a water well was. The official said that there was no well, and if she wanted water, she must go to a stream a few yards away. Before leaving, he told Father to come with him, so he could give us some cornflour and a bucket. Father was back in ten minutes. Mother took the bucket and Marysia and went to look for the stream. She brought back a bucketful of red water and said, "Are we supposed to drink this mud?"

Meanwhile, Marysia told us about the snakes she saw lying by the stream. When we heard this, we went up to Father and told him that we refused to sleep on the floor because a snake might crawl on us. Father went out. Soon he returned carrying a long board and other pieces of wood. These materials were for the bed extension. "Now we can all sleep across the bed like sardines in a can," Father said with a smile.

In the meantime, Mother managed to build a fire outside, strained the water several times through one of her towels, and cooked corn mush. Before going to bed, she brought another bucket of water so the mud could settle to the bottom by morning. Since there was no place to take a bath after a very long journey, we went to sleep just as we were, very tired and very dirty.

The next day after everybody went to work, Marysia and I went outside to look at our new surroundings. In front of the house was a small yard, fenced off by a thick wall from the street, making it cozy and private. To the left, far away, mountains rose high into the sky, and beyond them were more mountains. A huge, dark mountain was before us which seemed to be very close, but in reality it was about 60 kilometers away. To the right, there was a stream, which was rather a bubbling brook from which we had gotten water the previous night. There were no trees, not even shrubs, only dried grass covering the rolling hills. I was about to go beyond the wall to look at the street, when Marysia saw something in the yard. Thinking it was a snake, she became frightened and ran back into the house.

The following day, I woke up with a headache. When everybody went to work, I went back to bed. While I was resting, an Uzbek boy of about fourteen came in without knocking and began snooping around. I got up and told him to leave, pointing to the door. He said something which I didn't understand, and he didn't seem to understand Russian, but still kept looking around. I think I would have given him anything he wanted, if only he would go away. After a while, he left without taking anything. I locked the door behind him and went back to bed. By the time everybody came home from work, I was burning with fever. Mother cooked some cornmeal and offered it to me, but I couldn't eat it. Then Mother found her little treasure box, took out a fishhook, and went out. After a while she came back with two small fish and cooked them for me. Antek sat beside me and was practically devouring them with his eyes. When I refused to eat the fish, he asked Mother if he could eat them. She nodded "yes," and he quickly put them in his mouth, head, tail, and all, chewed once or twice, and swallowed. Mother now realized that something was seriously wrong with me and asked if there was anything I would like to eat. I told her that the aroma and taste of her sourdough pancakes haunted me all day long. Saying no more, Mother took her last new towel and went out to trade. She came back with a cup of "real" flour and made me a pancake. I tasted it, but it wasn't the same like the kind she used to make back home. Afterwards I didn't want anything and asked to be left alone.

In the morning, Olesia was sick and couldn't go to work. Mother went to the office to get a written excuse from work, one for Olesia because she was sick, and one for herself so she could take care of us. The office notified the kolhoz to verify that Olesia was really sick. The nurse took one look at us and said, "Typhus, typhus," and left. Soon she came back with an ox and a cart to take us to a hospital in Kitab. Mother protested vigorously, but the nurse insisted, saying, "There is an epidemic of typhus, and they must be quarantined."

The last thing I remember was Mother standing by the cart crying, saying that she would never see us again. I wanted to lift my head and tell her that I was not afraid of death, and that it wouldn't be so bad if I died, but I had no strength to say it.

The next thing I remember was being in the hospital, sitting on a chair, and a nurse shaving my hair off with clippers. On a chair next to me sat Olesia, and another nurse was cutting her hair with the scissors. Then the nurse told me to take my clothes off, except the slip. Having done this, she led us along a corridor and through one ward, then to a second ward where a few beds were still unoccupied. I only remember that our beds were next to each other.

Early the next morning a nurse took me to a smaller bed. We walked into the first ward. Then she stopped by a crib and told me to get in. I said, "But I am too big for a crib." She replied that I was the smallest patient there. I was too sick to argue and lay down. I also knew that they brought me my breakfast: a very small piece of bread and a plate of tea. Even if I wanted to drink that tea, I didn't know how I could manage without spilling it all over myself. I only took the bread and hid it under my pillow. As soon as I turned my head away from the tea, three other patients made a run for it. Only one got it and gulped it down, leaving the empty plate on my table. The same thing happened at lunch when they brought a plate of noodle soup, and at supper. The food for supper was the same as we had for breakfast. This went on for several days.

Then one morning a nurse came to change my bed because a doctor was coming. She discovered my bread. First she scolded me for hiding it, and then took it away. There were about five pieces. When I got back to my crib, I tried to figure out how many days I had not eaten. I began to calculate. Four pieces of bread meant two full days, the fifth portion I had hidden only that morning. And if I didn't eat that day, it would make it three days. My thinking was interrupted by the coming of a doctor. When I looked at him, I knew he was not Russian. He was tall with dark eyes and dark complexion. He wore a long rubber gown, long rubber gloves, a cap on his head, and had an odor of some disinfectant. He walked up to the crib and asked in Russian, "How are you feeling today?" I told him that I had a splitting headache and could he please give me something for it. "I wish I could," he replied. Then I told him that he smelled so awful it nauseated me. From then on, whenever he came he stood a little away from my crib. Several times I caught him looking sadly at me and nodding his head. Evidently there was no medicine to give. To my knowledge, no one was given any during my three-week stay in the hospital.

My head ached continuously and was very hot. Many times I asked nurses to put a cold compress, or just a wet rag on my forehead to cool it off, but I always got the same answer, "Seichas" (right away). At first I believed them, that any minute a nurse would bring something so cold that would not only cool my head but the rest of me as well. Day after day I asked them, but the nurses ignored my pleas. I wished I were at home, because I knew Mother would have taken better care of me. It seemed like the nurses were never there when I needed to go to the toilet. Soon after I was moved to a crib, I waited for hours for a nurse to come by, so she could show me where the toilet was and perhaps help me to walk there.

When I could wait no longer, I climbed out of the crib, and remembered from the first day that there was one somewhere along the corridor. I found the toilet, but the way back was the hardest. The corridor seemed so long, and the ward so far away. Many times I felt myself crumbling down, but I held on to the wall, telling myself, "It's not far. A few more steps, and you are there. You can do it." I was glad that my crib was by the entrance to the ward. I literally fell into it and then lost consciousness. The next thing I remember was a nurse waking me for supper. I looked at the small piece of bread, which was no bigger than my two fingers held together, then at the plate of tea and turned away, leaving the bread where it was. Another patient took it.

On the sixth day (if my calculations were correct), I woke up feeling thirsty. I drank the tea, but the bread I hid under my pillow. At lunch I had a few spoonfuls of soup, and again I drank the tea at supper. Little by little I began to eat. A few days later I not only ate my food, but also the food of other patients who were too sick to eat.

More and more patients were coming in. Soon there was a shortage of beds, and nurses put two patients in one bed. When they wanted to put a stranger in Olesia's bed, she objected, telling them that she had a sister there. "Put her with me and not a complete stranger." The nurses brought Olesia to my ward, then told me to go to her. "From now on, the two of you will sleep together," the nurse told us. Olesia was ecstatic, and so was I. I put my pillow at the foot of Olesia's bed and crawled in. It seemed like a pure luxury to be able to stretch my legs at last. In a crib, I could not do it for long because the crib ended in the middle of my calves. I had to pull my legs in because they hurt too much.

When more patients were brought in, they put them on the floor between the beds, and soon our ward became very crowded. Olesia and I ate the food that the sick refused.

When it came to eating other patient's food, there was an unwritten law among the recovering patients. No one touched the food until the patient looked at it or tasted it first and turned her head away. Then, and only then, the food became fair game for anyone to grab it. Those who were closer and quicker took it, gulped it down, and left the plate on the patient's table, or on the floor, whichever the case may be. It was the closest that we ever came to being like animals. Our feelings were dulled by our own sufferings and hunger so that we became indifferent to the pain and suffering of others. We thought of nothing else but food.

When Father sent us some bread, sometimes half a loaf, we didn't share it with anyone else. We ate it all. One day he sent a whole loaf, but we had received only half. We complained to the doctor about it. We even showed him Father's letter, where he had written, "I am sending you a whole loaf this time." The doctor told the nurses, "Whoever took it, must return it." The other half was returned to us. We felt neither guilt nor remorse. After all, we lived in a hungry world, a world of pain, suffering, and wretchedness.

I was recovering much faster than Olesia. She had to learn how to walk all over again, whereas I never had that problem, perhaps because no matter how sick I was, I walked to the toilet by myself. Seeing how well I was recovering, the doctor wanted to dismiss me. Olesia cried and implored him to wait and dismiss us together, telling him that I would get lost without her. The doctor agreed and allowed me to stay until Olesia became stronger.

A certain nurse, called Tania, who talked about my beautiful blond hair and was forced to shave it off, asked Olesia's permission to adopt me. Her argument was that sooner or later the doctor would dismiss me without her, and that I would be lost forever. "I will raise her as my own," Tania begged Olesia. "Only let me have her. I have means to support her, and will see to her education." Tania was very persuasive, telling Olesia all about herself and her husband who was a doctor, and how much she had grown to love me. Olesia, without mincing any words, flatly told her, "No. In the first place it is not in my power to grant you permission to adopt my sister. In the second, what would my Mother say if I returned without her?" Olesia said, and covered her face with her blanket, indicating the end of the discussion.

Finally the day came when the doctor dismissed us without any warning. Olesia asked him if there was any way to notify our Father. "He works in the vineyard somewhere in town, and we don't know the way home." The doctor told us that no messages could be sent anywhere from the hospital. Then a nurse came telling me that my clothes were lost. When Tania heard this, she went out and bought a brand new dress for me with lavender flowers. Another nurse brought somebody else's jacket and shoes.

Dressed in my new outfit, and before leaving the hospital, we stopped at the kitchen and asked the cook for some bread. The cook chased us away. There we stood, not knowing what to do when we saw Tania. Olesia asked her if she could manage to give me, not her, some bread for the road since we had no money. Tania told us to wait. It was the first and only time we begged for food. When Tania returned, she gave me a piece of bread wrapped in a napkin, hugged me tenderly, and walked away without a second glance.

We walked across the yard to the gate. The gatekeeper asked our names. He wrote them down and opened the gate to let us out.

There we stood, two destitute figures, wondering which way to go. Should we go to the right or to the left or straight-ahead?

First, we looked to the right, then to the left. There were not many people on either side. I was afraid of empty streets. Remembering that we had to cross the river over a wooden bridge, I suggested that we go straight ahead, hoping to find that bridge. "Besides, there are people on this street," I told Olesia. While she was making up her mind which way to go, I thought of my God, the God from my early childhood years. I said in my heart, "O God, don't let us perish now." Suddenly I was shocked and ashamed that I didn't think of him when I was so terribly ill. It took only a moment for Olesia to make up her mind, and she said that we would go straight ahead. We crossed the street, talking, and hoped to meet someone who understood Russian, so we could ask for the directions to the bridge and home. Then I asked Olesia, "Do you know the name of the kolhoz where 'our home' is? Because I don't." Olesia said that its name began with "Stary," old, but that she wasn't absolutely sure of the name. We passed a lot of people, coming and going, and men sitting on the sidewalk, giving us a sinister look. I felt with my arm to see if the bread, our priceless possession, was still there hidden in the lining of the jacket.

We kept on walking, glad it was daylight, when suddenly Olesia turned and cried out, "Antek! Antek! Where are you going?" She recognized him by Janka's jacket, which he was wearing at that time. Antek stopped, came to us and simply said, "I am taking some bread for you, but where are you going?" Olesia was so relieved at seeing Antek that all she could say was "Cud, cud!" (a miracle!). We both were aware of the fact that Antek knew the way home.

We passed the bridge and followed a beaten path. As we were walking, Antek told us everything that had been happening at home. He said that Mother cried for days after they took us away, and still cried whenever she thought about it. He worked in the fields when he became sick. Today was the first day that he felt better and was hungry. He told Mother he needed to go to town and see Father, but she forbade him and hid his jacket. Seeing that Janka was sick, he took hers. When Mother and Marysia went to fetch water, he left the house before they came back. Father bought some bread and told him to take half of a loaf to the hospital. He was on his way there when we saw him.

After a while, Olesia said that her legs felt like jelly, and she needed to rest. We sat down by the path and ate some bread. First, we ate the piece that Tania gave us, then Antek took out our half and cut off three slices. As we were eating, he began to laugh.

"What's so funny?" Olesia asked.

"Your heads," Antek replied. "You look weird without your hair." I lifted my hand and felt my head and said that my hair was growing back.

While we were walking, Antek told us the best news of all. He said that the Polish soldiers had found us. They gave Mother a little tea and sugar, and said that by the end of the next week we must be in Krasnovodsk, a port on the Caspian Sea. They would be waiting for us there. Then the soldiers asked Mother if she knew of any other Polish family living here nearby. Mother told them that, as a matter of fact, there was one. Three days ago they had buried two children. She even took the soldiers there, but came back all in tears; they'd found everybody dead. The soldiers stayed behind to bury them.

For about ten minutes, we walked in silence, thinking our own thoughts, when Antek broke the silence and told us that we were not far from home – just over the hill. We looked up, and there on the hill stood two lonely silhouettes. My heart jumped for joy, and I began to wave my hands and shout, "Mother, we are back!"

We came a little closer, and Marysia recognized us. She ran down the hill to meet us. Mother stood where she was, as though glued to the spot, and overcome by emotions, began to wipe the tears with her apron.

"Mama, we are back!" we both said at the same time, and ran into her outstretched arms.

"Thank God, you are back and safe," was all Mother could say at first.

The five of us stood on the hill for a while, just looking at each other. Mother had to touch us several times to make sure we were real and not apparitions. As she was touching us, she remarked, "How thin you are, nothing but skin and bones under those clothes."

Mother was thinner, too. Marysia was giving us side glances and finally said what she was thinking, "You look like boys without your hair." We all laughed.

The inspection of each other was over, and Mother led the way to the house, asking a thousand questions about the hospital and what it was like there. She wanted to know every detail about how we had met Antek. She was asking the questions so fast that we couldn't keep up answering them.

At last we came into the house and said hello to Janka, who was ill, barely acknowledged our presence, and closed her eyes. When we took off our jackets, Mother noticed my new dress and wanted to know how I got it. Olesia told her everything about Tania, how she had wanted to adopt me. It was Tania who bought the dress because my old clothes were lost. Mother nodded her head in approval of Olesia's decision and Tania's choice of the dress for me.

When Mother stopped asking questions, Olesia asked her one. "What were the two of you doing on that hill?" Mother explained that she was worried about Antek since he had been gone such a long time. She imagined all sorts of things happening to him: perhaps he was robbed and beaten up, or maybe he was too weak and had fallen some place on the road. So she and Marysia went up the hill to watch for him. They saw three children coming down the road and wondered who they could be. "As it turned out, they were my own children," Mother said.

It was late in the day, and Mother made some tea that the Polish soldiers had given her. Mother was saving it so she could offer us something special when we came home. We drank our tea with a piece of bread and, being very, very tired, we went to bed.

The next morning, every bone and muscle, especially our legs, ached so much that it was sheer agony to move. Mother didn't insist that we get up and told us to stay in bed and rest. For the remainder of our stay, we rested and recuperated.

The day before our departure from this small kolhoz, Father came home with some bread. Mother took an inventory of all the things that we had left. Our worldly possessions amounted to six blankets, four pillows and a small one, a tablecloth which we'd used the last Christmas at home, one unused bedspread (these two items Mother was saving for "the dark hour"), seven wooden bowls and spoons, one knife, scissors (which to this day are in Marysia's possession), about ten photographs of home, and a small black pot. There was no more change of clothes or underwear—whatever we had on our backs, that was it. Foodwise, we had a loaf and a half of bread and some cornflour. Mother decided to have only bread and hot water for supper and saved the cornflour for breakfast, so we could have something hot in our stomachs before we left.

In the morning Mother began to cook the mush and discovered that she had no salt. She was frantic about it, walking around saying, "What am I to do? There is no place to buy salt." Antek, hearing Mother complain and go on about the salt, took one of our rocks and said, "How much do you need?"

113

As Antek was chipping off a chunk of the rock, an Uzbek woman came by and asked Mother if she wanted to buy some milk. She spoke a little Russian and asked what Antek was doing. When she found out that it was salt, she told Mother she would trade the milk for a little salt. Mother agreed and told Antek to give her some. The woman was very excited and soon left. Five minutes later, there was a line in front of our house. Everybody in the kolhoz was there with milk, cheese, their kind of bread, which resembled tortillas, only thicker, and fruit. All of them wanted to trade their goods for salt.

Antek sat in the doorway, chipping away at our rocks, while Mother took the food. Some people came twice with diluted milk, but Mother took it anyway. Antek used up the last rock and told the people, "That's all of it." Everyone left, except one woman, who evidently had nothing to barter and sat in the yard while the trading was going on. She came up to Mother, making motions indicating if she could pick up small bits and pieces of salt where Antek sat. He even found a bigger chunk which had flown into the house and gave it to her. Thanking and bowing several times, the woman left.

On the last day of our stay there, we had more food than we knew what to do with. A surplus, and all Mother could say was, "All this time we had a goldmine and didn't know it. It is unbelievable that these people have no salt."

After we had eaten, Father took the bucket and other things which belonged to the kolhoz and returned them. He came back with an ox-driven cart and a driver. We took everything we owned, got into the cart, and left for Krasnovodsk without regrets. In fact, without as much as a backward glance.

It was drizzling when we arrived in Krasnovodsk, and a multitude of people were already there, sitting in an open field. We found a spot in the midst of them. Mother gave us blankets to keep from getting wet, while Father went to report to the headquarters. He came back with good news. We wouldn't have to wait here for days; we would leave by ship this evening.

Since it was already late in the afternoon, Mother told us to have something to eat. The rest of the food she gave to the children who were crying from hunger. Their mothers couldn't thank her enough, saying that it had been so long since they'd had a bite to eat.

Evening came, and we moved closer to the docks. I looked back, and I saw as far as my eye could see people sitting on the frozen ground. Children were crying from hunger and the cold, and I wondered when their time would come to leave the Soviet Union. Families with small children were first to board the ship. It was not a big ship, I thought, and would not hold our whole village, houses, roads, animals and all, remembering what Antek had told me so long ago.

Once on the ship, we were told to go below deck. There were two tiers of bunks, one on top of another. Mother and Marysia claimed one below, and so did Janka; the rest of us claimed the upper bunks. Soon the place was packed with women and children. Father remained on deck. I wanted to go there, too, just to see what I could see, but Mother forbade it. We made ourselves comfortable, and waited.

First the engines whined, then started. Their powerful roar was coming from below. The ship groaned and began to shake. Through a closed door, we heard a thousand voices singing, "Jeszcze Polska nie zginela," our national anthem. Mother said that the ship must have been leaving the port. It was taking us to Persia.

Later on that evening I had a stomachache, and decided to go to the toilet, which was on the upper deck. By then the ship was rocking back and forth. Twice I came close to the stairs, and twice I was forced to walk backwards. On the third try, I crawled. I reached the deck and, to my astonishment, there were so many people standing shoulder to shoulder that I could not see the sea, or anything else.

There was a long line to the toilets, so long that I thought everyone on deck was in it. I couldn't wait. As soon as the door opened, I ran in. The scene in the toilet could top Dante's Inferno. There was no privacy; several people squatted on the floor, and the human waste was everywhere. Luckily for me, a woman, who was using the stool, got up, and I quickly took her place before anyone else could beat me to it.

It took us all night to cross the Caspian Sea. In the morning we landed in Pahlevi, Persia (Iran). We had left the Soviet Union on

Good Friday, 1942, and arrived in Pahlevi, a Persian port on the Caspian Sea, the following day.

It was a warm spring day, and the sun was high above this ancient, yet all new to me, land. As soon as we were on the Persian soil, I could feel that this world was distinctly different from the one we had left behind.

After two years of hunger, cold, sickness, and life without laughter and the simple joys of childhood, Persia seemed like a paradise – sunny and bright, a dream come true. The feeling of gloom and oppression had gone, and so was the fear of hunger when I heard the Persian vendors crying in loud voices, Varonyie Yaytsa (boiled eggs); bulochki (rolls), and morozhnoe (ice cream)! These were wonderful sounds, and I wondered, "Why on the other side of the Caspian Sea was there hardly any food, whilst here there is such an abundance?"

The Polish soldiers were at the docks to meet us. They told us to get into the trucks and lorries and drove us to a beach outside Pahlevi.

During our short trip, I didn't see much of the port, and hardly anything of the terrain. The people in front of me blocked my view. It was the same way on the beach, all I saw were the backs and a conglomeration of footwear of the ragged and starved, the gaunt and the weary, young and the old people, like ourselves.

These thousands of people first gave thanks to God, then praised General Anders for delivering us from the "house of bondage," where so many had died, and so many still remained. "Who will remember them?" I heard someone say.

Then, above the noise of the crowd, I heard Father's voice, "Stay close to one another and follow me." He led us away from the crowd and the beach to a higher ground. We climbed a gently sloping sandbank. Overlooking the beach, there was a building. Father headed towards it. The building turned out to be more of a shack with three sides and a roof. "At least we will have a roof over our heads," Father remarked, surveying the structure of this shack. Mother spread a couple of blankets on the ground, and Janka, who was still ill, lay down, closed her eyes, and became oblivious to everything that was going on around her. Soon other people came, and women spread their blankets to claim their spots on the ground.

Then came the Persian vendors, carrying baskets full of colored eggs, bread-rolls, and meats. Seeing the eggs, I realized that it was Easter. While Mother was waiting to buy a few eggs and bread, I remembered an Easter of long ago, in another world, when I was about six years old.

We lived at the ranger's station by the river Lachowiec. Early on Easter morning, Father gently woke me up, and motioned with his hand to follow him. He led me to the kitchen. The aroma of spice and cinnamon still lingered in the kitchen from Mother's baking the previous day. A basket of colored eggs and a variety of sweet rolls and breads were on the table.

I was still sleepy-eyed and yawning when Father pointed to the floor and smiled. Suddenly my eyes were wide open. By the stove there were five little yellow ducklings. Surprised and delighted, I gathered them into my nightgown and brought them to the window for a closer inspection. Then I asked Father, "What do they eat?" Father gave me a roll and said, "Try this."

I sat down on the floor and shared the roll with the ducklings. After a while I fetched a clump of green grass and watched them climb onto it in a clumsy sort of way. I was so preoccupied watching the ducklings that I didn't hear Mother come in, until she said, "Christos Voskres," Christ has risen. At the time I didn't know what to say, so I repeated Mother's words, "Christos Voskres" (Christ has risen). This was an old Orthodox greeting among the people in the village on Easter morning. Evidently my answer pleased Mother, because she smiled and patted me on the head, then told me to be very careful with the ducklings since they had hatched only that morning. Mother busied herself with the lighting of the stove and with preparing Easter breakfast.

I was still in my nightgown when Father, Janka, Olesia, and Antek came in, wearing their Sunday clothes. For a moment I wondered if they were going somewhere, when Mother announced that breakfast was almost ready. But before sitting down at the table, Father said, "Come children, and join me in a prayer. It is Easter."

Janka, Olesia, and Antek were already kneeling down beside Father, who remained standing. Then he looked at me and said, "You, too." Reluctantly, I left the ducklings and knelt by Janka. After the prayer, I asked Mother if I could have my breakfast on the floor with the ducklings. Mother looked at Father and nodded "Yes."

When the breakfast was over, Father gave each one of us a couple of hard-boiled eggs. Then he said that we would have had an egg contest had we lived in the village. I asked him, "Tata, Daddy, what is a contest?" Father sat down beside me and showed me how to hold my egg, then he hit it with his egg. His eggshell broke, and he said that I had won his egg. Then he took another egg and told me to hit it with mine. This time my egg broke, and he said that I had lost and had to give him the egg. "Now try your luck with Antek or Olesia while I take these ducklings back to their mother."

When Father went out with the ducklings, Mother proceeded to tell us that in the village everyone, the old and the young, participated in the contest, to see who could win the most eggs. Also, she told us how one Easter, Father took only a few carefully chosen eggs with him and came back with a basketful. The way Mother described this egg-cracking contest sounded like a lot of fun, and I wished we were in the village then, so I could do the same. Antek took two eggs from the basket, and walking up to me, asked Mother how she colored the eggs.

"By boiling them with the yellow onion skins," she said, "something I learned from my mother." I looked at the eggs, and they ranged from light yellow to burned orange in color.

"Easter is such a nice and joyous holiday," Mother remarked as though to herself and began to clear the table.

"Mama, the reason we have so much food—is it because it is Easter?" Marysia's voice brought me back to reality. "And after Easter is over, will it all be gone?" Mother turned to Marysia, took her little face into her hands, and said, "From now on, we will have plenty of food, and we won't starve like we did in Russia." Mother said this with such a conviction that Marysia and I believed her. Probably the Easter of 1942 would have gone unnoticed by me, like the previous two, if it were not for the colored eggs, oranges, and other food the Persians sold us.

Towards the evening, when the sun was low on the western horizon, the Polish soldiers brought huge cauldrons of soup to feed the multitude of people. By the time we had ours and had eaten it, the sun had set. There were no lights, and we settled down for the night.

It was already dark when I heard a man's voice calling Father's name, "Józef Bogdaniec!" Upon hearing his name, Father got up and answered, "Here." Seeing that the man was a captain, Father saluted him, then apologized for not clicking his heels because he was barefooted. The captain wanted to discuss something with Father and suggested they take a walk. Father put on his shoes, and they left. Before falling asleep, I thought what an exciting day it had turned out to be. We were free again and there was plenty of food.

The sand we slept on was dry and warm, and the sky above was clear. I could see a few stars, twinkling in the night. But most importantly, we, Father, Mother, Janka, Olesia, Antek, Marysia, and I were together. Silently, I whispered in my mind, "Thank you, God, for everything."

I got up early the next morning and went outside to look around. There were people sleeping by the shack and on the sand, all the way to the beach. Here and there I heard someone silently weeping as though not to wake the others. I knew, without seeing, why they were weeping. One of their loved ones had died during the night.

I looked towards the west, and I saw a sea of tents. The people who were evacuated before us were in those tents. We were on the last transport that was evacuated that spring.

I was still weak from my bout of typhus ten days before, so I went back into the shack and lay down. Then my stomach began to give me trouble. I attributed the pains to the rich food I'd had the previous day. I made several trips to the latrine, which was nothing more than a hole in the ground with a few planks across it. During one of my trips there, I noticed that the people were going somewhere. I followed them. On the hill outside the camp, crowds had gathered to hear the Mass. It had been a long time since I had heard the Catholic Mass.

It was back in Łunin where I once went with Father to the little white church on the corner of the street, not far from the cemetery. The church was full of people from the periphery whom I didn't know. I sat beside Father in a pew at the back of the church. I could see the altar and a priest, but I didn't understand what was going on. Occasionally I heard the priest say, "Dominus vobiscum," or "Oremus," but I didn't dare ask Father what these words meant, not in the church. Before going in, Father told me that I had to be quiet and keep my eyes on the altar. I did just that, even if my eyes wandered from the cross above the altar to the holy pictures on the walls.

This Easter Sunday in Persia, I still didn't understand what was going on. I couldn't even see anything because of the people in front of me. So I stood in silence, trying to hear what was being said. Then the people began to sing, "Our free country return to us, O Lord." That meant the Mass was over, and the people started to disperse, going to their respective tents. I, too, ran "home" to tell Mother where I had been. At that time, I considered "home" was in the little shack on a beach by the Caspian Sea. Now I realize how important my family was to me. We were very close, supporting and looking out for one another. Thanks to my parents, we survived the worst and darkest days of our lives, just because we were there, sharing the same fate, yet encouraging us to go on whenever we were sick, hungry, or fed up with living in such misery. They often told us, "Never give up hope; live for today, and tomorrow will take care of itself."

Several days had gone by since our arrival in Persia, and my diarrhea did not improve; as a matter of fact, it got worse. My stomach refused to digest anything I ate. I didn't complain. In the daytime I continued to wander through a maze of tents, talking to other children and listening to their horrifying stories during their stay in Russia.

One girl with long braids, the color of wheat, told me that her mother had frozen to death when she'd gone to another settlement in search of food. The NKVD found her the next day and told her family that she had tried to escape because she had some bread in her pocket and no propusk (permit), to leave the camp. "Mama would never leave us," the girl said, wiping tears with a sleeve of her jacket which was several sizes too big for her. "She only went to find food for me and my little brother."

"My father died at work," said a boy with dark curly hair and blue eyes. "He was very sick, and we had nothing to eat. You know what the Soviets say, 'If you don't work, you don't eat.'"

Father and Mother
Teheran 1942

28 - August 1942
Nadia, Mother and Marysia

MINISTERSTWO WYZNAŃ RELIGIJNYCH I OŚWIECENIA PUBLICZNEGO

SZKOŁA

N.

ŚWIADECTWO SZKOŁY ZAWODOWEJ

Teheran - Iran 1942 - 1943
In this Chapel the children of Poland gave thanks
to the Mother of God for saving them during the
years in exile.

Antek in Palestine
Nazareth 29. 5. 1943

Antek 25.3.1943

Antek

Antek and Father 15. XII 1943
By approved military photographer

Pahlevi 1943 - Father and friends

Father in Pahlevi

Iraq 1943. Father gets a haircut.

My brother Antek in military
school circa 1943

Father and Antek 1944

Father and Antek, Egypt 1944

Antek meets Father in Tel-El-Kebir,
Egypt 13. IX. 1945

Egypt 1946. III Junackie
Gimnazjum Mechaniczne.

Italy March 1945.
Father and a friend from Poland,
W. Chilkiewicz.

The children who lost both of their parents were separated from the rest of us and lived in an orphanage. I didn't talk long to these children because I was afraid that the women who ran the orphanage would think I was an orphan also.

As I wandered among the thousands of people, I discovered that there were two camps: the "clean" and the "unclean." We were in the latter. In order to get into the "clean" camp, the people had to be deloused first, having all their hair shaved off, including the pubic hair, disinfected, and bathed.

When our turn came to be "purified," Olesia and I had no problems. Our hair was already cut very short when we'd had typhus. The so-called "nurses" (soldiers dressed as women) told us to strip, put our lice-infected clothes in a corner, and to proceed through a disinfection and showers. Afterwards, we received clean clothes, sandals, and blankets. Olesia and I were the first to be deloused, and we waited for the rest of the family. When Mother came out with Marysia, she was wearing a military uniform. We laughed and teased her about her uniform, saying that she tried to outrank Father. Mother calmly said, "Didn't you know I always outranked him? Now it is official."

Before going to our tent in the "clean" camp, Mother retrieved a small bundle she had buried in the sand. In it was the unused bedspread, tablecloth, photographs, scissors, and the little black pot. We stayed in the "clean" camp for about a week, then we were transferred to Teheran, the capital of Persia.

No sooner had we boarded a bus when Marysia said that she felt nauseous. Mother quickly took her out of the bus, and Marysia threw up two hideous, long, flat white worms. I saw them wriggle and squirm in the sand, until mother brushed them off with her foot to the side of the road. When they returned back to the bus, I asked Marysia how she felt. All she could say was, "Weren't they horrible looking things? Ugh!"

On the way to Teheran, there were high mountains with peaks reaching almost to the sky. For the first time in my life, I saw an olive tree, growing on the slopes of these mountains. We passed beautiful gorges and dense forests until we reached a great height on the edge of a precipice. When I looked down, I saw a winding river at the bottom of it. Later I learned that this was the Shah's road connecting Pahlevi with Teheran, which was open to traffic for a short time of the year.

I do not recall when we arrived in Teheran. I only remember wandering around the camp the next day as I usually did in a new place. I came to where the teachers were holding the school. A teacher asked my name and religion, then she told me to sit down on the ground and pay strict attention to what she had to say.

"Thanks to General Anders' efforts," the teacher began, "we are free people now. It was he who organized the Polish Army in the Soviet Union. Also, he persuaded Stalin to let the civilians be evacuated to Persia with the Army." The teacher said something else, but I do not remember what. I only remember writing the letters of the alphabet in the sand. Before dismissing the children, she said that we should come back to the same place the next day. I attended these classes for a few days until we were transferred to another camp.

In this camp there were a few buildings, but they were full of people. There was also a clinic, staffed by military doctors. Again I found a school, only this time there were chairs to sit on, and a blackboard. The classes were held in the open air. My teacher was a young man who taught us the Polish language and arithmetic. My Polish was not very good. I mixed a lot of Russian words with my Polish, and so did the majority of children in my class. However, I was good in arithmetic. The teacher was surprised at my knowledge of fractions. He told me that if my Polish language improved, he would transfer me to the second grade.

For several days I attended school with other children. Then, one day in the afternoon, I felt awful. I had a fever, my head ached, and a few red spots appeared on my hands and arms.

At the recess, the teacher wanted me to take charge of the children to see that they behaved themselves, didn't fight, or disturb anyone. I really didn't want the task. There were plenty of volunteers, yet he had chosen me.

When the teacher had gone, I told the children to be good because I didn't feel well. The children, who were the same age as I was or older, seemed to understand and were on their best behavior.

After school I came "home" to our tent. I told Mother I was sick and had to lie down. She took a good look at me and said,

"You and Marysia have measles." Mother took both of us to the clinic to see a doctor.

There were lots of sick children to see a doctor. While we waited, I lay down on the ground. Mother held Marysia in her arms. When my turn came to see a doctor, he told Mother that besides having measles, we both had pneumonia, dysentery, and dehydration. We had to be hospitalized. Without further ado, he told the medics to put us on a lorry and take us to a hospital. I faintly remember Mother, with tears in her eyes, waving goodbye just as the lorry was taking us away.

The hospital had to have been on the other side of Teheran, because I recall riding through the city with a beautiful, wide street, lined with green trees and shops. I liked the green trees. Marysia put her head on my lap and fell asleep.

We arrived at the hospital late in the afternoon. Our lorry stopped in front of a tent, and the nurses came and told us to get into the tent. Other nurses gave us hospital gowns and told us to take our clothes off, roll them up, and put our names on them.

First I took my clothes off, then helped Marysia with hers. By this time, I was exhausted. Before crawling into bed, I said to the nurse that no matter what happened, Marysia had to be next to me. "She is my baby sister, and I have to look after her." Having said this, I got into my bed and fell into oblivion.

I woke up the next morning, and my first thought was, "Where is Marysia?" I looked to one side and she was not there. Then I looked to my right, and Marysia was in a bed next to me. I was relieved, knowing that she was beside me. They did not separate us.

I don't remember what happened during the next few days. I only know that one morning a nurse told me to get up; she wanted to change my bed sheets. I got up, and immediately everything went black. I cried out loud, "I can't see!" The other children heard me and began to shout, "Can you see me? I am waving my hands." The children's voices were coming from every direction, but I couldn't see them. Then I heard a man's voice saying, "Don't make this child get up without my permission." The same voice snapped a few more orders. I felt a prick of a needle in my arm and a hand stroking my head.

After a while, the voice told me to open my eyes. I opened them, but still could not see anything. The voice issued an order to someone else, and in a minute or two I was told to drink something that tasted awful. Also, some ointment was put into my stuffy nose, which made my breathing much easier. Again the voice said, "Open your eyes and tell me if you can see." I opened my eyes, smiled, and recognized the doctor from the previous visits. The doctor put his four fingers in front of me and told me to count them. I counted, "One, two, three, four." He smiled and told me to go to sleep. But before I could go to sleep, I had to prove to the other children that I could see. Those who spoke to me, I had to tell his or her name and describe what each one of them was doing.

It seemed to me that the hospital was the place where the misery and suffering the children endured in the Soviet Union came to a climax. Death was all around me.

I recall one girl, who was older than I was, but who was very thin, virtually a living skeleton, and skin held her bones together. She had no muscle anywhere on her body for the nurses to give her injections. The nurses would come with a shot, look for a place, and seeing holes in her skin from previous injections, turn and walk away without giving her the injection. One afternoon her grandmother came to see her, bringing some peaches, cherries, oranges, and nectarines. Being on a bland diet because of the dysentery, I wanted to taste the luscious fruits, but the girl did not pay any attention to them. She made a motion with her bony finger for her grandmother to come closer. The woman put her ear to the girl's lips, but the girl, instead of saying a word, kissed her on the cheek and died. The grandmother called the nurses and, holding back her tears, silently walked out of the tent. I was deeply touched by the girl's love for her grandmother, and I cried for the girl who could no longer speak the words "I love you" to the only person dear to her.

On another occasion, I woke up in the middle of the night. The tent was dimly lit, but I could see a nurse walking by. She said something to me and quickly walked away. I was burning with fever. I touched the cross I had around my neck on a string, as I was accustomed to do upon waking, and found it very soft. I could bend and twist it into any shape I wanted. As I was flattening the cross on my chest back into its original form, I became aware of a commotion at the end of the tent, two beds away from me, where a girl, Krystyna, was. I knew her; we had attended the same school in the Camp 24, only she was in the third grade. She was a tall girl with long, blond hair and very pretty. Besides the nurses and a doctor, Krystyna's mother was there also. I caught sight of a nurse as she was walking by my bed, and I asked for a drink of water. When the nurse brought me some water, I asked what was happening to Krystyna. The nurse told me to be quiet and go back to sleep.

A few minutes later, I heard Krystyna's mother sob, Moja Krysia (my Krystyna). The doctor said something in a hushed voice to the mother and left. The woman began to sob louder, calling, Krysia, Krysia, but the nurse told her to control herself— "You will wake the other children," and led her outside. Before I fell asleep, I saw two men come in and take Krystyna's body away.

The next morning, the children asked the nurse, "Where is Krystyna?" One of the nurses told us that she was transferred to another tent. I was too sick to tell the children that Krystyna had died in the middle of the night.

During my five-month stay in the hospital, I witnessed many deaths of the children, who suffered from malnutrition and disease they brought with them from the Soviet Union.

The death of a little girl, who was no more than three years old, made the children cry. Her parents brought her to our tent after lunch. She was a beautiful child with dark hair and laughter in her eyes. Her parents and the nurses fussed over her, making her comfortable in the cot, while she talked to them. An hour before she died, she was lying still in her cot next to Marysia's bed. Suddenly she sat up, looked at her parents and said, "Mama, do not cry, look," and pointing with her thin arm somewhere above their heads, said, "God is looking at me." At this point Marysia, who was watching this scene, asked me, "What is she rambling about?, There is no one there." I put my finger to my lips. Marysia's eyes became big and round. She turned her head towards the little girl, who repeated again that God was looking at her. Then the girl stretched her little thin arm as though to take someone's hand, fell back on her pillow and quietly died. The heart-rending sobs of the little girl's mother affected us, and we began to cry with her. The nurses quickly ushered the parents out of the tent and tried to calm the children. Then two men, dressed in white, came and took the girl's body. I don't know where they took the bodies. Because of my illness, I was not allowed to walk outside the tent. For a long time Marysia was subdued. The death of the little girl affected her very strongly, and she remembers it to this day.

Although death was no longer a stranger to me, I always felt a great sorrow, and pangs of pain each time one of the children died, especially now, when we were free. I never thought, not for a moment, what I would do if Marysia suddenly died. She was so thin and weak that she couldn't walk to the toilet at the end of the tent, and I would carry her piggyback there, and back to her bed.

Several days had gone by since the death of the little girl, when an epidemic of mumps hit our tent. Marysia and I were transferred to another tent. I carried her piggyback to our new destination, and insisted that Marysia's bed should be next to mine. The new nurses were kind enough and allowed me to put Marysia down on an empty bed next to mine.

After we settled down, Marysia began to complain about the pain in her leg. I looked and saw a huge red sore on her thigh. I asked a nurse to take a look at it. The nurse brought some kind of ointment and bandages. After putting the ointment on the sore, the nurse bandaged it. Each day the nurse kept changing the bandages on Marysia's leg, yet never brought it up to a doctor's attention.

One day, a new doctor came to our tent and informed us that he was going to be our pediatrician. He was a young, local Persian doctor who spoke Polish and Russian. We learned, much later, that his name was Dr. Filipowicz. His father was a doctor in a Tsarist's army. For some reason his father deserted the army and came to Persia where he married a local girl. Our young doctor was his son, also a doctor with a family of his own. Meanwhile, he began to examine each and every one of us thoroughly.

When he came to Marysia, he noticed the bandages on her thigh and asked the nurses about it. The nurse said that it was nothing more than a sore. Nevertheless, he wanted to see it for himself. He cut the bandages and saw a swollen thigh, inflamed. Gently and lightly he pressed around the swelling, and suddenly the puss from the sore shot up covering his face and coat. Without a word, he went away and returned, washed, with his face covered by a mask.

He kept pressing until the pus was gone. Then with cotton swabs he cleaned the wound. I watched every move he made. Intuitively, he asked if I was her sister. I only nodded "yes." Then he asked if I knew what had happened. I told him that a nurse had given her an injection when we had first come to the hospital. The doctor nodded and told me to have a look. I looked. The hole in Marysia's thigh was deep, and I could see the bone. It was very white. Then he asked Marysia if she would like to see it, and Marysia had a good look at her own bone. Then I asked the doctor what was going to happen now.

"The wound will heal," he said, "but she will have an indentation there for the rest of her life." And indeed she has. The doctor reassured Marysia and me that her leg was going to be all right. Now that he knew about it, he checked the wound every day, telling me to look at it and how nicely it was healing. After several days, I could no longer see the bone.

By then, I had lost track of time and didn't know how long we had been in the hospital. The days turned into weeks, and weeks into months. Several times Father came to see us, bringing spring onions, for which we had an insatiable craving. He told us that Mother missed us very much and sent her love. On another occasion, Father brought news that in May, Antek had joined Junaki, a military school for young boys, and had already left for Iraq or Palestine. Before leaving, Antek was very sorry for not coming to see us to say goodbye. The next time we saw our brother was in England in 1948.

Each time Father came to see us, he always asked the nurses if he could bring us something extra. The nurses always replied that there was nothing we could have because our stomachs were not quite right yet. Then one day Father asked the doctor, "What can I bring my children?" "Because of a prolonged malnutrition, they became anemic. You can bring them some good red wine to build up their blood. Under a nurse's supervision, they can have a tablespoon of wine three times a day," the doctor replied.

The next time Father came, he brought two bottles of red wine. When Marysia saw this she asked for the bottle, which Father uncorked, and before anyone could say anything, she drank more than a tablespoon at one go, saying that it was very good. Father was very anxious and asked the passing doctor if this would have an adverse effect on the child. Smiling, the doctor replied, "No, only your pocket." From then on we had wine three times a day.

As time went on, Marysia was getting stronger. One day, as I was playing hand-made cards with other children, Marysia cried that she wanted to go to the toilet. I was fed up with carrying her piggyback there and back. I told her that she could make it on her own by holding on to the metal frames of the beds. Marysia tried. I kept a watchful eye on her as she walked, slowly progressing on her own to the third bed, and her knees began to buckle. I dropped my cards and ran up to her before she fell. Then I carried her the rest of the way. Each day Marysia walked farther and farther. She was getting stronger. She was determined to walk to the toilet by herself.

Soon I discovered that Marysia had made a pact with the nurses. When everybody was asleep, she would sneak out to the nurses' room and receive an additional tablespoonful of wine, sometimes an extra spoonful for the night. Marysia confided in me, saying, "I can tell you everything, but don't tell the others, as this is a secret between me and the nurses."

When Father came to visit us, he told us that he had been called up by the Army and would be unable to see us as often as he did. Just as he was leaving, Father said that Mother, Janka, and Olesia were transferred to the Camp Number 3. "Remember, Camp Number 3, should you leave the hospital before I see you again."

One day, the mother of my friend, Marysia Kusio, a very skinny girl, who was in a bed next to mine, came and brought burnt toast and spring onions. She offered some to me. I knew I could have these delicacies and accepted her kind offer. Mrs. Kusio gave me two burnt dry toasts and two green onions. Having in my possession the real food, I decided to eat it formally. I folded a blanket into a neat square, put it at the foot of my bed, placed a piece of paper as my plate, and then put the food there. The other children laughed at me for making such a big ado about the toast and green onions, but I proceeded as planned. I sat down at the "table," the Turkish style with my legs crossed, and began to eat the food like it was a real feast, savoring each bite. My feast lasted a long time because I chewed every bite no less than twenty-eight times. The results were outstanding – my diarrhea was checked.

The next day a new doctor came and, hearing the good news, decided to dismiss me but forgot to sign my chart. At the same time, he transferred Marysia to another ward. I felt it was my duty to know where Marysia was going to be, and asked the nurses if I could go with her.

The nurses took Marysia to a brick building, the town hospital, and placed her in a ward on the second floor with children of her own age. I stayed with her for a while until she got used to her new surroundings. Before I left, I told her to be a good girl and eat all the food and that I would come to see her the next day, and the next.

Perhaps it was the excitement of being dismissed, or the worry of Marysia being by herself in a strange place, that caused my temperature to rise that evening to about 103 degrees Fahrenheit. Despite the temperature, I felt fine.

The next morning, a different doctor came to check on us. The nurses told him that I was dismissed and would he, please, sign my chart. Noting the rise of my temperature as of the previous night and that morning, the doctor refused to release me from the hospital until he found out the cause of the sudden change in my temperature. He strictly forbade me to go outside, and said that I must stay in bed for at least three days. I was under constant surveillance of the nurses, and I couldn't sneak out from the tent to tell Marysia that I was still in the hospital.

During the next two days, my temperature began to decline. On the third day, it was normal. The same day before lunch, I heard Mother's voice asking, "Is Nadia Bogdaniec here?" I looked, and at the end of our tent, there stood Mother. As I ran up to her, I noticed how tired and worried she was. After giving her a hug, I asked, "How did you find me?" Mother replied that she had walked from tent to tent, asking for me. There were hundreds of tents, and she intended to stop at each of them until she found us.

I invited Mother to sit down on my bed so she could rest a while. No sooner had Mother sat down than she asked about Marysia. I told Mother about our separation which happened three days ago, and that I knew where she was.

"Take me to her, now," Mother said, standing up and ready to go. I found a nurse and asked for permission to leave the tent and take Mother to see Marysia. The nurse took my pulse and said I could go, providing I returned in time for supper.

Mother and I walked through a maze of tents until we reached the brick hospital. We walked into a ward, and, O God, I could hardly recognize Marysia. "How could she have changed so much in only three days?" I thought.

"Mama, Marysia was never that thin when she was with me," I said, as though apologizing for Marysia's present condition.

Marysia was very thin, only skin seemed to hold her bones together. She tried to get up when she saw us, but her strength failed her. She flopped back onto the bed, exhausted. I think Mother knew, and so did I, that Marysia was dying. I wanted to cry, but held my tears back and smiled at her. Mother, too, smiled and bent down to kiss her. As Mother was kissing her, Marysia's two thin arms encircled Mother's neck and in a barely audible voice said, "Don't leave me, Mama." Mother promised her that she wouldn't leave her, even if she had to sleep in the hallway outside her ward.

It was years later that I learned from Marysia what had happened. "When you left me that day... I was sitting on my bed when they brought us our so-called supper. It was a bowl of bland flour mixed with water – diet, they said. Cautiously, I tasted it when one of the girls opposite me said, 'Marysia, don't eat it, because if you do, your intestines will be glued together and you will die!' I barely swallowed a spoonful, thinking about my insides, and pushed the bowl away. In a flash the girl skipped to my bed, grabbed the bowl, and gulped it all down. I asked her, what about her intestines? 'Ah,' she said, 'I am older than you, so it is all right for me.' I suppose I believed her, because for three days I did not eat anything, and all the time I was hoping and praying that you or Mother would come and either stay with me or take me away from this diet. The night before you both came, the doctor and a nurse made a night round. They stopped at each bed, discussing each case. I pretended to be asleep when they stopped at the foot of my bed. Then I heard the doctor's sad voice saying that this one is also a hopeless case. It is only a matter of time, and she will die. When they left the ward, I sat up, clutched my hands into fists and whispered, 'I won't die, I won't die, you will see!' I don't remember anything else. Exhausted, I must have fallen asleep and the next day you appeared. Mother stayed, as you know, and dear Nadia, except for one boy and myself, the rest of them died. Some I watched die, others died in the night and only empty beds were there in the morning. Indeed, fate works in mysterious ways," Marysia finished her narrative.

Mother and I stayed with Marysia until a nurse came and told us the visiting hours were over and that everyone had to leave. Mother asked the nurse if it were possible for her to stay so that she could personally look after her daughter. The nurse was very indignant and told Mother to vacate the premises immediately. Mother left the ward, promising Marysia that she would stay, and sat down by the door. By then, the nurse had become belligerent and began to threaten Mother with orderlies who would forcefully escort her out.

However, fate had other plans. While Mother and the nurse were arguing, the Persian doctor walked in. First, he asked the nurse what the argument was all about. The nurse told him that this woman, meaning my Mother, refused to leave the hospital. Then Dr. Filipowicz asked Mother the same question.

Mother told him that under no circumstances would she leave her dying child. The doctor seemed to remember me and asked if this argument concerned my little sister. I said, "Yes."

To settle this argument between Mother and the nurse, the doctor suggested that he would take a look at Marysia. They walked into the ward, and I was right behind them. I stayed by the door, not to be in their way, or be told to leave. The doctor examined Marysia; he even remembered the wound on her thigh and wanted to see it. Then he told the nurse to bring the necessary papers for him to sign, allowing Mother to stay and take care of Marysia. He also authorized Mother to sleep in the bed next to her. Understanding Mother's concern, the doctor asked Mother if he could be Marysia's doctor, promising nothing. Mother agreed.

It was close to suppertime, and I had to leave. I told Mother that I would come to see her and Marysia the next day if my nurses would let me. I was very happy, perhaps ecstatic would be a better word to describe my feelings that Mother was now with Marysia. I knew Mother wouldn't let her die. Marysia was very special to me, and suddenly I remembered the day she was born.

It was a warm summer evening in June at the ranger's station. The fishermen stretched their nets on the grass in the meadow near our house. The cook had a nice fire going on the bank of the river Lachowiec. He was cooking something wonderful, and I was sitting close by, waiting with my little pot for the invitation to join them. I could hardly wait to taste the fishermen's stew. As I waited, the cook told me a story of the river, how the Lachowiec wanted to change the course of the mighty River Prypeć. "He turned and twisted here and there, and ended up flowing back into the Prypeć," the cook said, shaking his head. I loved these peaceful moments in summer with water gently lapping the bank of the river, listening to the fishermen's strange yet fascinating stories and legends. By the time he finished his story, other fishermen joined us, demanding their supper. The cook stirred the pot with a wooden spoon, tasted the stew, and said, "It is ready!" I was hoping to be the first to be served, when Father appeared and said something to the fishermen. They in turn began to shake his hand and slap him on the back. Then Father looked at me and said that Mother wanted to see me. Immediately, I ran to the house.

At first, no one seemed to be in the house. Then I heard Mother call me. I went to her. She was in bed. Mother smiled and lifted the bed covers. There beside her, I saw a little human being wrapped in a white blanket. Mother told me to unwrap it, and take a good look. I unwrapped the baby. Then Mother said, "Look at her hands and count her fingers." I counted to five. "Now, look at her toes and tell me how many toes she has." Again I counted to five on each of her tiny feet. Mother seemed to be pleased with my observations and asked me what I thought of her.

"Mama, she is so little that she could fit into the shoe-box Janka gave me," I said and ran out to find it. By the time I came back with the shoebox, Mother and the baby were asleep.

From then on, most of my time I spent by Mother's bed. Then one day Mother asked me, "What shall we name the baby?" Without hesitation I said, "Marysia." Mother asked why this name, why not, for example, Victoria?

"Oh, Mama, I know a song about Marysia," I replied, "and I will sing it to her." Whenever I rocked the baby, I sang that song. Sometimes I would go into the forest, climb a tall tree, and sing to my heart's content. It was a sad song, the kind one wouldn't sing to a baby, but I liked it. Being only six years old, I didn't understand why "Marysia" in the song committed suicide, or why she was in a hospital, and everyone was so concerned about her.

One day a lot of people came to see us. There were people from the village and the nearby stations. Also, there was the Orthodox priest who gave me only one piece of candy. I thought that he was very stingy because I was used to getting a whole bag from Commander Zajączkowski, who visited us regularly until the war began. Mother came and said, "It is official. We christened the baby Maria so you can call her 'Marysia.'"

Now, Marysia was very sick. The doctors transferred her to a ward of no return. As far as I knew, all the little children had died on that ward. I did not want my baby sister, whom I loved from the first moment I saw her, to die. It could not be. As I walked back to my tent, I became very optimistic because Mother was with her, and Mother wouldn't let anything happen to Marysia.

For the next few days I couldn't see Mother and Marysia. My fever shot up again, and the doctor forbade me to go out. I came to the conclusion that there was something sinister about the ward Marysia was in. I was there twice, and twice I came down with a fever. The doctor prescribed some medicine which made me sick. Then he told the nurses to give me the same medicine with milk and watch my reaction. Again I was sick. I threw up before I could get to the bathroom. After that, the doctor discontinued this awful tasting medicine, which I believe was quinine. I eventually became well again. A week or so later, I was dismissed from the hospital. This time I asked the doctor to sign me out.

Before going back to the camp, I went to see Mother and Marysia to tell them the good news. As I was coming up the stairs, I met Mother coming down, carrying Marysia on a pillow. I asked Mother why she put her on a pillow.

"I cannot carry her otherwise, or she may fall apart because she is so thin."

I lifted Marysia's blanket and saw that she was all skin and bones and no bigger than a pillow.

We went outside and sat down on a bench in front of the hospital. I told Mother that I was going "home" that afternoon. "But where is home if you are not there?" I asked Mother. Mama smiled. There is nothing as reassuring as Mother's smile, and

Mother's smile told me that I would be all right. Also, she instructed me how to find Janka and Olesia in the Camp Number 3, and that she and Marysia would join us shortly. I was so confident that it would be so, because Mother said so.

After I said goodbye to both of them, I went back to my tent. After lunch, I put on a dress and sandals given to me by a nurse. When a military truck drove up to our tent to collect the dismissed children, I got on it and told the driver to take me to Camp Number 3.

We rode through Teheran in a covered military truck. The children who sat in the back could not see anything of the beautiful boulevards of this ancient city. I thought it was the same street that I vaguely remembered, from when we rode to the hospital. This time I not only noticed the trees along the street, but also the huge posters of the Shah. He was so young and handsome, dressed in his uniform with lots of medals.

Somewhere on the outskirts of Teheran, the truck stopped and the driver announced, "This is the Camp Number 3." I and about five other children got off. At first I didn't see any camp, only a high wall with a gate at which sat a guard in the shade of an old tree. Later I found out that the guard was there not to keep the Polish people in, but to keep the Persian beggars out.

When I walked through the gate, the first thing I saw were tents. The place was full of them. Looking around, I noticed a pond to the right. A little brook emptied into the pond. On each side of this little brook were tents. To the left, there were fruit trees and pomegranate bushes. If it were not for the tents, the place would have seemed like the Garden of Eden. It belonged to a rich Persian who let the Polish refugees stay there.

I walked up to the first tent and asked a woman if she knew where Janka and Olesia Bogdaniec lived. As it turned out, the woman was Janka's close friend and took me to our tent. I looked inside, but no one was there. Still worse, nothing was familiar about it except a small bundle, the last remains from home, which Mother had saved from being burned while we were in Pahlevi.

I sat down by the little brook and watched the water run and bubble over the pebbles and stones. At lunchtime Olesia came by and was surprised to see me, exclaiming, "You are back!" I knew and felt that she was genuinely happy to see me. She put her arms around me and held me close for a moment, like she always did whenever I was frightened or sad.

Olesia and I were very close. As far back as I can remember, she always took care of me. Olesia was five years older than I. The three of us, Antek, Olesia, and I slept together with me in the middle. I recall how I used to beg her to rub my back before falling asleep. As I was growing up, Olesia was my idol. She was tall and willowy with golden-red locks and green eyes. Whenever I think of her, I have this beautiful picture of her before my eyes.

It was autumn, and the woods were ablaze with red maple, yellow birch, orange oak, and other trees, dotted here and there with dark patches of evergreens. I sat alone by the window, playing with my paper dolls, when I saw Olesia coming down the dirt road. She looked like a rusalka (naiad), wearing a white dress, adorned with red berries of the kalina (a guelder rose). The kalina red berries were in her hair, around her neck, and in her hands, which she held high above her shoulders. At first, I thought she hurt her hands and they were bleeding. I ran out to greet her and inquired what had happened, but seeing that it was only berries, I exclaimed, "You are beautiful!" Olesia smiled and said, "On your knees, you peasant, I am the enchanted princess of these woods."

And now, Olesia was still tall and slender but without her golden curls. Her hair was shaved off in the Kitab hospital when she and I had typhus. Releasing me from her momentary embrace, she suggested that we go to the place where she worked. Olesia took my hand and led me to the kitchen situated at the far end of the camp. Although I was not particularly hungry, she insisted I had something to eat. I sat down at a picnic table, and she served me some stew on rice. After I had eaten, Olesia told me that she couldn't spend the rest of the day with me because she had to work in the kitchen until suppertime.

I left the kitchen area and wandered off, surveying the camp. I found that the camp was walled in on all sides. There was no school or singular classes held anywhere. I saw many stalls with all kinds of fruit and sweets, but I had no money to buy anything.

The next day, Father came to see Janka and Olesia and was very surprised to see me. He was dressed in an army uniform. I asked if I ought to salute him. Father smiled and said it was not necessary as he was enlisted as a private. Father told me he came to say goodbye to us. His unit was pulling out in the afternoon. They were going to Iraq. He also said that we were in the hands of the British, and that they would relocate us. "When you are settled, look for me through the Red Cross," Father said. "Promise me that you will write to me."

Father wanted to find Olesia and tell her he was leaving. We walked to the kitchen and found her peeling potatoes. He talked to her for a while, then he said to me, "Walk with me to the gate."

On the way, we passed a fruit stall. I told Father I wanted to taste the grapes. He bought some and gave them to me. As we continued to walk, I said, "Of all fruit, grapes are my favorite."

When we reached the gate, a military truck was waiting. Father put his hand in his pocket and gave me some money, saying, "Buy whatever else you want to taste." I took the money, said goodbye, and watched him drive away in the truck. The next time I saw Father was in England in 1948.

It seems that the camp was divided into sections. When I returned to the tent, a woman in charge of our section told me to come to see her. A shipment of children's nightgowns had come in, and I could pick one for myself. I and about fifteen women arrived. As soon as the woman told us to take one gown per child, those women, like a pack of hungry wolves, rushed for those nightgowns, shoving and pushing, grabbing regardless of the size—the bigger the better—and in minutes all of them were gone, except one, the smallest that would fit a two-year old. It was left for me. The woman first looked at me, then at the nightgown, and without saying a word, handed me the gown she had chosen for her two-year-old daughter. The gown fit me perfectly. At last I had something to sleep in besides my slip.

It was sometime in September when Mother and Marysia arrived in the Camp Number 3. Although Marysia was still very thin, she looked much better and could walk a short distance. Mother warned us that we must never upset Marysia, doctor's orders, or she might get very ill. One day Marysia became upset and angry, all of her own, and her stomach began to swell. Even though I had nothing to do with Marysia's anger, Mother blamed me for her condition. Immediately Mother rushed her to a doctor, who told her that Marysia had a nervous stomach, a condition common in children who suffered malnutrition and dehydration.

I did not see Marysia and Mother for a few weeks. It was much later that I heard about her story in the hospital. The following is Marysia's story:

Nadia, I was very sad when you left the ward that day, but happy because Mother was with me. One morning when I woke up, there were Polish doctors and nurses in the ward, when the Persian doctor, Dr. Filipowicz, walked in, greeting everyone. Firstly, he made a round stopping at every bed, looked at the children, said nothing, until he came to my bed. After greeting Mother, he looked at me, smiled, and asked if my sister Nadia came to see me, and I shook my head. He then rejoined the waiting medical personnel, saying clearly, 'My colleagues, from now on, I will take care of the child Marysia Bogdaniec. I will expect all my instructions and orders to be carried out to the letter. As from today, she will have half a cup of chicken broth three times daily. After a few days a full cup of broth followed by a chicken wing. No solid food whatsoever. I will visit often, duties permitting, to see how she is progressing.' After this speech, the doctor said, 'Good day,' and left the ward. The relapse that I had when Nadia came to visit us, and Mother carried me on the pillow, I do not remember. Eagerly I awaited a visit by my handsome doctor Filipowicz—tall, slim, with kind blue eyes—although this meant painful injections into my thin thigh with saline solution, every day for the dehydration, I think.

One morning, as usual, Mother carried me to the toilet and brought me back to bed. When the doctor walked in, he picked me up, talking all the time until we came to the washroom. I was terribly embarrassed when the doctor looked down at my poo, looked at me, smiled, and said 'Good.' I also looked down to see what was so good about it. This time it was solid and darker in color, a sign that the dysentery was improving. He nodded this to the nurse standing nearby, and she pulled the chain to flush it. The doctor praised me, and after talking with Mother, he left.

For six months, the ward was my world. Here, suffering and death were regular visitors, where no one visited the sick children. The outside world I saw through a large window, when Mother carried me towards it to see what was going on outside. Down there I saw Polish soldiers and nurses going somewhere, but my eyes followed the children who were walking and skipping. I was thinking that one day, I will do the same. Meanwhile, I had to get healthier and stronger.

As the time went on, I accumulated a nice collection of toys, including seashells, pebbles, and playing cards, all brought by kind nurses. But who gave me the nice, beautiful doll, I do not remember.

My health was improving daily, but I was still unable to walk. One night, I awoke feeling very hungry. Everybody was asleep, and so was my Mother. Silently, I moved to the edge of the bed towards a small cupboard where Mother stored food. I leaned towards it and managed to take out some breadrolls, boiled eggs, and grapes, and placed them on the blanket on my lap. For a while, I just looked at the food. Then I tasted a bit of everything and finished with the sweet white grapes. I was happy. I meant to put the leftovers back into the cupboard, but I fell asleep. When I awoke in the morning, Mother stood by my bed, looking very worried. Then my doctor came. Mother told him about my feast during the night and was very sorry for not waking up to stop me from eating so much food. The doctor smiled, sat on my bed, and asked me if I enjoyed it. I explained to him that I was very hungry, and this was my best lunch. The doctor assured Mother that all would be well, and that I was now on the road to recovery.

One day when the doctor came and, as usual, sat on my bed, I crawled towards him. He took me onto his lap, and I put my right hand around his neck, and looked into his kind eyes. I asked, 'Will you truly make me well so I can walk and skip like the children I saw out of the window?' The doctor hugged me and said, 'Dear child, when I make you well, you will dance your life away.' I hung my head and said nothing because the word 'dance' meant nothing to me. I did not know its meaning. Oh, if he only knew...

Meanwhile, the children continued to die. Some died during the night. Some, I watched die. To take my mind off death, Mother would talk to me, tell stories, play cards, and tell fortunes with cards. One day I was happily playing cards when the doctor arrived and asked me what I was doing. 'Telling fortunes,' I replied. 'Oh, doctor, shall I tell you your fortune?' and I quickly spread the cards on the bed. Pointing at hearts, I said that soon I will be well, will walk again, and will leave the hospital to join Father, who is far away. The doctor smiled and said that I was *telling a fortune for myself and not for him. 'But doctor,' I quickly replied, 'it is thanks to YOU that I will walk and run again, and I will never forget you.' Holding the deck of cards in my hand, I asked him to pull one card and he pulled out a diamond. 'This means you will be very rich,' I told him. The doctor patted my head and said, 'You're a wonderful fortune teller.' He was a good doctor, and for him I did everything he asked concerning my health. Afterwards, Mother picked me up, put my feet on the floor, and told me to stand on my skinny, wobbly legs. I obliged. Soon, holding Mother's hand, I managed to make a couple of steps.*

I was getting stronger each day. The day came for me to be discharged from the hospital. Dr. Filipowicz came to say goodbye, and was pleased with my recovery, and I thanked him most warmly. The nurses also wished me well. All my toys I left behind as I no longer needed them, except one, the beautiful doll. On the day that we were leaving the hospital, I carried the doll in my hand, when one very pretty nurse asked me to leave it with the rest of the toys. I refused, as this was the only toy I wanted to have with me as a memory of my stay in the hospital. But she continued her pleas, on and on and on. In the end, I almost threw it into her outstretched hands, and without a word I walked towards the door and Mother, neither turning back to look at the nurse, the doll, nor the empty ward. Mother did not interfere; the decision was mine and mine alone.

Many years later, thanks to Nadia, I have a collection of beautiful Barbie dolls, which to this day adorn my bedroom.

Over the years, when I visited Nadia in Albuquerque, I would receive from her many Barbies and also pretty dresses for them, which Nadia made from pieces of fabric. Every time Nadia presented me with a Barbie, such as 'Christmas Carol,' 'Swan Lake,' '50th Anniversary,' to mention a few. I would hug and hug Nadia, saying, 'Thank you!' During my many visits to Albuquerque, I met wonderful American people, Nadia's friends, among them professors and doctors, who made my visits truly wonderful. As a thank you, I wrote a few articles with photos of them to the 'Polish Daily' in London.

*

Soon after our arrival, the liquidation of the Camp Number 3 began. The Polish soldiers arrived in the military trucks and lorries, and told the people to pack and get into them. We picked up our blankets, and one small bundle, the remains from Poland, and left the camp with its fruit trees, pond, and little bubbling stream where I spent hours just sitting, watching, and listening to the whispers and rustle of its waters.

We left Teheran and drove for a couple of hours over a barren and dusty terrain, until we arrived in Ahvaz, Persia. Again Mother claimed the spot in a huge brick building by spreading the blankets on the floor. For our evening meal, we received some canned cheese and crackers, compliments of the British, and washed down with water from a tap.

A few days after our arrival in Ahvaz, the epidemic of the pinkeye broke out among the people. It seems everyone had it, except me. Perhaps it was due to the fact that I slept on the ground outside the building since it was too stuffy and hot inside. Then, one morning, I couldn't open my eyes. My eyelids were glued shut. I didn't panic; I'd known it was a matter of time before the infection would hit me. So far I'd had everything else that was going around, only now it was pinkeye. I rubbed the dry matter of one eye, just enough to see, and went to a water tap and thoroughly washed my face and eyes. For the next several days, I stood in line at the eye clinic to have my eyes washed and drops put in.

In the meantime, Marysia used to lead Mother to the clinic, but since both had the eye infection, neither of them could see very well. Marysia didn't see a big hole in front of them, and they both fell in, scraping their knees on sharp stones. I was already at the clinic when I saw them coming with dirt all over them and bleeding. I gave them my place in line and asked what had happened to them. "There is nothing worse than the blind leading the blind," Mother said.

I don't exactly remember when or how we left Ahvaz. I only recollect that we arrived in Karachi, India (at that time Karachi was in India) by ship. Somewhere outside Karachi was our camp. My memories of our short stay there are very sketchy. We were served soup with "worms," or macaroni floating in the grease on top of it. The British soldiers showed us the outdoor movies. We slept outdoors, again on the ground, and watched the beautiful night sky. You could clearly see the Milky Way with its millions of twinkling stars, and I wondered before falling asleep what those stars were made of. Now I realized how much I missed my brother, Antek. He was no longer there to ask such important questions, such as, what was beyond those stars, or why did they flicker in the nights, or why we can't see them during the day, and I would fall asleep, listening to the weird laugh of the hyenas and other strange noises in the night.

We didn't stay very long in Karachi. Soon the trucks arrived and drove us back to the docks. On the streets of Karachi, there were lots of sick natives, just sitting or lying on the pavement. Also, there were many beggars who came up to our trucks. Baksheesh, or alms for the poor. I wished I had something to give them, but we were so poor that we had nothing to give.

At the port, we boarded a British ship. This one was much bigger than the one on which we had crossed the Caspian Sea, and I thought that perhaps our whole village would fit into it if all the houses were compacted into neat cubes.

On this ship, we were at liberty to roam its decks. My friend Zosia and I were amazed at the number of lifeboats. They were everywhere, on the deck we were on, and also on the upper deck, and we wondered if we would have to use them. After all, we knew the war was on, and what if our ship hits a mine?

Towards the evening our ship pulled from the shore. I was standing alone watching the port fade away, when a British sailor walked to me, said something which I didn't understand, took my hand, and forcefully led me to the upper deck. First he showed me the lifeboats and what was inside them, talking all the time. I assumed he was explaining that these boats would be used in case of emergency and what we must do. Being ten years old, I was naturally curious and ran from boat to boat to see if any of them were different from another. After looking at several boats, I concluded that they were all the same, with oars, life jackets, and a few things stored under the seats. On my way back to the lower deck, the sailor blocked the narrow passage between the boats, catching me in his arms as I tried to run past him. Then he knelt down, put his head on my stomach, and began to feel my buttocks and legs with his hand. I sensed his sinister motives and became frightened. With all my might I pushed him, and he fell backwards. I jumped over him and ran away. When I was already on the lower deck and among other people, I looked back. The sailor was running, took two steps down the staircase, but changed his mind and disappeared on the upper deck. I stood still for a moment, took a deep breath, and being no longer afraid, went to the place where the rest of the family was. I told Olesia about the horrifying experience. She was sympathetic and caring, and said, "Never trust a stranger, and, from now on, always stay with your friends or me. The man is obviously a child molester." I didn't know what that meant and didn't ask her to explain it to me. I only promised that if I ever saw that man, I would point him out to her. But as it turned out, I never saw him again.

As we sailed over the Arabian Sea, other British ships joined us. There were destroyers and mine sweepers in front, on both sides, and astern our ship. The convoy stayed with us during our voyage over the Arabian Sea and the Indian Ocean. Then one morning, I noticed that the ships had disappeared. A few hours later, we arrived in Mombassa, East Africa.

On the whole, our voyage from Karachi to Mombassa was very pleasant. There were no storms to make us seasick. We had plenty of food to eat and water to wash in. The British even provided individual towels. My friends and I watched the fantastic sunsets which can only be observed at sea. We saw the schools of porpoises, jumping over the whitecaps as the waves were breaking, and we wrote our memoirs. My friend Zosia, who was older than I, told me to write everything down, read it, and remember and tell my children and grandchildren about it. For a long time, even while in Africa, I continued to write all my experiences, good and bad, funny and sad, about my school years and friends, but the notebook got lost in a shuffle from place to place, which is most regrettable.

Looking back on those horrendous years, the question frequently crossed my mind: How and why did we survive? Was it because we inherited a family quality of resolution and determination? My Father certainly manifested these qualities. Was it due to the care and dedication of our parents to the family and health matters? Perhaps it was a combination of both factors.

On reflection, I decided that it was a combination as expressed, plus good luck in choosing the right company, that determined our fate.

Whatever the explanation, I am grateful to Almighty God for the result. I am here to tell the tale.

CHAPTER 6

Africa and the Camp Koja
September 1942 - February 1948

Everyone was on deck, watching the strange and mysterious land, never before seen by us, called Africa. The port Mombassa seemed very large, the biggest city I had seen so far. We passed many ships from different parts of the world, sail boats, and plain boats. Along the shores grew tall coconut palms, gently swaying in a light breeze. My recollections of actual docking and getting on a train are dim and sketchy.

The next thing I remember is being on a train, which was taking us into the interior of Africa. We had no idea where we were going. On our way from Mombassa to Nairobi, Kenya, we stopped at some small town. The natives were just as curious about us as we were about them. Some of them had pieces of ivory pierced through their noses. Others had such heavy earrings that they pulled down the outside skin of the ears, making the heavy barrels hang below their shoulders. Only a few men wore shorts or pants; the rest wore long caftans. The women had pieces of material wrapped around their bodies, while children were naked.

After the natives had taken a good look at us, they disappeared and soon reappeared, bringing bananas, oranges, pineapples, and other fruit, not yet known to us. Mother traded my one and only nightgown for some bananas and oranges. One woman in our car traded her scarf for a papaya. All of us were curious about this strange fruit and watched her cut it open. When she cut it, she was very disappointed and said, "It is a rotten pumpkin!" Feeling cheated, she threw it away when the train pulled out from the station.

The train sped on through a magic world, grass-covered, vast savannahs, dotted here and there with herds of zebras, giraffes, lonely rhinos, and lions. The animals seemed to be in reverie, to be going somewhere over this great expanse. The sight of these magnificent animals evoked sheer delight from all of us, but they seemed oblivious of us or the train, and with a graceful gait, kept on going.

We stopped in Nairobi, the capital of Kenya, long enough to have something to eat, and then sped away into the night.

The next day we arrived at a small station, Mukono, in Uganda. By the time we got off the train and boarded the awaiting buses and lorries, it was almost noon, very sunny, and very still in this small town. Sunshine lay on the ground in shafts and gold plaques between the houses. The natives came out to look at us, but they didn't trade their wares or produce with us.

We drove for several hours to our final destination. On our way, we passed a few small villages. The houses were round, made of mud and straw. The women in their sarong-type skirts and naked children stood by the roadside and watched us drive by. We didn't stop anywhere., Tthe drivers seemed to be in a hurry to get us somewhere as quickly as possible.

We were the first transport to arrive in this exotic country. There were 300 of us – the people, mainly women and children – who in 1940 were deported from Poland, survivors of labor camps and prisons in the Soviet Union.

Upon arrival at our final destination, we saw a huge lake and mysterious green jungles. The driver told us to get out of the bus. We picked up our belongings and stood beside the vehicle, gaping at the surrounding wilderness. Before us was a lake, which seemed further away than I thought at first, jungles, hills, two mountains, and tall grasses obscuring any other detail. There was nothing of the familiar civilization.

Surveying the situation, some women began to cry, saying, "They brought us to the end of the world. How are we to survive in this wilderness? We shall certainly perish here, and the world will never know what happened to us!"

I was so busy looking at what was before me that I didn't notice the huts especially built for us. As a matter of fact, hardly anyone saw them. The tall elephant grass hid them from our view.

The sun was hanging low over the lake. The British administrator, talking through an interpreter, said that there were only thirty huts. Since there were three hundred of us, he had to allocate ten people in each house before it got dark. None of us understood why this Englishman was so anxious to house all the people before sunset.

Mother, not giving in to hysterics like other women, found another family of five, Mrs. Zalega, a widow with four children, Janka, Marysia, Edward, and Veronika, and claimed the nearest hut on the edge of an empty space. As we walked into the hut, I noticed that it had been constructed in a hurry. It was made of bamboo and mud, with holes in the walls so big one could put a fist through them, and anything could crawl in very easily. The roof was thatched.

Entering the front door, there was a "common" room, with a table and two benches. To the left and the right, there were two other rooms with five beds in each of them. Mother chose the one on the left and Mrs. Zalega moved into the right one. The beds had wooden frames, ropes for springs, lumpy cotton mattresses, and mosquito nets. Each post of the bed had holes for the bamboo sticks on which to hang the mosquito nets. In each bedroom there were two windows without panes, and one in the common room. Also, there were two heavy, solid mahogany panels for each window, which I couldn't lift. The door was also made of mahogany and had no lock.

As soon as the sun went down, it became totally dark. Since there was no electricity or lamps, we had no other choice but to go to sleep. And thus ended our first, very exciting day in the camp situated on the shores of a big lake.

Before falling asleep, I listened to the noises outside. It seemed as though nothing slept during the night here. The rough grunts and snorts of various animals came from the lake, but what sort of animals? In the jungle, the exotic birds cawed and cried in shrill voices. Some sounded like the moans of human beings in pain. All this was at once scary, foreboding, and wonderful, and I was glad to be in this mysterious land where the days were warm and the nights cool. I pulled a blanket over my ears to shut out the noise and fell asleep.

When we awoke the next morning, the sun was up. Mother had built a fire in front of the hut and was boiling water in her little black pot. Standing near the fire, Marysia and I looked around in awe and wonder at this new place. The rays of the morning sun touched the tips of the tall grass over which I could only see the roofs of other huts. I felt some sort of relief, freedom and excitement, and I was eager to explore our temporary "locality." Here was the beginning of a new life – free from oppression, cold, and hunger. Here we didn't have to worry about food, clothes, and health. We left these responsibilities in care of adults. "Here is going to be a good life," I thought.

My thoughts were interrupted by Mother's voice, telling me to go and wash, pointing to an empty space between the houses. At first I couldn't see anything where Mother was pointing, then I saw a pipe with a tap sticking out from the ground where the grass was much shorter and greener, as though someone had mowed it a few days ago. I splashed water over my face and head and came back to the fire to dry. Marysia did the same. Soon Janka and Olesia joined us.

Between the houses there was also a latrine. It was a deep, oblong hole, enclosed by bamboo walls with a straw roof. Wooden boards with a square hole made up the floor. Behind our latrine, there was a tall palm tree and a huge termite mound.

By then, other people were up and about. They also made remarks about the tall grass, which was obscuring their view of each other, and what was hiding in it. The last words frightened me. Did they imply snakes, I wondered? The thought of the unknown and unseen terrified me, and I made up my mind not to wander through the grass alone.

After a breakfast of tea and rusks of bread, I ventured away despite my fear of snakes. Next to our house was a flat, vacant plot with several deciduous trees, and the grass was not so tall. I looked at the nearest tree and thought, under this tree I would read and study when school started. I walked further on, to the edge of this plot, and saw more trees, thick, lush, green vegetation, and that the terrain was gently sloping toward the lake. As I was about to turn around and go home, my eye caught a movement in the trees. I froze and watched. There were monkeys, sitting on the branches and grooming each other. Some jumped from tree to tree, just having fun in the cool of the morning, as the air held a divine, sweet freshness. The monkeys seemed to be aware of my presence and began to show off, swinging from branch to branch, on one hand, or just hanging by their tails. I laughed and applauded their superb acrobatic performance.

I returned to the hut and found a teacher taking down the names of the school-age children. The teacher told Mrs. Zalegas, three children, and me that the following Monday we should come to a place at the end of the row of houses, where there was no grass but sand, for our first day of school.

The rest of the day I spent exploring the area close to our hut. I even walked through the tall grass to meet our neighbors. In the first house the women seemed discontented and bewildered. They couldn't come to terms with the reality of our surroundings. It was the first time they had been in complete wilderness. They kept repeating, "How can we survive here?" As the women were complaining about such primitive conditions, I thought, at least we didn't have to sleep on the ground, as we had done in so many other places. Here, each one of us had a bed, pillow, blanket, and mosquito net. But most important, it was warm here.

In the next house I was surprised to see my school friend from the camp "Listvinnitsa 22," Leokadia Gnutek. She was a tall girl, about my age, and very polite. Together we walked to the place the teacher designated as our school.

Within a day or two, since our arrival here, the natives distributed a few tools – an axe, a hoe, and a shovel to each house. These tools served not only as something to dig or chop with, but also as our weapons. Soon afterwards the natives brought kerosene lamps and containers of kerosene. Looking at our lamp, I told Marysia that our countryman Lukasiewicz was the first one to invent such a wonder. Marysia opened her eyes wide and said, "Really? A Polishman?"

Janka took it upon herself to inspect the lamp. She checked all the mechanics, filled the lamp with fuel, trimmed and shaped the wick, and lit it. Everything worked fine. In the meantime, Mother and Mrs. Zalega quickly decided that the best way to use the lamp would be by rotation. One evening the Zalegas would have the lamp; the next evening we would have it. This system worked until we moved. There was, however, one drawback to this system. When the Zalegas had the lamp, we were in the dark and had to go to bed early. Candles were not available. Even if they were, we couldn't buy them. We had no money. Mother, however, had a brilliant idea.

From neighbors, Mother learned that there was a man in the camp who was a welder by occupation. He was too old and physically impaired to serve in General Anders' army. There was a handful of such men in the camp, unable to be in the army due to age or being physically unfit. So Mother took an empty can of beans and went in search of this welder. When she came back, she brought a kopciuszek (something that produces a small flame). She filled it with kerosene, put a piece of cotton rope inside as a wick, and lit it. "And there was light!" This little flickering light allowed us to read and do our homework. Besides, we didn't have to go to bed after the sunset. Only much later, however, the kopciuszek caused me a big fright.

Within a few days of our arrival to this wilderness, the natives built a temporary chapel on the empty plot beside our hut. It had three walls and a roof, and in the middle was an altar made of two boards. The following Sunday the priest said Mass. It was Thanksgiving service. Mostly, we gave thanks to God for delivering us from the hands of Stalin, the land of imprisonment, and forced labor. After the regular sermon, the priest enlightened us about our whereabouts.

He said that we were now in Uganda, British Protectorate in East Africa, and that our camp was called Koja (pronounced "CAH-juh"), built especially for us on the northern shores of the Lake Victoria. The capital of Uganda is Entebbe, and Kampala is a commercial city sixty miles away. Like Rome, Kampala is built on seven hills, with a good hospital. The spoken language there is Swahili.

During our five-year stay in Uganda, I learned at school that we were about 4,000 feet above sea level. Our camp was on the fabulous Lake Victoria. Besides being the second largest body of fresh water in the world (the first is Lake Superior in the USA), the lake is also the source of the legendary River Nile. Uganda lies in the heart of the tropics, actually astride of the equator, where the climate is pleasant with temperatures ranging between 60 to 100 degrees Fahrenheit. Our camp Koja was cooled by the breezes from the lake. From my personal observations, I learned that there are two rainy seasons: one in spring, the other in autumn. The rainfall is plentiful, and it keeps the country lush and green. In Uganda, it is always summer with little change in the temperature from season to season. During the dry season, the vertical sun is so hot that we could not stay outside between 11am and 2pm without a hat or a cork helmet, designed especially for the tropical climate. Many times I carried my books on top of my head because I forgot to take a hat with me in the morning.

The beginning of our life in these surroundings was very hard. Everyone managed as best as they could. We cooked our food gypsy-style – a few stones for the hearth, and Mother's black pot hanging on a few sticks over the fire. The aroma of the cooking soup enticed all sorts of insects: mosquitoes, gnats, moths and whatever else that was flying by. It was Marysia's chore to fish out with a spoon all these insects. After a while, Mother stopped her, otherwise there would be no soup left.

The natives brought huge, weather-beaten logs, covered with moss and the unknown-to-us African flora, and unloaded them close to the houses. Women and young boys chopped the logs with axes into small pieces for firewood, because every able-bodied man, and boys over 18 years, joined General Anders' army.

The camp was divided into sections. Each section had a leader appointed by the administration. The leader's responsibility was to inform the people about where to get food provisions, clothes, garden tools, meetings, and information in general.

For us children, it was a real paradise. Unrestrained children ran wild over the camp and stood in lines for provisions: bread, flour, sugar, cooking oil, powdered milk and eggs, and bars of yellow, strong-smelling soap. On Fridays, we had dried fish, mostly kippers, meat twice a week, which we had to carry under a cover because hawks with their telescopic eyesight swiftly dove in on us and stole the meat from an uncovered plate. One day, a hawk had brazenly stolen the uncovered meat from my plate. The result was that we had no meat for a few days. Mother was understanding and did not scold me for the loss of the good meal.

Life started to improve. The natives built our kitchens behind the houses. It was a small shack with three walls, a straw roof, and a wood-burning stove with a five-gallon square can for an oven. When our stove was built and Janka lit a fire just to see if it "worked," Marysia came in a little later and, seeing a shiny new oven, put her hand inside the "oven" and seriously burned the palm of her hand. We had no medication whatsoever, so Mother put a cool wet cloth on her palm, changing it often. In time, Marysia's hand healed without a scar. Very often, from the straw roof lizards used to fall into uncovered pots of soup or potatoes. Some missed the target and sizzled on the hot plate. To avoid the unwanted extras in our meals, we covered the pots tightly.

By the kitchen, we stacked firewood. Under these stacks lived various snakes that used to frighten our chickens. One day, by chance, we happened to see a long snake slithering out from its hiding place, heading for the chickens. To save them and their eggs, we had to kill it. Such incidents with snakes occurred all over the camp. One man, who lived two rows below us, caught and hung three big snakes when they got into the coop and attacked his chickens during the night.

Just as the bright day declined, and the sun set in the blue, calm lake, a ten-foot snake was crawling along the wall of our house. Mother and Mrs. Zalega panicked. One grabbed a hoe, and the other an axe, and cut the poor snake in half. The half with the head slithered into the tall grass, and the other half they threw into the latrine. That night we closed the windows with the mahogany panels, barricaded the door, and put mosquito nets over our beds, tucking them well under the mattresses.

The next morning I got up before anyone else did and lit a fire in our new stove. Watching the fire, I remembered that I did not bring a kettle with me. On my way to the house, I was humming, skipping, and jumping. Then I saw the other half of the snake which had run away the previous evening. I almost stepped on it, and I let out a terrifying scream, waking not only everyone in our house, but also the neighbors. Within seconds, Mother, Mrs. Zalega, and others were by my side, armed to the hilt with hoes, shovels, and axes.

"What is the matter?" they all asked at once.

"Look! There it is," I said, pointing to the half of the snake as it crawled along the wall towards the door with its guts trailing behind it.

"This snake is either looking for its other half or is determined to get into your house," said Mr. Gnutek, one of the few men in the camp who was too old to serve in the Polish army. He walked up to the snake, and with one swing of an axe, chopped its head off. Janka came with a shovel, picked up the head and the rest of the body, and unceremoniously dumped them into the latrine. Before the kind neighbors left, they advised me not to get up at sunrise, or I might encounter something more dreadful than a snake.

Using garden tools and axes, we began to change the complexion of our camp. First, the women made paths between the houses. They landscaped their front yards. Marysia and I walked from house to house just to admire the designs the women had made. Neither we nor the Zalegas had any talents in landscaping, so our yard was rather plain. We only cut the grass and planted some flowers and vines by the front porch. Marysia and I constructed a bench on our porch by hammering stakes into the ground for a frame and weaving the bamboo cane over it. These skills and techniques we learned from the natives. We were proud of our bench, because it did not collapse when Mother sat on it.

Once the mud walls were dry, the natives came and plastered the inside and outside of the huts. Also the natives tied the straw mats to the rafters of the ceilings to stop rats and lizards falling on us during the night. Under the circumstances, the British authorities tried to make our lives as comfortable and bearable as possible.

Soon the natives came and cut the grass on "no man's land." Now that we could see our neighbors, we became a much happier people. Although there was no traffic, such as we know it now, we made a street in front of our row of houses. Occasionally, a truck with straw or firewood would drive over our street, causing some excitement among the children.

Walking and running, most of the time barefooted, we soon realized that it was not in our best interest. Something was causing a great discomfort under our toenails. By word-of-mouth, we learned that a certain species of fleas liked to get under the toenails and leave a bagful of eggs to incubate. The infected area itched and hurt unbearably. Some people went to the first aid hut for help. We resorted to a home remedy. Before going to bed, all ten of us would sit in the common room and do a "flea operation." First we dipped needles in kerosene, punctured the fleabags, squeezed the eggs out, disinfected the wound with kerosene and bandaged it with clean rags. This "flea operation" became a ritual in the early months. Eventually we became immune to this affliction. The only other time a flea made its presence known to me was under my fingernail while I was in the hospital, sick with malaria. I lost count of how many times I had malaria in five years.

After a few days of delay, we finally met our teacher at the place she indicated. There was no grass but lots of sand. The teacher told us to find flat stones, the ones we could sit on, and a small stick resembling a pencil. According to her directions we placed our stones in a circle, sat down, and smoothed the sand in front of us. With a stick, we wrote our names and where we were born. The teacher walked around and wrote our names in her notebook. She was the only one with a real pencil and paper. Afterwards we had lessons in arithmetic. Then she read a short story and asked questions about it. The teachers thought that we had already lost too much time of learning and couldn't afford to lose any more. For this reason, the teachers set up schools and held classes wherever it was possible. Our parents admired the dedication of the teachers. We, on the other hand, would have rather played, or watched the natives build more huts, or listened to their singsong of counting to ten in Swahili, than attend classes in the open air and write with a stick in the sand.

The teachers continued to hold classes in the open air for some time, while the natives were building our school. In the meantime, we filled out the Red Cross forms to find Father, and let him know our new official address: The Polish Settlement Koja, PO Box Kampala, Uganda, East Africa.

One day at school, my teacher noticed that I always wore the same dress, which was worn-out and thin from everyday wash and wear. The teacher asked me if I had something else to wear.

"All I have is this dress, slip, and panties," I replied, showing her my underwear. "When Mother washes the dress, I walk around in my slip, and when underwear is washed I walk in my dress."

"Go to the Red Cross hut and ask the lady there to give you another dress," the teacher said. "And tell her I sent you."

After school I went to the Red Cross hut. Marysia was keeping me company. She wanted to see what the Red Cross looked like. Literally, she followed me everywhere. At the reception window, I told the lady in charge that the teacher had sent me here to ask for a dress because I had only one.

"Have you any money?" the lady asked me.

"No," I replied.

"Doesn't your father send any money?" she asked again.

"How can he send us money if he does not know where we are?" I replied.

"When your father sends the money, bring it here, and then, and only then, I will give you a dress," said the lady and turned her back on me, indicating that our conversation was closed. No money, no dress – it was that simple.

I walked away from the Red Cross hut a little disappointed. I had hoped to get another dress, thinking, "How rich I will be having two dresses like other girls." Marysia took my hand and squeezed it, looked at me, and in silence we returned home.

I continued going to school wearing the same dress and no shoes. The teacher guessed that the lady at the Red Cross did not give me a dress. She only shook her head and said, "Your mother had no money. What a shame that the Red Cross won't give anything for free for those who need it most."

One Sunday after Mass, Mother and two other women decided to explore the area outside the camp. Marysia and I tagged along. Mother took with her two dresses which were too small for Marysia, just in case she found something worth trading for. On our way, we passed the newly built hospital – two buildings made of mud and straw, one for the adults and the other for the children – and followed a road westward toward the jungle. About a mile or so from the camp, we found a well-trodden path to the right. We followed it. As soon as we entered the lush green vegetation, we came upon a native family. They lived in a small, round hut with a thatched roof. In the yard, there were banana trees with clusters of ripe bananas hanging from them, a few coconut palms, and orange trees. The naked children played outside the hut. Upon seeing us, they ran into the hut. Soon, a tall man with gray hair, wearing a gunny sack, carrying a long, sharp knife, came out and greeted us in Swahili. Mother and the other two ladies answered, "Dzien dobry," good morning, in Polish. When we saw the long knife, Marysia and I hid behind Mother. We were frightened a little. We didn't know what to expect from the natives on our first encounter with them. Marysia and I became more frightened when the man pointed with the sharp tip of the knife to his teeth, which were loose, saying, "Bananas, bananas." Mother showed him the two dresses and said, "Dresses for bananas." The man inspected the garments, went to the nearest tree, cut the cluster of bananas down, and gave them to Mother. He took the dresses and disappeared into the hut. One of the ladies helped Mother carry the fruit back to the camp.

On the way, the women talked about the natives and how civilized they were despite the nakedness of the children and their mode of dress. Marysia and I listened carefully to their conversation and were greatly relieved, knowing that we had nothing to fear from the natives, and that we could explore the surrounding area of the camp by ourselves.

One evening, Mother and Marysia went to see Mother's friend. Across the path lay a huge log, overgrown with moss and creepers. Mother stepped over it with ease. Marysia, trying to be grown-up, did the same. Her short legs couldn't span the log and brushed against it. In that instant she felt a sharp prick. After a while Marysia couldn't walk and told Mother. By the light of the nearby house, Mother looked at her leg. Under the right knee, the skin was swollen and black. Mother returned home, carrying Marysia, saying, "Marysia was bitten by a snake. She needs to go to the hospital at once." Olesia, who was already in bed, dressed quickly, took her little sister on her back, and like a gazelle, ran swiftly over the tall grass and fields until she reached the hospital. I was right behind her. Mother followed breathlessly at a slower pace. The hospital was a quarter of a mile away from our hut. By then

Marysia had broken out in a cold sweat and started to whimper. When we reached the hospital hut, Dr. Bulba was still there, making her evening rounds. A nurse called her, and Dr. Bulba practically ran to the Nurses' Room where we were. The doctor took one look at Marysia's leg and told me to go away. As soon as I came outside, Mother was only a few yards away, almost running. Anxiously Mother asked about Marysia. I pointed to the hut, and Mother quickly went in. Soon I heard Marysia scream. After a while, Olesia came out and told me that Dr. Bulba firstly tied leather belts above and below the swelling, cut it open where the snake bit her and squeezed the black liquid until red blood flowed.

It was a moonless night. Darkness enveloped us, yet we waited by the entrance of the hospital hut, hoping to learn something about Marysia's condition. A nurse, who was Olesia's friend, came out from the ward, and in a whisper told us that the doctor decided to keep Marysia in the hospital overnight. Olesia asked if we could see our sister. She agreed, and we followed her. As we walked in, I noticed that the ward was dimly lit. Under huge mosquito nets lay patients who suffered from malaria. The nurse stopped at Marysia's bed and said, "Here is your sister." In a barely audible voice, the doctor was saying something to Mother. I overheard Mother saying that she would stay with Marysia overnight. Although the light was dim, I could see that Marysia's breathing was shallow. Her eyes were half closed, yet she managed a faint smile when she recognized us. Mother looked at us and said we should go home.

"There is nothing the two of you can do for Marysia," Mother said as a matter of fact. "I will be with her for as long as it takes."

Olesia and I left the hospital and walked towards a dirt road. It was a longer way home than the one we came on, carrying Marysia. We reached the road and began to run. It was dark and scary, and we wanted to get home as soon as we could. No one was in sight. All we saw were the kerosene lights shining through the windows of the huts as we passed them.

We were out of breath when we reached home. It was dark and quiet, and Janka was not in yet. I undressed and quickly got into my bed, asking Olesia to tuck the mosquito net under my mattress.

"Are you thinking what I am thinking?" I heard Olesia's voice in the darkness. I whispered back that I was thinking about Marysia and Mother and how strange and quiet our home was without them. We both said a prayer for Marysia's speedy recovery and went to bed.

The next morning, before going to work, Janka woke me up, saying that my breakfast was ready, and that I mustn't be late for school. By the time I washed and dressed, Janka and Olesia were gone. Janka worked in a sewing workshop, and Olesia in the fields, planting potatoes, cabbages, and many other vegetables to supplement our diet.

When I came home from school in the afternoon, Mother and Marysia were home from the hospital. Marysia was resting on her bed with a bandage on the leg where the snake had bitten her. Mother, too, was resting, exhausted from carrying my sister such a long distance. I was happy to see them, and the room didn't seem so empty. Being separated from Father and Antek, it was important to me now that we stayed together. I was willing to carry out their slightest wish, even cooking and doing the dishes myself. Soon Marysia was well again, and she followed me wherever I went. I asked Marysia if it hurt when the doctor cut the swelling, because we heard her scream.

"Oh no!" she replied. "But when I saw the doctor take out a penknife and heat it over a naked candle flame, I knew what she was going to do with a hot blade, so I screamed."

A few months later, Dr. Bulba came to see us to say goodbye, because she was called to serve in the army somewhere in the Middle East. Seeing Marysia well and jumping around, Dr. Bulba only then told Mother how serious Marysia's condition had been and that she had feared for her life. The doctor explained that the poison was strong and unknown, spreading quickly. The options were to wait until morning to see if her treatment worked, or take Marysia to the hospital in Kampala, a 60-mile drive over dirt roads in the night for treatment or possible amputation of the leg. A drive to Kampala was out of the question. There was no vehicle available, and besides, the doctor feared that Marysia would not survive the long journey. Having said this, Dr. Bulba looked at Marysia's leg and smiled, then said goodbye and left. We haven't heard anything about her whereabouts since. To this day Marysia has two teeth marks below her right knee.

One evening I had to finish my homework by the small flickering light of the kopciuszek. It was a pleasant evening, and a gentle breeze was blowing, moving the curtains back and forth. Mother was dozing on her bed. Marysia, as always eager to learn to read and write, was sitting by and watching me write. I was so engrossed with my math problems that neither I nor Marysia noticed how far the breeze was blowing the curtains. Now and then the light flickered, but I was used to it. Suddenly, I heard Marysia's strange, "Ooooh!" I looked at her, but her gaze was fixed at the ceiling. I followed her eyes. Oh my God! The curtains were on fire. The flames were almost reaching the loosely hanging straws of the ceiling. One more second, and the whole house would have been engulfed in flames. Without hesitation, I grabbed what was left of the curtains and pulled them down, crunching them into a bundle to put the rest of the flames out. In the process, I slightly burned my fingers. Mother was on her feet asking why the room was full of smoke. We explained that we had almost burned the house down by accident. Mother took the remains of the charred curtains outside, and upon return asked me if I'd burned myself putting the fire out. By then I was a nervous wreck; I did not realize that my fingers were burned until I looked at my hands. Suddenly they began to hurt. Mother brought a small bowl of water and told me to wash my hands, so she can look at them. There were only a few blisters, nothing serious. Mother put something on them and told both of us to go to bed.

For a long time I couldn't sleep. I was too upset. I thought of all the "ifs." What if I froze like Marysia, and didn't react as I did? What if the hut did catch on fire? Where would we spend the night? Such thoughts occupied my mind, each one more frightening than the previous one. It was almost dawn when I finally fell asleep. The next morning I went to school as usual, but the memory of that almost would-be fire remains with me to this day.

Within a few months, women, walking to the chapel, began to complain to the men about eerie and spooky noises coming from a tree. It was the same tree, close to our hut, under which I thought I would read and study. The men, who lived not far away, did not take the women's complaints seriously, because they never heard anything and dismissed the stories of ghosts as pure imagination.

Then one day, a man walking by this tree and happened to see something big crawl into it. The incident was reported to the authorities. Soon the men arrived with axes, shovels, and hoes, accompanied by an Englishman with a rifle. Women and children gathered around to see what the men were up to. Marysia and I also became curious about the commotion which was going on so close to our house. The men found a hole at the bottom of the tree. Unable to dig deeper, they decided to smoke "it" out, whatever it was. Somebody lit a handful of straw and stuffed it into the hole. Everyone was watching and waiting. Soon we heard a big commotion inside the tree. Everybody present waited with bated breath. Suddenly a big lizard majestically crawled out, dazed by the smoke and the sun. The men began unmercifully to hit the lizard with axes and shovels. Then the Englishman came up to the poor animal, put his foot on its back, and started to take aim with his rifle. The lizard thrashed with its tail in all directions, and even bit his suede shoe. Then a rifle shot rang out.

Marysia and I talked about this incident, and we felt sorry for the magnificent lizard which could not escape into the thicket and find another home. For a long time everybody talked about this event, and the stories about ghosts haunting this area ceased.

Shortly afterwards Marysia joined the kindergarten playgroup. The Head of the group was Miss Lucyna Derkacz, now Mrs. Kaminska in Leicester, England. After a few days of crying and wanting to go home, Marysia settled in very well and enjoyed being with other children, learning all sorts of songs which she would sing at home, driving us mad.

Suddenly, or so it seemed, it was Christmas. How could there be Christmas without a Christmas tree? My friends and I decided to go to the nearest jungle to look for fir trees. To our surprise, we found the jungle so densely overgrown with brush and intertwined with vines and creepers that we couldn't penetrate ten feet into its interior. Besides, we couldn't see any evergreen trees even from a distance. Disappointed that fir trees did not grow in this part of Africa, we cut down a few small deciduous trees. We thought that if we decorate them with some ornaments, we could pretend they were real Christmas trees.

We brought our trees home and put them in water in a corner of the common room. Marysia helped with decorations, making a chain by gluing pieces of paper and rags. From long strips of paper, I made a few stars, the kind Mother taught me in Poland. To make these decorations, we used my notebook on which I did my homework. It did not matter that something was written on this paper; I could not spare a clean sheet of my notebook. Paper was also difficult to get in those first few months. The glue we made by mixing flour and water.

Mother and Mrs. Zalega pooled their food resources together and made soup and Polish "pierozki," stuffed with cabbage and potatoes. Meanwhile we, the children, waited for the first star to appear in the sky so we could eat the Christmas Eve supper after having fasted the whole day. As soon as the sun went down, the first star appeared in the sky. We ran into the house, shouting that we saw a star. The table was covered with the embroidered linen tablecloth which we used in Poland so long ago, and which Mother was saving for the "darkest hour" during uncertain times in the USSR. Mother brought the soup, and Mrs. Zalega brought "pierozki." We all sat down at the table and together said a prayer, thanking God for His blessings and asking Him to look after us in the future. There was no opłatek, so we shared bread. After we had eaten, we sang Christmas carols far into the night.

On Christmas morning, there were no presents under the tree for any of us, except for Marysia and little Veronika Zalega. Her older sister Janka and I made rag dolls out of scraps of material. Both girls were delighted with these dolls and kept them for many years.

By the time the New Year came around, our Christmas tree was a sorry sight to see. We forgot to water it. The leaves wilted and shriveled up, and it was no longer green. It was impossible to keep it until the 6th of January, as the Polish tradition demanded. The day after the New Year, we took it down, saving all ornaments for the next year.

To make our first Christmas and New Year special, teachers and other talented women organized a show. Olesia and Marysia took part in this spectacle.

By the lake, the men built a stage with a wooden platform. Several kerosene lamps hung in strategic places illuminating the stage. The people came and sat on a side of the gently sloping hill, looking down to the stage. Mother, Janka, and I were sitting close to the stage. The curtains opened, and for the first time in this far corner of Africa, under the starry sky, resounded Polish poetry, songs, and dances in colorful national costumes. After the introduction, the kindergarten children came out with Marysia somewhere in the middle. They wore white dresses and white caps with bobbing cotton balls, representing snow and snowflakes. These children did not know what snow was, what it looked and felt like. They were too young to remember it from Siberia. Older students recited a few well-known poems and excerpts from "Pan Tadeusz" by Adam Mickiewicz, the celebrated Polish poet. Then Olesia appeared, dressed as a boy, and danced the Hungarian "czardasz" with her partner. They received the loudest and longest applause. Everybody seemed to enjoy the play, although many cried, wishing they were back in Poland.

To this day I am amazed by the speed the Polish authorities organized schools, kindergarten, library, and books in our camp. Years later I learned that it was the same in all other camps in Africa and India. It was General Anders' vision to create a "little Poland," and to educate the youth so they becaome true Poles, ready to return to a free Poland.

Marysia admired Miss Lucyna Derkacz, her kindergarten teacher. Every time Mother visited Lucyna's mother, she would drop whatever she was doing and go with Mother so she could see Miss Lucyna. Mother's friendship with Lucyna's family goes way back. The Derkacz's lived in the village Srebrynica, about three kilometers from our village Łunin in Poland. In Koja, they lived only three houses from us. For some time Mother complained about pain in her legs. When Lucyna's mother came to see us and learned about Mother's pain, she suggested soaking Mother's legs in a salty water. I happened to hear their conversation, and every evening I would sponge Mother's legs with warm, salty water. After two weeks of this therapy, Mother said that her legs didn't ache anymore.

As the days went on, we received pocket money monthly of 10 Ugandan shillings per grownup and 2.50 shillings per child from the British government. With this money, the British authorities allowed us to trade with the natives at the market by the main gate only. The natives built stands where they brought their fruits, vegetables, and chickens. One day Mother decided to go to the market and buy a few chickens. When she left, I told Marysia to collect four strong poles, straw, bamboo, and bast. She should get these things where the natives were building new huts. "With these things we will build a chicken coop," I told her. Marysia nodded her head "Yes." True to her word, all the materials were waiting for me. We decided to build it on the south side of the kitchen, thus saving ourselves making one extra wall. We pounded the stakes into the ground, made walls of bamboo, covered the roof with straw, and made a door that could be opened and closed. It was a miracle we did not get hurt during the construction. Before Mother came home from the market, we had finished the coop, cleaned up the mess, and waited. After a while, we decided to go and meet Mother, just in case she bought more than she could carry. We met her outside the camp, loaded down with bananas, pineapples, oranges and three chickens. Mother was pleased to see us. I took the bananas and pineapples from her, and Marysia carried the oranges. The chickens looked pitiful, panting with their beaks open, and Mother carried them upside down by the feet.

"Mama, we have a surprise for our chickens," Marysia blurted out enthusiastically before I could stop her. Mother was too tired to ask any questions. All she wanted was to get home and rest. As soon as we came home, we showed her our surprise. "This is really nice," Mother said with a smile. "Thank you, the chickens thank you. Now go and get them some water. I am sure they are as thirsty as I am."

While Marysia ran to get some water, Mother released the chickens and examined the coop. I have to admit it was rather wobbly. "Next time, make the door a little wider so I can get inside and clean it," Mother said thoughtfully. The chickens very quickly settled in.

On the third night, a big storm woke me up. I could hear the rain beating hard against the straw roof of our hut and the crashing of branches of a fallen tree nearby. I thought of our chickens in their feeble coop that we built. "Are they safe?" To block the fury of the storm from my mind, I turned my thoughts to a more philosophical matter. I contemplated, if Mother didn't marry my Father and I was not born, the world would not and could not exist without me. Because I existed, therefore, the world existed. Being still egocentric at the age of eleven, I concluded that the world was very lucky to have me. By the time I worked it all out, the storm subsided and I fell asleep.

When I got up the next morning to light a fire in the stove, I noticed that several trees were uprooted, and that our chicken coop was down with the chickens still inside it, cackling loudly.

On the way to school, other children and I just had to walk on the trunks of the fallen trees which were blocking our way. About five of us lined up and started to walk on the wet and slippery bark, saying that the first one to fall off is a "rotten egg." The girl, Leokadia, who was walking right behind me, put her hands on my shoulders to regain her balance. This unexpected touch caused me to lose my concentration, and my foot slipped. I straddled the tree, scraping my left knee on a rough bark. It began to bleed profusely. I told the girls that it was an unfair fall, and they should not call me the "rotten egg" or clumsy. I ran back to the house, ripped a narrow strip from an old sheet, bandaged my knee, rejoined the group, and together we went to school.

On the way back from school, I stopped at the First Aid station and asked a nurse to look at my wound. Taking off the bandage, the nurse pulled it off, causing it to bleed again. She put some white ointment on a piece of gauze, telling me that this would prevent the gauze from sticking to the wound, and bandaged it with a surgical bandage. As I was walking out of the door, the nurse told me to come by every day to have the wound checked.

The same day in the afternoon, Marysia and I rebuilt the coop. Having now some experience, the coop was sturdier with lots of straw on the roof and a wider door. Proud as peacocks, we called Mother. She examined it carefully and complimented us, saying, "It seems to me that you have learned something from the first one, because this one is much better." We beamed with pleasure. As the years went by, we built many chicken coops without any supervision from Mother. Now, I realize that Mother was a wise woman, because she allowed us to make our own mistakes and watched us to see if we had learned from them.

When I stopped by the next day at the First Aid station, there was a different nurse. She took the bandage off and tried to determine what kind of ointment had been previously used. The white cream mixed with blood appeared black. This new nurse dressed my wound with the black ointment. From then on, the nurses used this black cream each time they changed the dressing.

A week later, my knee began to ache. Each day before sunrise, I would wake up in agony. Yet I did not complain to the nurses. I was confident that the pain would go away very soon, if only I remained patient. "After all, the nurses were taking care of me," I thought. It was almost two weeks since I had scraped my knee, and, as fate would have it, I came down with malaria and had to be hospitalized. After the terrible chills were over, and I was thrown into a high fever, I pushed all the blankets off, exposing my bandaged knee just as a doctor was making his morning rounds.

"What is the matter with her knee?" the doctor asked the nurse.

"It is only a scratch," she replied. The nurse tried to convince the doctor that it was nothing serious, just a scratch, and that they were capable of dressing it themselves. But the doctor insisted that the bandages be removed so he could see it for himself. Because of the high fever, I had my eyes closed, appearing to be asleep while this conversation between the doctor and the nurse was taking place.

"Oh my God," I heard the doctor gasp. "Don't you know that this is a tropical wound, and that the child may lose her leg?" At this moment I opened my eyes and asked him, "What is the matter with my leg? It has been hurting for some time now, and does it mean you will have to cut it off?"

"No, no! Nothing as drastic as that," he replied. "Your leg will be as good as new by the time you leave the hospital." After these reassuring words to me, the doctor turned to the nurse and told her to bring several things. The nurse brought a tray full of bandages, bottles, and bowls. The doctor mixed a solution, washed the wound, and told the nurse that this must be done three times a day, and no more ointment and bandages. By the time I recovered from malaria and left the hospital, my knee stopped hurting. The inflamed, nasty looking wound started to heal, forming a scab over the raw flesh. Upon dismissing me from the hospital, the doctor said, "Next time you scratch, cut, or hurt yourself in any way, come to me first." Despite my promises to follow his advice, I did not live up to them. When I cut my foot on a sharp stone, it was a deep, ugly wound. I just washed it in dirty water, put my shoes on, which immediately filled with blood, and bravely without limping, tried to walk in front of Mother. Yet, I did not go to the First Aid or the doctor. But when Olesia noticed the deep cut on my underfoot, she sent me immediately to the hospital for treatment. It is amazing that I, and many others, survived all the things that had happened to us when we were growing up in the tropics.

In 1943 more Polish refugees arrived in Koja. Like us, ten of them had to live in one house. They, too, complained about primitive conditions and wilderness. First we listened sympathetically. Then we told them our tales of woe and what it was like to be the first in this settlement. They even had jobs waiting for them.

In a short time the camp looked different. There were fields of potatoes, cabbages, cucumbers, and beetroots. A profusion of flowers adorned the fronts of houses.

In one of the transports of refugees were Mrs. Korzeniewska and her small daughter Marysia. Mother invited them to live with us, and they shared Janka's and Olesia's rooms. The two Marysia's became close friends. After several months they moved to another house with more space.

Evidently, the British Administration decided to keep women busy. Making bricks was a good therapy for the body and soul. Olesia quit her job in the fields and joined other women making bricks. With bare feet, skirts tucked up at the waist, they mixed clay with chopped straw until the mixture was suitable for filling in the brick forms. After a while, they made a stack of bricks. The priest had convinced the Polish Administration that we needed a church. Mr. M. Makowski, the architect, drew up plans for the church, but there was no transport to take the bricks to the location, nor the workers to build it. Once the permission was granted, we formed a human chain from the place where bricks were made to the top of the hill, where the church was to stand. I was in the middle of that chain, taking a brick from one and passing it to another. Every able body was there to help. Those who knew anything about brick laying, mixing mortar, or digging foundations were eager to help. When the church was finished, it was tall with three walls, a gabled-pitched roof, and covered with straw with a cross on top. We had three priests: Godlewski, Gruza and Myszkowski. In this church many children including Marysia had their First Communion. Our teachers formed a school children's choir of which I was a member. There was also a grownup choir of talented people with exceptional voices. Their singing, especially of the Polish Christmas carols, always filled me with exaltation.

Olesia continued to work making bricks. She befriended a Jewish lady, and described her as a nice educated lady whose husband was a medical doctor, had two children, and was eager to contact her husband. When the other women heard this, they laughed, saying, "Have you ever seen a doctor's wife having her legs knee-deep in mud, making bricks?" Every day most of the other women made fun of this Jewish lady. Such remarks were breaking Olesia's heart, because she knew how kind this woman was.

One day Olesia told Mother that this lady liked to smoke, but had no money to buy cigarettes. Mother gave Olesia some money. In the newly opened shop, one could buy a packet of five cheap cigarettes, such as "Stork" or "Elephants." One day Olesia asked if she could bring this lady home for lunch. Mother agreed.

On that day, I came home early from school, because a snake crawled into our classroom and the teacher, unable to control the screaming pupils, dismissed us. When I came home, Olesia introduced me to Mrs. Melzak. The woman was of medium height, and very thin with dark hair and a warm smile. For lunch Mother served "golabki," stuffed cabbage leaves, potatoes, and cold tea. Mrs. Melzak told us about their experiences in the Soviet Union. She worked in a kolhoz. Her children, Lilianna and Bronek went to a Russian school. Her husband, a medical doctor, was not allowed to practice medicine in the kolhoz, or anywhere else, but was forced to live as a lumberjack in the Siberian forest. Because the doctor was in good physical shape, strong and healthy, the commandant of the camp told him that he would make a better woodcutter than a doctor. Now Mrs. Melzak was trying to find his whereabouts. Soon it was time for both of them to go back to work. Mother packed the leftovers into a small pot and gave it to Mrs. Melzak. "It is for your children," Mother said. From that day, Mrs. Melzak was a frequent visitor in our house. She was a very handsome woman, intelligent, and spoke a few languages. One Saturday she came to see us, beaming with good news. Her husband, Dr. Melzak, after finding out her whereabouts, was coming here, to Koja, to work as a medical doctor for the refugees. Mother was very happy for her and said that as soon as the doctor arrived, she would have many friends. Mrs. Melzak shook her head and told Mother that no one will be such a good friend like Mother.

Sometime that year, a shipment of shoes arrived to outfit every man, woman, and child in the camp. Our section leader was a man who was physically unfit to serve in the army. He announced the place where the shoes would be distributed. We went to the designated house and waited for hours to get new shoes. When our turn came, the man told us bluntly that he had no shoes for us. Mother did not argue with him, and we left.

On a Sunday, there was a dedication ceremony of our new church. All the British dignitaries, including the superintendent of the camp, were invited to attend. After Mass, I waited until the people had gone. I wanted to look closely at our church and the altar. By the time I was ready to go home, the sun was high and hot, and so were the pebbles and sand around the church. Since I was barefooted, I tried to avoid the hot stones by jumping on clumps of grass. Suddenly I heard the interpreter's voice. "Little girl, come here." I looked up and saw Mr. Sadowy standing with other men, beckoning to me. I skipped over to them and politely said "Good morning." The interpreter told me that the superintendent wanted to know why I was barefooted. I simply told him that I had no shoes.

"How can it be that you have no shoes? Didn't the head of your section give you any?" asked the interpreter.

"He said that he did not have any shoes for us," I replied. For a while he talked with the British Administrator and, taking out his notebook, asked the name of our section leader. I told him. Mr. Zadworny wrote something on the pad and told me to go home. He also said, "Be careful not to burn your feet on hot stones." By the time I got home, I had dismissed the whole incident from my mind.

Late that afternoon, we were all at home when our section leader, Mr. Zadworny, showed up carrying a bag of shoes to our house, apologizing to Mother for the oversight. He dumped the shoes in the middle of the room and told us to choose any pair we liked. Mother, in turn, politely but sternly thanked him for his concern, saying that we would not need his shoes, because as soon as her husband sent some money, we would buy the shoes. Then she bid him good day. Mother was puzzled by the man's action and asked all of us if we had complained. I explained to Mother the incident I had had with Mr. Sadowy, the interpreter, and the Englishman. I did not complain; I only answered their questions, that's all. Mother smiled and remarked, "Now I know why he came to our house and was so polite."

About a week later after the incident with the shoes, we finally received a letter from Father. Mother, Marysia, and I were sitting on the porch when Olesia came running and shouting.

"Mama, Mama! A letter from Father!"

Mother took the letter, looked at it, turned it over several times, and opened it. For a fleeting moment I felt sorry for Mother because I knew she would have liked to read it herself, but she could not read or write. It was not her fault that she was illiterate. Although she had money when she was young, her stepfather did not believe that a girl should have an education. He only sent his sons to school.

"Read it to me," Mother said and handed the letter over to me. As I unfolded Father's letter, I found a Postal Money Order. I was very excited at the prospect of having a new dress and a pair of shoes. Mother took the money order away from me and insisted that I read the letter.

Mother, Olesia, and Marysia became very quiet as I began to read Father's letter. Now I cannot repeat verbatim what Father had written. I remember he wrote that from Teheran he was shipped to Quisil Ribat in Iraq for military training. He and other Polish soldiers lived in tents which they pitched on the sandy desert, and that it was very hot there. He also mentioned something about General Anders' orders on behalf of the Commander in Chief that they should not antagonize the Soviets in any way, and they should not even talk about their hardships in the Soviet Union.

In his book, *An Army in Exile,* General Anders writes:

In accordance with a wish by the Commander in Chief I issued an order to my troops and warned them that they should not only refrain from any activity directed against the Soviets, but that they should also not talk about their dreadful personal experiences. With an exemplary sense of discipline the soldiers have complied with this order. They did not wish to do anything which could render the whole problem more difficult and have an ill effect on the fate of our next of kin who still remained under very precarious conditions in the USSR (P. 137) (Macmillan & Co Ltd., London 1949).

I remember vividly that first letter. Father wrote that many soldiers burned their notes which they wrote about their life in the USSR. Father concluded his letter by saying, *We must never forget what had happened to us. And even though we are out of Stalin's reach, we must remember our relatives in Poland and the people we left behind in the USSR.*

"Co to znaczy? What does it mean?" I recall asking Mother after I finished reading the letter.

"It means, for example, if Father wrote about our life in Russia, Stalin could put your aunts, uncles, and cousins in prison, or ship them to Siberia, or kill them. Besides, Stalin doesn't want the world to know what it's really like in his Soviet Union," Mother replied. "And remember those thousands of people sitting on the shores of the Caspian Sea on the 'other side' when we left? They may never get out if everyone starts writing about their personal experiences in the Soviet Union."

Although I didn't say it out loud, I was glad to be in Africa where it was warm and with plenty of bread, fruit, and vegetables, rather than in the "rai rabochikh," workers' paradise. Even the Russians called it so, ironically. I thought, "In Africa I am not starving nor shivering from cold."

My thoughts were interrupted by Mother as she asked me to read Father's letter all over again. I obliged and started from the beginning, "My dearest wife and children."

With the money Father sent us, Mother bought me a pair of white tennis shoes and a brand new dress through an acquaintance of hers who went to Kampala in an ambulance. I must admit that I never again went to that lady in the Red Cross to ask for a dress. I avoided her for five years. Whenever I saw her, I would run into a side street just so that I wouldn't have to curtsey and say, "Good morning" or "Good evening" to her.

Father wrote as often as he could, informing us of his whereabouts and the people he had met from our part of Polesie. I did not know most of them, so Mother explained who they were, where they lived, or how they were related to us. In one of his letters, Father wrote that he had made contact with Antek, and that we should hear from him soon. When we received Antek's letter, he was in Palestine, attending a military school for boys. He even enclosed a photograph of himself. Looking at the photo, Mother was pleased that he looked so well – a little different, more mature in his uniform, and happy. Whenever it was possible for him to obtain some Polish books of literature and poetry, he would send them to me. He even sent me a little atlas, which stimulated my interest in geography in general. I used to trace our journey from Poland up to Archangielsk, down across the Soviet Union to Uzbekistan, Krasnovodsk, across the Caspian Sea to Pahlevi, Iran. From Pahlevi to Teheran, then Karachi, India (now Pakistan), across the Indian Ocean to Mombassa, Kenya, and to Uganda, until I stopped at the northern part of Lake Victoria, not far from Kampala. Then I would look where Poland was, and think of a long journey we would still have to make to reach our home in Polesie. I believed Father when he wrote, "Once the war is over and Poland is free, we will return home." I had no reason to doubt his word. After all, we were on the side of powerful Allies such as England and the United States, who promised to keep a free and independent Poland. These promises kept our hopes and morale up, and we, in turn, kept the Polish speech, traditions, and culture which historically began at the end of the 10th century under Prince Mieszko I.

The same year (1943), we applied for permission to move to another house. Mother reasoned with the authorities that it was no longer necessary to live in such close quarters. There were still plenty of empty houses after the arrival of new refugees. The authorities granted our petition to move.

We moved to a new house. It was lower down the slope and closer to the lake. The house had an odd number, 47/1, and it was the first in a row from the main street.

The first thing Marysia and I did was to build a chicken coop for our chickens. As usual, Marysia collected the building materials, while I prepared the place by the kitchen. It was our third try at chicken coops, and we built it well, and before the sunset. When the sun was low over the lake, we helped Mother bring our chickens from the Zalegas.

In this house, Mother, Marysia, and I had a room all to ourselves. Janka and Olesia shared the room to the left. The window panels were covered with burlap, as was the door. It was easy for anyone to get inside by cutting the burlap. To make our room comfortable and fit for doing my homework, we traded one of the burlap panels for a mahogany one to serve us as a table. We pounded the four posts into the dirt. Marysia was bravely holding each post while I, with the blunt edge of an axe, pounded the posts in. To this day I can't believe that Marysia trusted me so completely that I would not hurt her hands! After several trials, we finally had a solid table under the window.

There was a lot of work to be done, but we really liked our new house and the location. We did our laundry in the lake, and swam in it. When the British found out that people swam in the lake, they forbade us to do anything in the lake. Warning signs appeared on the shore of the lake: "Swimming in the lake is strictly forbidden." Then the natives arrived and put a big water tank and a tap across the street from our house. A little later, we had laundry rooms with running water. This was a real luxury indeed.

A few months had gone by when Olesia began to complain about her lumpy mattress. For the next few days, Olesia insisted that, due to the lumps in her mattress, she did not sleep well. Finally mother stripped her bed and lifted the mattress. Under Olesia's bed was a big termite mound. We were all surprised that in such a short while, the termites built their castle under the bed. The natives came and removed the mound with the termite queen. After such excitement we settled down, hoping that it was the end of the "invasion."

In our rooms, we had no such luxury as clothes closets or wardrobes. We just hammered a long stick into the wall and hung our clothes on it. I remember the look on Olesia's face when one day she took a white, silky dress that was hanging against the wall. Olesia was aghast! Instead of a dress she held up for us to see a "blouse" with a "lacy" hem. Olesia had tears in her eyes. We, on the other hand, laughed at the audacity of the termites.

From time to time, Marysia and I would rearrange our room. Mother's bed always remained in the same place, at the door. The most difficult and consuming work was moving our table. One day we placed our beds together so the loving sisters would be close to one another, or so we believed. Watching us at work, Mother didn't say a word, only waited to see how long this happy arrangement would last. Of course it didn't! Two days later, we disagreed on something and immediately the beds "flew" in opposite directions. Soon we were friends, but we never put our beds together again. When lime was available we whitewashed the walls, inside and outside of the hut, to keep the bugs from invading it. It helped a little, and the camp looked very pretty in the bright sunlight.

About a month after we had built the chicken coop, Mother's and Marysia's hushed voices awoke me in the middle of the night. I was fully awake when I heard a chicken and the chirping of baby chicks. I asked what was the matter. Mother told me to come quickly and help save the chicks from ants. In no time I was by the chicks. The poor things were covered with small black ants. Mother had already cleaned the mother hen and placed her in the middle of the ring made of rags soaked in kerosene. This was to keep the ants from making a second attack. Each chick, free from ants, we gave to its mother, and it quickly disappeared under the hen's wings. We saved all the chicks, except one. It died in my hand from multiple bites to its eyes and neck. The hen and the chicks spent the rest of the night with us.

"Mama, how did you know that there was something wrong in the chicken coop?" I asked Mother. "Yes, how did you?" Marysia echoed. Mother told us that she heard the chickens were restless and made a lot of noise, especially the mother hen. So Mother took the lamp and went to see what was going on. "Perhaps the snakes or wild animals had gotten into the chicken coop," Mother said. When Mother opened the door, she immediately saw that the hen and chicks were covered with ants. Gathering the chicks into her nightgown, hen under her arm, Mother brought them into our room and began to clean the hen first. At that point Marysia awoke and started to clean the chicks, talking in a hushed voice to them.

In no time, cats and dogs appeared. Marysia had a black and white kitten, and looked after it well, always giving the best chunks of meat to the cat. I also had a stray, a longhaired cat. The cats multiplied and a "cat-catcher" was roaming the camp. The man would skin a cat or a dog, then spend a long time at the lake, catching crocodiles. When the news spread that a crocodile was killed, a long line of people would walk to the place to see the great reptile. A new fashion evolved: snakeskin bags, belts, and shoes.

One day, the natives brought a galvanized bathtub. We had no private bathroom, or a big enough room to put it in. Marysia and I decided to place it among the bushes behind the house. We thought that if we ever wanted to take a bath, we would hang large sheets on those bushes for privacy.

As it happened, we wanted to take a warm bath, a change from a cold shower. The question was how to heat the water. The solution came quickly to us – let the sun heat the water! For several hours we carried water by the buckets. We filled the tub about half full, then we had to stop. We were worn out from running back and forth with buckets. The next day, when I came home from school, we tested the water. It was warm. We hung sheets and blankets on the bushes, brought soap and towels, undressed, and hey! What luxury! It was the first and the last time we took such a bath. It was simply too much work and trouble to fill it. It was still harder to empty it. We could not turn the tub on its side to let the water flow, so again out came the buckets. Enough was enough. We went back to taking cold showers, which were strategically placed between the houses. The tub became a flower garden.

One evening, Mother went to visit Mrs. Korzun and her daughter Wanda. As usual, Janka had the lamp. Janka was a seamstress, and she sewed for her clients in the evenings. That evening, one of her clients, Mrs. Hayduk, was with Janka. Marysia and I were in our room, in the dark (Mother told us not to light the kopciuszek while she wasn't there). It was still too early for us go to sleep, and we were bored to tears. Then I had a brilliant idea.

"Let's play ghosts and scare Janka and her guest," I said. Marysia agreed. Without making any noise, I gave Marysia a piece of paper and told her to tear out two holes for the eyes, one for the nose, and one for the mouth large enough to stick a tongue out. I did the same for myself. Then I found two white towels – one for Marysia and one for me. Then I explained to Marysia that we would only show our heads through a doorway. We got ready. Marysia's head was lower, and mine was just above her head. Mrs. Hayduk was walking around the room, talking very fast about something that happened to her. When finally Mrs. Hayduk saw us, she stopped walking and talking. She placed both her hands on her chest and could only say:

"Oh, Oh! Janka, there are ghosts in this house." Janka calmly responded, "Oh I bet there are two of them." By the time Janka picked up the lamp and told Mrs. Hayduk that she would show her these ghosts, we had hidden our masks and towels under the mattress, jumped into our beds, and pretended to be sound asleep. Janka marched into our room with the lamp, and Mrs. Hayduk was a step behind her. First, Janka was looking for our masks by lifting our blankets. Then, holding up the lamp, she closely examined our faces. It is so difficult to feign sleep when you are frightened, but we had no choice. We knew Janka would punish us for frightening her customer. Meanwhile, Mrs. Hayduk was whispering that we couldn't have done this joke. "Look, they sleep like little angels." Mrs. Hayduk was convinced that what she saw were real ghosts. After they left, we let out a big sigh of relief. Eventually we fell asleep.

In the back of our house we planted banana trees and pineapples, just to see if they would grow, which they did. We also planted manioc and flowers. We used the roots of manioc to make pancakes, desserts, and starch.

In the shade under the manioc bush, my friends and I would sit embroidering or crocheting. Most of the time I read aloud interesting books, or our assignments from school. Marysia was constantly present, listening to what we had to say. We often asked her to bring us a drink of water or tea, just to get rid of her. But she learned quickly. She would run as fast as she could, get what we asked for, then run back, spilling most of the water. Marysia didn't want to miss anything.

My friends and classmates lived next door to us. There was Zofia Glowacka, who lived with her father. Her mother died in the first year. Then there were twins, Aldona and Izabella Fijalkowska. They lived with their mother and brother Ryszard, sharing the same house with Zofia. Bronia Bura lived behind them with her sister Bogda and mother.

One evening, Bronia and I decided to shower together. Bronia said that she was going to get her soap and towel, and that we would meet in the shower. When I came there, I heard the water running in the shower. Naturally, I assumed that my friend was there and boldly walked in, saying "Jamboo" in Swahili. Suddenly I saw a naked woman run past me, screaming at the top of her voice. By the way, I was wearing a black dress. I was shocked. I ran after her, apologizing and trying to calm her down by saying that I didn't mean to frighten her and that I thought it was my friend in the shower. I was hoping that the woman would hear me and stop screaming before the neighbors came out, armed with hoes, shovels, and axes. The woman stopped just in time. I went ahead and took a long shower, waiting for my friend, but she did not come. The next day before classes, I asked Bronia why she didn't turn up at the shower. Bronia told me that her mother had a job for her, and by the time she finished, it was too late. Bronia didn't think I would wait for more than an hour.

Down the street from us lived Karolina Mariampolska with her mother. Karolina was better known as Linka. Her mother called her that and so did her friends. Linka and her friends were our role models. They were beautiful, smart and full of self-esteem. To us, Linka was Dorothy L'amour after we saw the movie "Road to Morocco." My friends and I wanted to be just like them. We made a pact that we would study hard and be the best we could be, so younger girls would look up to us like we did to Linka and her friends. As of this writing, Linka lives in London, England, and was married to Ryszard Kaczorowski, former president of Poland in exile, who is now deceased.

As we settled into our new home, Marysia decided to go to a "real school." She was bored in kindergarten, because she knew all the songs and the alphabet.

"Now I want to learn how to read and write," she said with determination. For days we listened to her reasons for wanting to go to school, and we were fed up with her. In vain we tried to reason with her that she was not yet seven years old, the official school age.

One day, Mother asked me to take her to the principal. At first I was reluctant to do so. But the thought of having peace and quiet in the house convinced me to do as Mother asked. When Marysia heard the good news, she was in seventh heaven.

"Tomorrow you are coming with me, but don't cry if the principal says 'No,'" I cautioned her. The next day, Marysia put on her best dress, white socks and brown shoes, tied a ribbon in her hair, and kept looking into a mirror, asking me endlessly if she looked presentable.

"Why the sudden interest in your appearance?" I asked.

"Well, if the headmaster sees me looking my best, he will NOT say 'No'!"

When we came to the office, I explained to the principal why we were there. He looked at both of us and said, "If Marysia wants to go to school, by all means she should go." He wrote a note, instructing me to take Marysia to the headmistress, and she was then admitted to the First Grade. From that time on, we had peace in the house. Marysia began to play with her new friends and no longer followed me everywhere. As soon as I joined the Girl Scouts, she wanted to do the same. Only this time she could not become one; she was too young and too short. Once my troop leader explained this to Marysia, she lost interest. A little later, she joined Pszczolki (Honey Bees), a group for very young girls.

The natives continued to clear the rest of the hill and built more huts. There was no variation in architecture. All huts looked alike with three rooms and little porches over the front door, kitchens in the back, and outdoor latrines between two huts. Soon more refugees arrived, totaling about 3,000. They were all from Eastern Poland, deported in 1940 to Siberia. Each family had an interesting story to tell about their experiences in the labor camps or prisons in the Soviet Union, Urals, or Kazakhstan. No one wrote anything down or published their stories. But as the time went by, they put aside their dreadful memories and began to gossip and bicker. In other words, women began to lead a normal life.

When the local market opened, most people had chickens, ducks, cats, and dogs. Young girls and women were working in the fields and the brick kiln, others in the hospital as nurses, cooks, secretaries, and teachers.

In 1944, Miss Maria Mayakowska came to live with us. She shared the room with Janka and Olesia. We liked her. We didn't call her Miss Mayakowska all the time, only Miss Maria. Miss Maria spoke fluent English, and she liked to go exploring with us. Sundays were the best days for taking trips outside the camp. Saturday was too busy for us. In the morning we had to go to school, then there was homework to do, then cleaning the street of grass which had grown tall since the previous week, and then getting our dresses ready for Sunday.

While exploring the jungle, we found a huge tree that six of us couldn't circumvent. We saw beautiful flowers in the distance which we were unable to reach – maybe just as well. They could have been poisonous. We saw huge ants, about an inch long, standing guard over smaller ones as they migrated, carrying their eggs. We didn't disturb them. We were a little afraid of so many ants of different sizes.

One day the natives brought a huge snake – a boa constrictor – to our camp. The men tried to tell us something. Finally an interpreter came and explained that this snake had attacked one of their women. Such snakes live in these jungles, they told us while pointing across the water. Our photographer, Mr. Gebis, came with his camera and took pictures of the snake. I, too, had a photo taken with this snake. Actually, thanks to Mr. Gebis and Mr. Stelmach, we have many photographs from Koja. For a while we stopped going into the jungle. During that time we were bored on Sundays, our only free day of the week. But the mysterious jungle enticed us.

Our spirit of adventure and exploration of our new environment was with us from the beginning. Sunday morning after Mass was the best day for exploring the jungle. One day we found signs of a path, and we followed it, going deeper into the jungle and its mysteries, until we came upon snakes sunning themselves in the middle of the path. We threw several stones at the snakes to make them go away. We quickly passed the place where they lay and waited up on the other side to see if the snakes would return. They did. They stretched themselves and went to sleep. We continued walking and saw the most beautiful butterflies and flowers, which we were unable to examine because they grew far away from the path. We walked for miles until we came to a plateau and saw a building – a bungalow – with manicured lawns, and a veranda with wicker chairs and a table. By then, we were tired and thirsty. Someone must have heard us, because a native manservant in a white uniform came out of the bungalow. He greeted us courteously. We said in Swahili, "Lleta mi madi," indicating we wanted a drink of water. He invited us to the veranda. Soon another servant came with a tray of glasses of cool water. For a while we played on the terraces, and walked down the long, steep path to the lake. In the distance we could see white sailboats. On the horizon was Kampala, which seemed to be so much closer to get to over the lake, rather than a 60-mile drive over land. When we returned, the servant invited us to look inside the house. He opened a door to the living room. There were armchairs, sofas, tables with lamps, carpets, and pictures on the walls. To us it seemed like a palace. Once we found this place, we used to go there more often than to any other place. We learned that the bungalow belonged to the two Englishmen, and only once did we meet these elusive gentlemen. Because the house was white, we called it a "White House." Miss Maria used to go there with us. One time when she was with us, we met the Englishmen, the owners of the "White House." Since she knew the English language, the gentlemen invited and entertained her for a couple of hours.

One day, as I was coming home from my friend's house, I noticed two black cars parked in front of our house. This was most unusual. Cars just did not drive on the streets of our camp, but only trucks full of straw and bamboo, and occasionally an ambulance collecting and driving sick people to the hospital. I ran home. Loud voices were coming from behind the house. Not wasting time, I jumped through the window and saw two Polish and two native policemen, a terrified native holding some clothes, and Marysia clinging to Mother's skirt, crying loudly. When I came up to Mother, I noticed another man, who was the British Consul. I learned later that his name was Mr. Coleman. Mother, with her hands at her back, stood still. Sobbing, Marysia told me that these people came to arrest Mother. I heard Mother explaining to the Consul what had happened, and she told the Polish interpreter to say exactly what she said because our friend Miss Maria, who was in her room, spoke English, and could translate for her.

"You know very well, Mrs. Bogdaniec, that close contact with the natives is forbidden? We caught this man," he said, pointing to the frightened native, who was still holding his clothes, "and he tells me you gave them to him. Is this true?" Mother admitted that she paid the man with clothes for chopping a pile of firewood because she had no money.

"But it is not allowed to employ natives by individuals," the Polish policeman was shouting, "and for this we came to take you to jail!" Marysia, upon hearing the word "jail," burst out crying.

"For the first time in two years I am unable to cut the firewood. I asked this kind native to do it for me, so the children can have hot food. And for this you want to take me to jail?" Mother asked loudly, and extended her hands before them. "Look, this is the reason I was unable to chop the wood myself." Mother's hands, due to some infection, were swollen and black.

"I know that you tell General Anders and our husbands in Italy that we have a good life here. We don't have to work because the natives do it for us. But, as you know, I have ways and means to transmit this incident to my husband, and then we will see," Mother finished her story and started to cry. The interpreter translated well, because Mr. Coleman came up to Mother, put his hand on her shoulder and said that everything would be all right, and no policemen would enter her house ever again. The police released the terrified native with the clothes and let him go. Then the Consul said something to the policemen and drove away. We were so relieved that we started to cry for the sheer joy that Mother had not been arrested.

True to his word, we had no trouble with the police. However, Mr. Coleman visited our house a few times. One day, Mother was embroidering a cushion when she heard a knock on the door. There stood Mr. Coleman saying, "Motor-car." The way he was pronouncing "motor-car," Mother understood that he wanted a "motyka," a hoe. Seeing him rather shaken and slightly bruised, Mother invited him into the house, brought him a hoe, saying, "motyka." At first Mr. Coleman seemed surprised, then he began to laugh and laugh, then sat down at the table on which was Mother's embroidery. At this moment Miss Maria came in and gladly did the translating. Mr. Coleman asked Mother if she would embroider six cushions for him. Mother agreed and set her price. After they made a deal between them, Mr. Coleman asked Mother to come with him. A few yards from our hut was his "motor car" in a ditch. Finally, Mother understood that his "motor car" was not a "motyka," but a car. Mother went to a house where single men lived and asked them if they could help this Englishman. The men pushed the car out of the ditch. Mr. Coleman thanked them and drove away.

About a week later, there was a knock on our door. Mother opened it. Before her stood Mr. Coleman, the British Consul, with a big box. Mother stepped aside and he walked in, placing the box on the table. Marysia, standing in the doorway, was first to go to the box and open it. Then we heard her "Oooos!" Curiosity overcame us. Everyone had to see what was inside. There were chocolates, candies, cookies, biscuits, and tins of something. It was a generous gift. We had to taste everything. After a while, Mr. Coleman produced a green bottle and suggested that he and Mother have a drink. Mother declined, and told me to go and ask Mr. Glowacki, our neighbor, to come over. Then, Mother told Marysia to bring two aluminum mugs. The two men sat on a porch and, raising their mugs, drank toasts, first to Mother's health, then to each other, and everyone else they could think of. The more they drank, the better they understood each other. Mr. Coleman spoke in English, while Mr. Glowacki spoke in Polish. I don't know how long the two gentlemen sat on our porch. I only know that the next morning we found an empty bottle and two cups on the bench. In England I learned that the liquid in a green bottle was Gin. From that time on Mr. Coleman would stop by and look at Mother's hands to see if they were healing properly. Occasionally, he would say to Mother "motor car" and point to her hoe. They both laughed. One time, he drove us to a jungle, but the car wouldn't go as far as we wanted it to.

When I learned enough English at school, I would ask Mr. Coleman for the journals he no longer needed. I was collecting pictures of film stars for my scrapbook. At that time, the girls were collecting film stars, and boys, postage stamps. If Mr. Coleman could not bring the journals himself, he would send them by Miss Maria or Janka. Needless to say, I had the best album of film stars, which later I sold for five shillings to my good friend Stasia Michno.

We were getting used to our surroundings and the way of life. The camp was getting bigger since more refugees had arrived. From the highest point where the church was, one could see that our camp Koja lay on the shores of the Lake Victoria. It was a huge, gently sloping hill, crisscrossed by dirt roads, dividing the camp into four sections. The church was visible from all directions. Close to the church was a community hut with a radio. In the evenings, people would gather there and listen to the world news at 6 and 10 p.m. Facing the church was a huge water tank. The water was pumped from the lake, purified, and pumped into taps and showers strategically placed all over the camp. The doctors stressed the point that we should not drink water from the taps, but that we should boil it first. Much later, I finally understood why there was an urgency to boil water first.

One day, as I was walking home from my friend's house, I had to go by the water tank. The men in charge of the water tank opened the valves to let the water out and clean the tank. Where the water spilled, I saw small fish, tadpoles, frogs, snakes, and other creatures jumping, crawling, or wriggling on the grass. Seeing these creatures for myself, I drank only boiled water.

On the north side of our camp was Mountain Giletta. At the foot of this mountain was our cemetery, enclosed by strong concrete walls. A monumental cross faced the entrance with the inscription:

Here lie Poles enroute to Poland.

On one unkempt and lonely grave grew small tomatoes. One hot day Zosia and I were coming down the mountain, and had to pass the cemetery. We were very thirsty. We walked into the cemetery just to say a prayer for the dead when we saw ripened tomatoes on a neglected grave of a man who was the first to die. We ate some to quench our thirst. Afterwards, we began to joke with each other. I told Zosia that if his ghost came to haunt me, I would tell him to go to her. Zosia didn't like my joke. She didn't want the ghost to come to her in the middle of the night. It was getting dark. We ran home without looking back to see if the ghost was following us, demanding his tomatoes.

On All Souls Day, especially in the evening, the cemetery became a place of prayer and worship. On each grave there were several candles, flickering in the cool air, giving the graveyard an eerie fascinating appearance. A long procession of people with lit candles moved like a glowing river over the dirt road, then around the graves, adding mystique and reverence to the place.

Whenever anybody died, the Scouts, boys and girls, were notified to dress in the Scout uniforms and escort the dead to their

Koja 1.8.1943 Janka, Nadia, Mother, Olesia and
Marysia

Our typical huts

Koja - makeshift chapel

Koja - Polish Church

Koja - Construction of our huts

Women working in vegetable garden - 1943

Father   Mother

Janka   Olesia

Nadia   Marysia

1943 - Zalegas and our family

Our first hut and kitchen.
Veronika Zalega and Marysia with dolls

Koja - Christmas card

1944 - Kindergarten in Christmas play

May 1946 - Janka, Miss Maria, Marysia, Mother, Olesia,
Nadia and Mrs. Korzeniewska

Our hut No. 47/1 - Janka

Janka and Miss Maria

1945 - Marysia, Mother and Crocodile

Janka on Lake Victoria

1946 - Marysia and Nadia

Marysia with my cat

Janka, Mother, Mrs. Korzeniewska,
Marysia and Marysia K.

Best friends
Marysia B. and Marysia K.

Nadia and Olesia

From left, Aldona, Ryszard, and Isabela
Fijalkowski, my friends and neighbors

Janka and her friend Maria

My English tutor Captain Kozlowski
and a child in 1948

My sisters Janka and Olesia in Camp Koja

Standing - Mrs. Korzeniewska and Mother; Sitting - Nadia, Marysia K., Olesia, male friend and Janka.

Girl Scout Camp Katosy

Nadia and Girl Scouts on a picnic in 1946

1946 - Girl Scouts meeting   Nadia

Girl Scout parade - Nadia, first right

Bronia Bura, Nadia Class 2 dressmaking - 1947

Koja - Kindergarten

Józef Bogdaniec, Zygmunt Metelica Ancona
Italy 1946

1947 - Nadia, Iza, Zosia Glowacka Fijalkowska

Nadia and Boa snake

Miss Maria Majakowska

1947 Olesia

Olesia

1946 Namilyango

Dr. Melzak (right) with nurse.

Hospital Team - Koja

My friend
Bronia Bura - 1946

My friend
Zofia Glowacka

Marysia and Fr. Myszkowski

Teresa Labocha and Marysia

Polish settlement Koja, nr. Kampala, Uganda East Africa
1942-1948

Koja 1943 - Funeral of Mr. Maksymowicz

Polska Y M C A

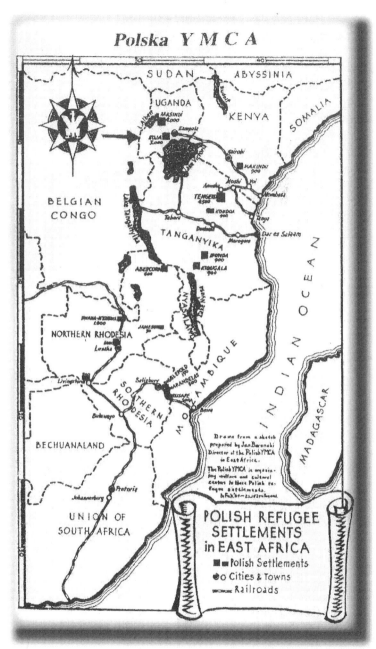

POLISH REFUGEE
SETTLEMENTS
in EAST AFRICA

■ ■ Polish Settlements
● ○ Cities & Towns
━━ Railroads

This map appeared in the Polish Daily newspaper in London on 6 July 1992
Original source: "25 years with the Poles" by Paul Super Memorial Fund Inc, New
York 1947

resting place in the cemetery. Since I was a Girl Scout, I participated in many funerals. By the time we left for England in 1948, there were about 100 graves. Not long ago I read about the cemetery in Koja. It appears that during the reign of Idi Amin, president of Uganda in the 1970's, the cemetery was partially destroyed. A huge bulldozer was sent to rip the walls apart and level the graves to the ground. The bulldozer broke its teeth on the wall, and the natives refused to work further, saying that the Slavs' ghosts were guarding this Polish graveyard. Not long ago, Marysia told us that Fr. Jan Marciniak, with his students, received permission to rebuild the cemetery at the expense of the present Polish government.

The Post Office was functioning well. Miss Wanda Maksymowicz was the Head of this service. She lived with her father, who died soon after our arrival in Koja. All Scouts escorted him on his last journey. The Administration imposed censorship on incoming and outgoing mail. Most women didn't like it at all. The reason for the censorship was because the war was still going on. Whenever I wrote letters to Father or to my brother, I tried to write clearly and without mistakes.

Next to the Post Office was the R.K.O., the Cultural Center. There meetings, concerts, and dances were held. The Center also served as a movie theater. We would use some of our pocket money to watch movies there. We saw films such as "Tarzan" with Johnny Weismuller, and "Road to Morocco" with Bob Hope, Bing Crosby, and Dorothy Lamour. These were our favorites. We also liked "Ali Baba and 40 Thieves." We saw many musicals and western movies. The children's favorite was Roy Rogers and his horse "Trigger." Although we didn't understand English, we enjoyed the movies very much. We had a little help from Lilka Melzak who wrote summaries of the different movies in Polish, which were projected on the screen before the movies started.

In due course, a proper hospital was built with buildings for children and adults. We were plagued by malaria. Everybody, sooner or later, came down with this awful sickness. In the beginning we had to drink the "quinine." It was very bitter, and no matter how much water one drank, the bitter taste lingered in the mouth for a long time. Only the very sick received quinine in tablets. The rest of us had to drink it in a liquid form.

There was only one road that led into the interior of Uganda and to Kampala. Where the boundaries of our camp ended, there were a fence and a gate, guarded by the Polish and native police. Along this road were the British and Polish Administrative buildings. All the rules and regulations concerning us came from these offices. For example, swimming in the lake, dealings in black market with the natives, walking without a hat between 11:00 AM and 3:00 PM, all were strictly forbidden. Due to constant malaria outbreaks, we had to wear long sleeve shirts and pants after the sunset. Curfew for young people was set for 8 p.m. Non-compliance with these rules was punishable by a fine or dismissal from school. A trip to Kampala was possible only by a permit from the administration, and only in the ambulance with a sick patient who had to be hospitalized in town. The women who went to Kampala had a long shopping list for themselves, friends, and neighbors. On top of the list were items such as fabric, shoes, thread, needles, and yarn.

The market was by the main gate. The natives brought their produce, fruit, and chickens. It was a long way to carry our purchases. Each time Mother wanted to go to the market, she would tell us to meet her on the way back.

There was a time when thieves stole all our pots and pans. We had to report this theft to the authorities before we could get new ones. In the box of new cooking utensils there was a big teakettle. We would make tea in this kettle in the morning, put it on the dirt floor in the common room, and have something refreshing to drink for the rest of the day. Occasionally, we made cold coffee from fresh coffee beans. It was thick, black and sweet. It had the most delicious taste.

When the second Christmas came around, Marysia and I cleaned the area and swept around the house to make the place look more festive. We sat on the porch, scanning the sky for the first star. Janka and Miss Maria were in the kitchen, putting the last touches on Christmas Eve supper. Mother and Olesia were setting the table. Suddenly Marysia said, more or less to herself, "How can Santa Claus deliver presents to so many children in one night? It must be by magic," she concluded. Then I asked her if she wanted to hear another magic story that happens only on Christmas Eve. She nodded yes. I told Marysia that once I heard grown-ups say that at midnight on Christmas Eve, all animals could talk in human voices. Marysia's eyes opened wide, and all that she could say was, "Really?" At that time she was six years old, and like most children her age, she believed almost anything she heard.

During the evening meal Marysia said that she was going to stay up until midnight so she could hear her cat talk and asked Mother to wake her should she fall asleep. The poor child made a great effort to stay awake until midnight. She suggested we take a long walk and listen to carolers. Then she asked Mother to tell her the story of Christmas not once, but twice. On the second time around, Marysia fell asleep.

When she awoke the next morning, she began to cry, blaming Mother for allowing her to fall asleep, and now she had to wait until the next Christmas Eve. Marysia went on and on, crying all the time until I told her that my friends Iza, Aldona, Zosia would soon be there on the way to the church, and they would think she had received only twigs instead of presents from Saint Nicholas. At first, Marysia pretended she did not hear a word I had said, but then she quickly splashed some water on her face, put on a new dress, and kept asking me if she looked pretty.

The following year, we had to take the English language at school as a subject. From the beginning we found English very difficult to learn. We couldn't understand why vowels sounded differently in some words. For example, take a word "sit," then add "e" at the end—"site"—then the "i" sounds differently than in "sit." At first, we thought it was impossible to learn English.

When more refugees arrived in our camp Koja, Captain Kozlowski was among them, except he didn't look like a refugee. He wore a military uniform. Captain Kozlowski lost one eye to cancer, and for this reason he was discharged from active duty in the Polish Army.

In time Captain Kozlowski passed the word that he would tutor students in English for a small fee. Mother, always thinking ahead, arranged that I would attend his classes. At first, I rebelled and refused to be tutored. However, Mother put on pressure. Finally, I agreed to go and attend his lessons just to stop Mother talking about it.

My first meeting with the Captain was very pleasant. He introduced me to his students. One was a judge who was too old to serve in the army. The other one was an accountant. He was a young man with diabetes. I enjoyed studying with them. Then I talked my friends into coming to the class. All the Captain's students met at his house. We became very fond of the Captain, because he took time to explain certain aspects of the English grammar.

One evening I came a little earlier than usual. The judge was sitting at the table, reading the assigned text. When the judge saw me, he asked, how did I manage to go to school, do my chores, and know the material which the Captain assigned to us. He told me that he reads a dictionary every day, but remembered only a few words. (Now that I am his age, I appreciate his statement.).

The rainy season had started. During this rainy season, there was not much to do. We had no electricity, no telephones, no radio, no television, and only very few had manually-operated gramophones (record players). On such days, we usually asked Mother to tell us some tales of the days gone by. Mother always had interesting stories to tell, and this time the story was quite different from all the previous ones.

We gathered in one room, as we had only two rooms for the five of us. As the rain was steadily beating on the straw roof, and in the light of the kerosene lamp, Mother began to tell her story. First, Mother told us what the ancients had said to her about curses. "Don't curse or cuss anyone or anything, because you don't know what curses could do." This story was passed on from generation to generation until it came to Mother. Mother then said, "Now I am passing this on to you. The story starts long, long ago when curses walked on earth. There was one woman who liked to swear and curse whoever crossed her path. This woman married a widower with two children, about eight and ten years old. As a stepmother, she didn't like the children and was very mean to them. She beat them and punished them severely. She often put them to bed without their supper. One day, the stepmother sent the children to fetch water from a well. She gave each child a bucket and said to hurry. The stepmother didn't like their attitude and the looks on their faces as they were walking out of the house. She cursed them by saying, 'May you turn into stone.' Some time had passed, and the children did not bring the water. The stepmother became angry and went outside to punish them. She was dumbfounded when she saw two stones and an empty bucket by each stone." Janka got up and took the lamp and left. Olesia, on the other hand, was wondering if the stepmother could turn the stones back into children. Marysia was in a land of her own, sound asleep. Because Mother told us many stories from the Bible, I thought that if Lot's wife could become a pillar of salt, then anything is possible.

Another day, I had to go to my English tutoring lessons. It was raining very hard, and the Captain asked us to wait to go home until the rain subsided. We sat around the table, and Stasia, my classmate, asked if anyone knew any good ghost stories. We waited in anticipation. For a while no one spoke. Outside the rain was coming down by the buckets. Finally, Captain Kozlowski cleared his throat and said, "When I was still a young lieutenant, I saw something that could be classified as a ghost story."

He told us that when he was on maneuvers, recently promoted to a lieutenant, a platoon to which he belonged came to a small village late in the evening. His commanding officer issued an order to the troops to pitch their tents on a field outside the village. Leaving a sergeant in charge, the three of them went to a manor house situated on the edge of the village to ask the owners if they could spend the night there. Two ladies, a mother and a daughter, lived in that house. The daughter was very apologetic for not being able to accommodate them for the night, because there were no suitable rooms in the house. However, seeing how disappointed they were, she offered one room, saying, "It is haunted." The officers did not believe in the supernatural and accepted the room. The lady led them upstairs and unlocked the door. The room was empty, devoid of all furniture, except for one portrait of a woman, hanging on a wall. They put their portable army cots up, washed, and got ready for bed. The three of them sat on their cots, discussing plans for the next day. Somewhere downstairs they heard a clock strike twelve. Suddenly they noticed a movement in the room. The portrait was moving along the walls. They turned their heads when it was behind them. Stricken with awe, they watched the portrait glide along the walls until it came to its original place and clicked back on its nail. They were stupefied, and waited for about a half-hour longer without saying a word to each other. Since nothing else happened, the captain bid them goodnight and went to sleep. They left the next morning and said nothing about the moving portrait to their hostesses.

When we asked Captain Kozlowski for an explanation of this phenomenon, he had none. He only said, "If it had not been for the turning of my head, I would have thought it was only an illusion." Needless to say, we were a little scared after hearing this story. The accountant volunteered to walk us home.

It was drizzling when we left the captain's house. Later, it rained in torrents during the night. It rained the next day, washing the dirt underneath the boards of our latrine and filling it with water to the top.

One day, during this rainy season, I was walking home from school when an ambulance passed me by. Through a window of the ambulance, I caught sight of Mother's face. I became very concerned about her. When I had left for school, she had been well and in good spirits, so why was she rushed to the hospital, I wondered. I ran home to find out what had happened. I found Marysia sitting on her bed, crying quietly.

"What happened to Mother?" I asked breathlessly.

"Mama went to check on the latrine after you left for school, and when she stepped on the boards they gave way and she fell in," Marysia replied between sobs and continued, "At that moment Mr. Glowacki was on the other side and, holding his trousers, ran out and called for help. With the help of the neighbors and the rope they pulled her up. Then the ambulance came and took Mama to the hospital. I was crying and wringing my hands, not really knowing how she was, when one woman looked at me and said 'Poor little orphan, crying so bitterly.' They did not let me see Mama!"

"Oh my God, how awful!" was all I could say, imagining Mother falling into the latrine full of human feces. "Thank God Mr. Glowacki was there to sound the alarm."

"When the neighbors came," Marysia continued, "they didn't know what to do, how to help Mama. Some came with a ladder, shovels and hoes. Mama had to tell them that the ladder was useless. There was no room for it, and asked for a rope, and that's how they pulled her out. One neighbor wanted to take me with her when the ambulance left, but I refused. I told her that you would be home soon. Besides, I wanted to cry by myself."

I gave Marysia a big hug and told her that Mama was going to be fine because Dr. Melzak was a friend and would take good care of Mama.

Instinctively, I knew we had to do something before we could go to see Mother in the hospital. I said, "Let's clean up the room, so that when Mama comes home it will be neat and tidy." In two hours, we changed the sheets on every bed, washed them, and hung them to dry under the roof because it was still raining. We washed every dish and pot we owned, and still had time to clean out the chicken coop.

"I think it is time to go and see Mama in the hospital," I said to Marysia. To save our shoes, we walked barefooted, ankle deep in the mud. There were three hospital buildings with two wards in each one. We inquired in each one until we found the ward where Mother was. A nurse told us that we could not see her now, as she was very ill and asleep. I asked the nurse where Mother was. She pointed to the right, where the bed was screened off, and told us to go home. We tried to sneak in and see Mother, but it was futile. The nurses kept a very close watch. As the nurse was coming out from behind the screen, I caught sight of Mother for a brief moment. Her stomach was bloated, swollen twice the normal size. I knew Mother's condition was very grave. Very worried and disappointed, we returned home.

The rainy season was over, and after three weeks, Mother came home. Our home was happy again. Mother improved and even told us about her treatment in the hospital. It was due to the care of Dr. Melzak that she got better. In the meantime, the natives repaired our section of the latrine with much longer boards.

We had not heard from Father for about three weeks. Then he wrote from Naples, Italy, saying that the 2-Corp under the command of General Anders had joined the Allies in the fighting against Nazi Germany in Italy. Father believed that as soon as they had defeated the Germans, they would go to liberate Poland. As I read on, Father reminded us that this was not the first time the Polish soldiers marched from Italy to Poland. About 150 years ago, General Dabrowski organized Polish Legionnaires on the Italian soil and led them to Poland. Father hoped that they would do the same under General Anders. Father was very optimistic in his letter.

As I recall, most of the women received similar letters from their husbands. The optimism was running high. It affected everyone in our camp. Everybody smiled. Hope of returning "Home" was revived. Whenever a group of women met, they talked about nothing else, but returning "Home." Several women came to our house with yards of material, asking Janka to make them new dresses. They wanted to look nice when they returned to their homes.

As I was doing my homework in the next room, I could not help but overhear them talking about their homes in Poland. One woman said that the first thing they would have to do was replace a broken windowpane in the kitchen. Another one said that a few bricks in the oven needed to be replaced, and so on. For a moment they were back in their homes, visualizing what needed to be done. Their enthusiasm and longing was infectious and filled me with nostalgia. I imagined myself sitting in our orchard and listening to the concert of bees as they flew from blossom to blossom of our flowering fruit trees. It was a beautiful picture in my mind.

Being a Girl Scout, I attended almost all our meetings and practiced marching with the whole troop. On special occasions and national holidays, we marched in parades.

One day our troop leader announced that older Girl scouts were planning to take us to a camp for two weeks. The girls would arrange the transportation to the camp, tents, food, pots, and pans, and a guard. The camp Katosy was about 60 miles from Koja. I went!

When we arrived at our destination, there was a clearing devoid of trees and bushes, surrounded by jungle and close to the lake. We unloaded the truck that brought tents and blankets and all other necessities. We pitched our tent and made beds on posts, high above the ground for safety. Later, we helped collect wood for cooking and the campfire. After we had eaten, we sat and sang a few songs, and went to our tents to sleep.

Within about a half an hour, our beds collapsed in our tent. There was a big commotion. It was dark, and we couldn't see anything. As we were trying to sort out our bedding, the older girls came with lamps. They helped us to settle down and make our beds on the ground. By the time we crawled into our beds, the wind was picking up. The pole in the middle of the tent was swaying too far in the direction of the blowing wind. Being tired, we didn't worry about it and went blissfully to sleep. Just before dawn, our tent fell on top of us. Fortunately, no one was hurt. We crawled out from underneath the tent and waited for the sunrise.

When the sun rose, older girls awoke the rest of the camp and escorted them to the lake to wash. The leader in charge came over and told us that we were excused from all activities that day. We had to put up our tent, so that we would survive the biggest storm, and make our beds close to the ground. We did such a good job that we had no problems with the tent or beds until it was time to break camp and go home. The rest of the time we spent exploring, hiking, and practicing, sending and receiving messages in the "Morse Code." When our turn came, we cooked for the whole camp.

When I came back, Marysia welcomed me by hugging me and holding my hand, asking endless questions about my stay in the scout camp. I learned that she with her group were going for a week to a camp in Namiljango, an English Mission, a few hours ride from our settlement. When Marysia returned, she told me all about the adventures they had experienced. They did not sleep in a tent but in a large brick building. There was running water for washing and civilized toilets. At the local museum there were hundreds, no, thousands of beautiful butterflies neatly stored in trays, each fixed with a pin through its body. Marysia did not like it, because she believed these pretty butterflies must have suffered before they died. The food was good, and she added, "Just imagine how many different tasty dishes can be made from corned beef!"

During school vacations, Mother taught me how to embroider in cross-stitch. Many times, sitting in the shade of a tree behind the house, Mother would ask me to fill in the background between the designs which she had already embroidered. I would do it for a while, then stop and read a book. "Only one chapter," I used to tell Mother.

"If you must read, read it to me also," she said, meaning that I should read aloud. I read Daniel Defoe's novel "Robinson Crusoe" in Polish translation. I would take books out of the library and read to Mother our Polish classics, such as the well-known "Quo Vadis" or "Trilogy" by Henryk Sienkiewicz, and many others.

Even though Mother was illiterate, she taught me to appreciate art, music, architecture, science, and even engineering. Her embroidery, with various patterns and color schemes, was astonishing. She would look at a picture long enough, and then – presto! There was an elephant, a giraffe, the animals she had never seen. Mother even entertained the idea that I could become a violinist and made arrangements for me to take lessons. But I was too stubborn to comply. Besides, I had no ear for music. Mother talked to me about love and compassion and the sexuality of the world. Yet she never talked about sex or menarche when I was growing up.

The vacation came to an end, and I went back to school. As usual, notebooks, pencils, and erasers were scarce and hard to get. Then one day, our school received these items and small pads from some organization. The teachers were supposed to distribute these gifts among the pupils. My teacher started to give them out by calling each name in alphabetical order. At first, I was puzzled why she skipped my name. I was the second on the list. I looked at her, and she gave me an angry, piercing glare. I was positive that I had done nothing to offend her. I was not talking in class, my homework was done, and I had answered all questions she asked. "What did I do?" I asked myself. When she handed out these gifts to all students, there remained a few spare ones. But instead of giving me one, she gave them to the girls in the front row. Suddenly my classmates realized what had happened. The teacher had singled me out for no apparent reason. They were appalled and wanted to share their gifts with me. The girls who received two gifts offered one of them to me. The teacher did not say a word; she only stared at me, and I stared back at her. Holding back the tears and praying for the bell to ring, I said to the girls, "No thank you. I will do without them." At that moment the bell rang. I ran outside and let my suppressed tears flow. I cried all the way home. I threw myself on the bed and began to sob. Mother asked what had happened. I didn't answer. I did not know what to tell her. Should I tell her that my teacher humiliated me in front of my classmates, I wondered? I decided to keep silent and continued to cry. I can only guess that Mother went next door to my friends, hoping that they knew what had occurred. A few minutes later Mother came back, sat down beside me, and said, "Don't cry.

Don't waste your tears on such trivial things. Look at me, I have lost my home, livestock, land, and all the rest. No amount of tears can bring them back. What's important is that I am alive. As long as you are alive, you can hope and have far better things in life."

"Mama," I said between sobs, "I am not crying because I didn't get the pencils or the erasers or the pieces of paper. I am crying because my teacher singled me out and hurt me, and I don't know why!" When Olesia came home from work, Mother told her how my teacher slighted me in front of the whole class.

At suppertime Olesia shed some light on this matter, and believed that she was the cause of my misfortune. At that time Olesia was working for the School Administration. Olesia told us that my teacher came into her office and demanded that she should issue her something classified. Olesia refused. She could not do so without written permission from her boss, Mrs. Delawska. The teacher called Olesia an illiterate peasant from Polesie, and said that she would get even with her. Olesia then told me not to worry for she would take care of this matter. Within a few days, the teacher's attitude changed. She became extremely kind towards me. I, however, no longer trusted her, and became a model student in her class. I did not want to give her any excuse to belittle me again.

Antek did not write as often as Father did. He wrote mostly about school and what he did in his spare time. One letter stands out in my memory. He and his friends wanted to prove to themselves that a scorpion would commit suicide if it couldn't find a way out of something. They made a ring of fire and put a scorpion in the middle. The scorpion ran around several times, and unable to escape the flames, he killed himself with his own sting. I think my brother wanted to shock us with such a tale.

Before Easter, Father sent us a card. It was a beautiful card, depicting a basket of Easter eggs with delicate designs, highlighted with gold and glitter. In reply, after I had written what Mother wanted to say, I asked Father to send more of such cards and a fountain pen. Soon we received a package with yards of silk and a coral necklace for Mother, and to my delight, a fountain pen with a gold tip for me. I was the happiest child in the neighborhood. I immediately tried it out by writing a letter to Father, thanking him for such a wonderful gift. Since we had to write with ink pens at school, my papers no longer had ugly ink blotches.

In the following months, Father's letters came from different parts of Italy. In one, he wrote that he was at Monte Cassino, and how proud he was to see the white and red flag of Poland flying over the old Benedictine Monastery, the stronghold of the Nazis in Italy. We had already heard this news on the radio, that on May 18, 1944, Polish soldiers, with the help of the allies, defeated the Germans at Monte Cassino and opened the road to Rome.

We celebrated the good news with the Mass. The priest, Father Myszkowski, reiterated all the events from the beginning of the war to the present, and ended his lengthy sermon with these words:

"We rejoice with our Allies that the war is over, but there is no victory for Poland." These words brought tears to the people's eyes, and they cried in silence. When the Mass was over, the choir sang the Polish, British, and American national anthems.

A few months later, or so it seemed, I met Captain Kozlowski on my way home from Kasia's house. He asked me to join him, the judge, and the accountant for the six o'clock news. To tell the truth, I didn't really want to go with them and listen to something as boring as the news on the radio that was full of static and unfinished words. My first impulse was to say, "No, thank you," but I agreed, providing that I could bring some of my friends. The captain agreed. I only convinced Stasia, my classmate and participant in Captain Kozlowski's private tutoring, to come with me.

When the broadcasting of the news began, the voice was fading in and out, muffled and static. At first, I had to listen carefully to get the drift of what was being said. After a while, my thoughts wandered as I watched the faces of other listeners. They were serious, not a smile on any of them, a few with closed eyes, intensely listening to the news. Suddenly their expression changed, became more alert. I stopped wandering and listened. I caught the name of Churchill, the Prime Minister of England. Something he had said had alerted the people, something about the Curzon Line as a new boundary between Poland and the Soviet Union.

"What is the Curzon Line?" I whispered to Stasia. She did not know either and suggested we ask the captain. As soon as the broadcasting was over, we asked him to tell us about the Curzon Line.

"In 1920," the captain began, "Lord Curzon, the British Secretary of the State for Foreign Affairs, proposed a line, running from the Polish-Lithuanian border, through Brest (Brzesc) to Czechoslovakia. It was only a tentative armistice line to prevent Polish-Soviet hostilities. You should know from history that in 1920, the Red Army was at the gates of Warsaw, and we pushed them back. Always remember that the Curzon Line was never the Polish-Soviet border."

"Why is this line so important now?" I asked the captain.

"I don't know what transpired between Churchill, Stalin, and Roosevelt at the Teheran Conference in 1943, but my guess is that Churchill made an agreement with Stalin that the new Polish-Soviet frontier will be along this line," the captain replied.

"If this is true, then I will be in Russia," I said, having some concept of the geographical location.

"Me, too," said the captain sadly. The judge and the accountant echoed in unison.

For a time we walked in silence. Stasia and I fell behind the three gentlemen, allowing them to discuss the latest developments without any interference from us. They talked about the allies and politics in general, analyzing the news which now I hardly remember. The conversation stopped when we reached the captain's house.

After that fateful broadcasting, everyone in the camp was depressed. Churchill's stand on the Curzon Line as the new frontier between Poland and the Soviet Union was a staggering blow to us. All the people in the camp were from the Eastern Provinces of Poland and dreamed of returning there soon. When women, Janka's clients, came to collect their dresses, they asked each other, "How can our ally do such a thing to us – give our homes to Stalin? What will become of us?" One woman said that America would stand behind us. Our last hope! Sitting in another room, I could hear them saying, "Yes, America is our friend and will not allow this to happen." And thus a new hope and trust in our ally was born. When the women left our house, they seemed to be in better spirits.

"Yes, America," I thought. "What do I know about America? America is the champion of liberty and the oppressed. Kosciuszko and Pulaski fought for her independence. Pulaski died at Savannah, Georgia." Yet America seemed so far away.

The year 1945 was full of surprises. One day I stopped to listen to the six o'clock news at the radio hut by the church. I was on my way home from a friend's house, and the unusually large crowd that came to hear the news intrigued me. Despite the static and the fading of the speaker's voice, I could make out that the news was about the Yalta conference. As far as I could make out, the Big Three—Roosevelt, Churchill, and Stalin—agreed that the Polish Eastern frontier would be along the Curzon Line, and that Poland would receive territories in the North and West.

"This is a direct contradiction of the Atlantic Charter," the reporter said. Suddenly, from the midst of the crowd, I heard a woman's voice. "They sold us out!" Another woman took up the cry, "We are betrayed by our allies. Sold out!" A woman in front of me began to cry, "My God, what will become of us?" Other women expressed their feelings, saying that they wouldn't go back to Russia, and they kept repeating, "Sold out! Sold out!" Such an outburst from the crowd made it impossible to hear the rest of the news, so I left.

I walked slowly down the hill, feeling sad, very sad, as a matter of fact. I had to admit to myself that we would never go back home. I tried to remember what our home looked like. It was whitewashed on the outside with sparkling windows, a closed-in yard, a water well by the big gate, an orchard with apple, pear, and plum trees, Mother's herb garden, and Janka's flower beds. Behind the orchard, there was a barn. Sometimes in summer, we slept in this barn on the fresh-smelling hay. Next to the barn there were stables and a pigsty. I wondered whatever happened to our cows, horses, pigs, geese and chickens. Next to the kitchen there was a large pantry with barrels containing flour, millet, sauerkraut, salted pork, wheat and rye for the next spring's planting, and a sack full of flax seed. Braids of onions and garlic hung on the wall. A small barrel of salt, jars of honey, dried mushrooms, parsley, and dill stood on the shelves. In the kitchen was a big brick stove. It was my favorite place. It was the hub of our life, and we spent a lot of time there. Mother cooked and baked in this stove. We took our weekly baths by the warm fire, and had our meals at the big table by the window. On and on my mind brought back pictures from the past.

Some months later, we were faced with a new crisis. Far into the night, the natives beat their drums every day as a means of communication, and it continued for many days and nights. We saw the natives cross the lake in long boats and disappear behind the jungle. Out of curiosity, we asked one native what it all meant. The tall Negro with a necklace of 10, 5, and 1 cent coins tried to explain to us a little in English and Swahili that they had some grievances against the British, and if the British refused their demands, then the natives would "Chyk, chyk Polanda," meaning us, and then he ran a finger across his throat. His words frightened us, and we wondered why they would want to slit our throats. We hadn't done anything to them. We lived with them in peace. They worked in our camp, and we traded with them unofficially. The British, however, took their threats seriously and brought in the British and Sudanese troops from Entebbe, Uganda's capital. With the coming of troops, all activity ceased in the camp. The school was closed, and so was the marketplace where we bought the local produce and chickens. The natives who worked in the camp disappeared one by one. All of us stayed at home. A meeting was called, and Mr. Sadowy, the interpreter, suggested that women should patrol their neighborhoods during the night. Mother thought it was a ludicrous idea because what would a woman do if a native should jump out from the bushes and slit her throat before she had a chance to scream for help or wield an axe! Nevertheless, Mother complied with this order and, taking turns with Janka and Olesia, patrolled our section of the street, armed with an axe and a shovel.

During the whole week, day and night, we heard the ominous beating of the drums. It was very frightening.

On a fateful day, Janek, my classmate and neighbor, came running into my hut and said that the British troops had opened fire on the natives who had gathered by the main gate. Several of them were killed. I asked him how he knew. Janek answered that he and some of his friends had hidden in the bushes and saw what happened.

"The soldiers fired the machine gun, and some of the natives were killed," Janek said. As Janek was talking, I was thinking –

what else could the British do? They were protecting us from any harm. How could they tell the Polish soldiers somewhere in Italy, who gallantly fought for everybody's freedom, that their families were massacred in the camp in Africa?

One of the victims was a "Boy," a domestic, who worked for Dr. Melzak. This I know, because Dr. Melzak stopped to see if Mother was alright after her fall into the latrine, and told her about the incident. He missed the "Boy," and asked Mother if she would mind if he asked Olesia to help his wife with household chores and cooking. From then on Olesia worked for the Melzak family and became a fantastic cook.

I don't know what kind of an agreement the British made with the natives. Soon after the incident, the natives came back to work in our camp. Within a few days, the British troops left. Our school was opened again, and so was the marketplace. Again, we lived in peace and harmony with the natives until we left for England in 1948.

We hardly saw Olesia. She was happy with Dr. Melzak's family, and often returned home late. One day she brought a few, almost new dresses which Lilka had outgrown, and Mrs. Melzak thought we could use these garments. Trying them on, Marysia was ecstatic as they fitted her perfectly. She ironed each one carefully and hung them by her bed, which was right under the window. During the night, not only were all her dresses stolen, but also a blanket off her bed. The burlap in the window was cut, and nobody heard anything. The police were notified, but no one was caught and no stolen goods were retrieved. Marysia cried bitterly for the loss of these pretty dresses. Also, she had nothing to wear to school that morning. Without a word, Janka pulled a tablecloth off the table, sat at her sewing machine, and presto! Marysia had a new dress.

On November 20th, 1947, there was a tragedy. I remember this date not because it was the wedding day of Princess Elizabeth (now Queen Elizabeth II), but because of the tragic death of a sixteen-year-old boy, Franek (not his real name), on the Lake Victoria. Yet, these two events are inseparable in my mind. Whenever I think of one, I also think of the other. I recall my remark to a friend, "People in England are celebrating the wedding of their princess, but we are mourning the death of our friend."

On this particular day, it was hot and quiet, just like any other day. No one was in sight, and everything that lived hid in the shade and waited. I, too, sitting on the porch, waited for the sun to tilt more to the west, so I could go and play with my friends. But the burning sun seemed obstinate and hung over the lake like a hot furnace, torturing us with its heat. As always, the lake was tempting, enticing—its cool waters virtually begged us to swim in it. Yet, the lake was dangerous. Besides the crocodiles, hippos, snakes, and leeches, there were millions of microbes, hazardous to our health. To check the children's health, the authorities ordered them to go to the hospital for blood tests. The results of the tests showed that some contracted amoeba, others bilharzias, among them Marysia. She had to attend the hospital for injection treatment three times a day, for three days.

Suddenly, a terrifying scream broke the silence. I immediately was on my feet and ran barefooted in the direction of the scream, towards the lake. Those who heard it were running also. We came to the spot where we thought the scream came from, not far from my house and a little to the left, where the monkeys usually played among the tall trees, where we found three terrified, shivering boys standing by the shore.

"What happened?" a woman asked the boys.

"A crocodile...snatched...Franek," one of the boys replied in a trembling voice. As soon as the boy had said this, four men ran to the boats. Within seconds they were on the lake, heading towards the jungle. With their oars, they searched for the crocodile and Franek. When the men were out on the lake searching, I heard another woman ask the boys how it had happened. Janek, my friend and neighbor, who had slightly recovered from the shock, began to relate the incident. Everyone became quiet, and I moved closer to my friend.

"We were walking along the shore," Janek began, "and we were hot and sweaty. Franek suggested that we cool off in the lake, only to wash the sweat and dust off. We intended to do just that. Once in the water, we felt great. After a while, Franek challenged us to a swimming race. We raced. In no time, Franek was way ahead of us. When we realized that we couldn't catch him, we slowed down, and that's when we spotted a crocodile, heading straight for Franek. We screamed, 'Franek, a crocodile, turn back!'

When he turned around, we knew he had heard us. We then swam to the shore. When we looked up, the reptile was upon Franek. With its tail, he flipped Franek into the air, and that's when Franek let out a blood-curdling scream. The crocodile opened his huge mouth, caught Franek in the middle, at the waist, and slowly disappeared under the water with Franek in his powerful jaws. We couldn't help Franek; it happened so quickly."

The news of Franek's untimely and terrible death spread like wildfire throughout the camp. A huge crowd gathered around the boys. Every newcomer wanted to know what had happened, and the story was repeated several times. Someone asked whether the boys knew that it was forbidden to swim in the lake, pointing to the sign which clearly stated: Swimming in the lake is strictly forbidden.

The sun was hanging low over the lake, but the crowds were still waiting for the men in the boats who had temporarily disappeared behind the jungle. As the sun started to sink into the water, we saw the men coming back. Their boats were empty. They didn't find Franek's body. They said that at dawn they would go out again.

The following day at dawn, a large crowd gathered at the lake. The men returned empty-handed. The priest then asked everyone present to come to the Church and pray for the repose of Franek's soul. It was not surprising that many people came to the church. We all knew Franek and his two sisters. The youngest one, Anna, was my classmate. They were orphans. Their parents had died in Siberia in a labor camp. Franek, being the oldest, kept the family together. He took care of his sisters and didn't allow neither himself nor his sisters to be placed in an orphanage and brought them to freedom. The people in the camp admired him for keeping the family together.

After the requiem Mass, Father Gruza led the procession to the same place where we found the boys at the lake. He said some more prayers, then we threw flowers into the lake – Franek's grave. Everybody was deeply moved and had tears in their eyes, including myself when this strange funeral was over. I do not know what happened to his sisters after we left for England.

The two years 1946 and 1947 were years of uncertainty and expectations for all the people in our camp. Naturally, the people were concerned about their fate. I often heard them say, "What will happen to us now that the war is over? Where will we go?"

These concerns and worries spread even to our classrooms. The same questions we asked our teacher, Mrs. Szablewska, who taught us the Polish language as well as Polish history. The teacher told us that she had heard on the radio that Churchill was urging all the Polish people to return home and start rebuilding Poland. When she said this, many hands went up. The teacher chose Irma, a tall girl with dark, curly hair, to speak. Irma spoke for all of us when she said, "Did Mr. Churchill forget so soon that he and the President of the United States gave our part of Poland to Stalin as his rightful share of the spoils of war?" We were reminded by the teacher that Churchill and Roosevelt compensated Poland's lost territory in the East by moving Poland's border to the West, thus giving Poland back her ancient territory, and that's where Churchill wanted us to go. Before we could say anything, she quickly added, "Soon a representative from the United Nations Relief and Rehabilitation Administration (UNRRA) will come to assist those who want to go back to Poland." On this note, she terminated our discussion and began to teach history.

After school, we talked. My classmates wanted to go to America. In fact, everybody wanted to go to America. Personally, I didn't think that I would ever go there. I imagined myself settling someplace in Africa, where it was not too hot, living in a little white cottage with beautiful lawns and trees around it. To me, America seemed so far away and too good to be true.

One late afternoon, the head of our section came to our house to inform all the grown-ups about a meeting.

"You must all attend this meeting tonight. A representative from UNRRA will be there." I did not go to this meeting. Besides, someone had to stay with Marysia. I was happy to stay at home because, as I said to Marysia, we would have the kerosene lamp all to ourselves to read and do our homework.

The next morning Mother told us about the meeting. The UNRRA man talked for a long time. He was very convincing how much Poland needed us, and urged us to return. All we needed to do was to sign up, and he would do the rest. He did not convince Mother at all. Mother said if we couldn't return to our Home, we would stay here in Africa. Within a few months, those families who decided to return left our camp. Among them was Marysia's friend Wacka Piotrowska, who promised to write from Poland. Marysia never received a letter from her.

We moved to another hut vacated by a family that went to Poland. It was closer to the administration offices by the main road. We settled in very quickly. We had two rooms, and a kitchen, as usual, at the back. The third room had an entrance on a side and there lived Mrs. Czerwinska. Each time we moved, we always took our chickens with us. Once again, Marysia and I had to build a chicken coop. This time, we had experience behind us. Besides, we were much older and stronger. As usual, Marysia collected all the necessary materials while I was in school. By sundown, we constructed a magnificent chicken coop. It was sturdy and spacious with a very wide door.

By this time Olesia was working at Dr. Melzak's as a cook. Janka did the dressmaking and managed to go in the ambulance to Kampala for special shopping. Marysia was still a tomboy, but liked her school. She still insisted that I read aloud interesting books. I had a lot to study, and having private English lessons, there was not much time left for leisure reading. Trying to encourage Marysia to go to the library and read for herself, I would start to read a book, then stop at the most interesting place. Marysia would plead with me to continue, but I was adamant. Giving the book to her, I suggested that she read it herself. That was a good idea, because my sister was so interested that eventually she began to use the library.

After a few weeks of our settling down, it seemed that the house was haunted. Every night, Mother and Janka heard strange noises during the night, such as a drake pitifully crying, or a violin playing a mournful tune. Even Mrs. Czerwinska was frightened by these noises. Mother and Janka talked about it each morning, asking each other, "Have you heard the noises?" I was skeptical about the whole situation, because I didn't hear anything, nor did Marysia, and we dismissed it as a figment of their imagination.

Then one day, Janka decided to exorcise this ghost. Just before sundown, she took a stick, whispered something over it, and began drawing a line around the house, walking backwards and mumbling all the time. She also cautioned us not to step over the line, or the spell would be broken. Of course, we did not dare to disobey our older sister. Years later in Long Eaton, England, Marysia asked Janka what she was whispering over the stick. "A prayer of our Father, you silly girl," Janka told her.

The next morning, we discovered that the termites had built their "castle" near the wall by the door. Mother submitted a report to the office that the termites had invaded our home. A team of natives with picks and shovels arrived and began to dig deep to get to the queen. As they were digging, they uncovered a skeleton of a baby. The white bones frightened them, and they ran away. Soon the natives returned with a policeman, who put the remains in a bag, and told them to finish the job. From then on, neither Mother nor Janka heard any strange noises in the night. The bones were eventually buried at the cemetery.

After we did all our chores and got ready for bed, we would ask Mother to tell us something about her childhood. Mother obliged, and we listened attentively. Very often I would read aloud. One evening, I started to read a very interesting book by the light of the kopciuszek. Because of the poor light, I told Mother that I had to stop. I could barely see the letters. Evidently Janka was also listening in the next room. Suddenly, she came to our room, carrying the lamp, and asked me to read for a while longer. No one wanted to go to sleep until they knew the end. I finished reading the book just as the dawn was breaking.

Homework usually took up a lot of my time, and it had to be written in ink. Notebooks and paper in general were hard to get, so tearing out a page with mistakes was considered wasteful. Yet, to submit a paper with too many scratched out words was almost inadmissible.

While I was doing my homework one afternoon, Mother went to see somebody, and Marysia, being bored, decided to do some mischief. As I was writing, she quietly sneaked behind me and pushed my elbow. My pen slid across the page over everything I had written. I looked at her and tore out the page. It must have pleased her, because she was laughing uncontrollably. I started to write on a new page, but also kept my eye on Marysia. When I saw her sneaking up behind me, I pretended to write. She repeated this trick several times. When she realized that I was not tearing out the pages, she became angry, very angry indeed, almost on the verge of hysteria. In a barely audible and strange voice I heard her say through clenched teeth, "With this axe I will kill you!" I turned around and saw Marysia. She was holding the axe with both hands. She had a strange look in her eyes that frightened me. No time to reason with her. I calmly stood up, took a few steps towards our bedroom, and quickly jumped out of the window. I ran along the dirt road, and Marysia ran after me with the axe.

As I was running, I thought, "Why am I running? I am six years older than she is, and why do I let this little squirt chase me with the axe?" I stopped, turned around, and dared her to come to me. I saw the madness disappear from her eyes. She dropped the axe. Now frightened, she turned and ran home. I caught up with her and spanked her hard. "I will tell Mama on you!" she cried. "Good, but tell Mama why I spanked you," I replied.

Many years later, when we met in England and remembered this incident in Koja, Marysia told me, "I often reflect and shudder when I think about it. Would I have struck you with that axe if you hadn't jumped out the window? Probably I would have at that precise moment. Many years later, the thought of what could have happened gave me many sleepless nights, trying to work out why I had this 'blackout?' Is it by chance that I have a 'king's' malady in my genes? I just don't know what I would have done if you were not with us. And I with the stigma of a murderess. It seems my Guardian Angel saved you and me," Marysia concluded and gave me a big hug.

Towards the end of 1947, we heard on the radio that those who do not want to return to Poland would go to England, as long as they had a sponsor. By then Father was in England, in a hostel near Shrewsbury in Shropshire, working on a farm, and Antek was somewhere in the south of England. We had sponsors.

In view of this new situation, the English language became mandatory in all classes. Soon Marysia was singing "London Bridge is falling down," and asking why the London Bridge was falling down. She seemed to be very happy to go to England. Marysia would tell me that she would live in a nice brick house with a slate roof, not thatched, a garden, and a pond with a fountain. I was amazed to hear of her dreams. It seemed out of context.

Meanwhile, life continued as usual. Besides listening to stories, fairy tales, or reading aloud, another favorite pastime for us teenagers was walking up the main road, around the church, and down again to the only electric street lamp by the RKO community hall, to see who was dating whom. By this light, boys and girls met, paired off, and walked away. Those of us who had no dates walked in a group of three or four behind them. We didn't stand a chance of having dates our own age. Older, or more aggressive girls dated 15-17-year-old boys. Boys who were 18 were drafted into the Polish army and shipped away.

The curfew was at 8 pm. Every evening, a bugle sounded at exactly 8 o'clock pm as a signal for us to go home. Afterwards, a policeman and teachers patrolled the streets. Those who were caught had to stay one hour after school for a week. We were careful to comply with this rule, because no one wanted to stay after school.

At the end of 1947, we heard that we would be going to England. The elite families of the officers left earlier. We were the "others" and did not know when we would leave Uganda for England.

With the beginning of the year 1948, life continued as usual. The school had just begun, and all children were encouraged to attend classes. I made up my mind to be one of the best, or even the best student in my class. I had all the textbooks because most of my classmates did not want to study. They dreamed of a new life in England. Students were out of control, and this frustrated our teachers. Then, one day, Mrs. Szablewska thundered at us, "Stop this dreaming of marrying some lord or count when you get to England, and start paying attention to your education." The girls lowered their heads and giggled.

A few days before our departure for England, the Scout Leader proposed that all Girl scouts should meet for the last time. We decided that the meeting would be a special one. Those of us who wanted to make our last meeting a memorable one learned and rehearsed new songs, and searched for funny jokes and sketches. When the time came for us to meet, we had everything ready, including wood in the middle of a vacant plot, stacked scout's style for easy lighting of the fire. We also invited the general public.

Just before the sun set in the waters of the lake, all Girls and Boys Scouts gathered in troops, not far from the vacant plot. Then troop after troop marched in and encircled the unlit stack of firewood. Before we sat down on the grass, I noticed that Mother and Marysia were among the spectators. They had come early to claim a place close to the fire.

A few minutes later, our Scout Leader and some dignitaries from the Administration came and joined our Circle. We greeted them with our Scout Salutation: "Czuj, czuj!" (like "hip hip hooray"). More than a hundred voices answered, "Czuwaj!"

The Scout Leader stepped forward and introduced the guest of honor who would light the fire. In a minute or two, the logs burst into flames, illuminating the faces of the Scouts and the spectators. We then began to sing our traditional song, "Plonie ognisko," (The fire is burning), a song we always sang when the fire was lit. Then we sang an old song, "Beyond the River Niemen," in which a girl asks her lover why he has to go beyond the River Niemen and what lures him to distant lands. A girl perhaps?

One of the Troop Leaders introduced a variety of entertainment. First came the comedians, then singers. There were soloists and duets, followed by folk dancers, who sang as they danced. In whatever I took part, Marysia and Mother applauded very loudly.

The Scout Leader thanked the performers and made a speech. She reminded us how hard it was here in the beginning and how far we had come. Through perseverance and hard work, we turned wilderness into blooming gardens, and after suffering, we became a healthy and organized society. She also said that we had always hoped to return to our homes in Poland, but that was not to be, not yet. The Second World War had reshaped not only the lives of two generations, but also the borders of our country. Now we must go where destiny leads us. She wished us a safe journey wherever we may go. On this note, the Scout Leader rejoined the circle. At the same time, we linked our arms with each other and began to sway from side to side chanting, "We are going to America."

During this chanting, I realized that I had no desire to go to America, but to school. Would I be able to finish my education in England? Perhaps go to a university? What is it like to sit in on a lecture and listen to some learned professor talk about wondrous things, I mused. In the meantime, someone stirred the embers in the fire, and thousands of glowing sparks flew into the dark sky. I kept my eyes on them. Some died quickly, and others rose high into the sky and disappeared. "It is like wishes," I thought. Some are fulfilled immediately, others come later. I did not know it then that my wish to go to a university would come true, some 30 years later, in America.

Only embers were glowing now. The Troop Leader gave us a signal to stand up and close our last general meeting with a song. We sang to the melody of "Taps."

> *The night comes. The sun has gone from the hills,*
> *From the fields, from the seas.*
> *In a quiet sleep, rest ye now, God is nigh.*

Afterwards, we marched in silence from the field in the same order as we came in. The full moon, which seemed much bigger here than in any other place, was hanging over us, lighting the way home. Above, in the dark velvety canopy of heaven, the stars sparkled in an astounding splendor. It was a night full of memories, happiness, and sadness at the same time, but also of expectations.

In February 1948, Mother was notified that we would leave Koja on the next transport, and that we should go to the hospital to be inoculated and vaccinated. Our arms and bottoms ached for days. Meanwhile, Mother's immediate worry was to buy some luggage. We took almost everything, except the little black pot, which had served us faithfully for such a long time, and gave it to a native as a present from us.

The whole camp, those who were leaving and those who were staying, was giddy with excitement. At long last, we were going to a civilized world, to England, of all places! But one thing marred our happiness. Mother was told that Janka, who was over 21 years of age, would not go with us. To this day I do not know who instigated this rule. Mother, of course, was furious with the authorities and refused to leave without her oldest daughter. Mother told them that she managed to bring all her children through Siberia, Iran, and Uganda, and what would she say to her husband when she arrived without Janka? Eventually, Dr. Melzak intervened and assured Mother that Janka would go on the next transport and would join us in Mombassa.

The day before our departure, I took a cold shower, as was my custom, and washed my hair until it squeaked, because I had no idea when I would be allowed such luxury again (a hard lesson from previous journeys). As I was dressing, Mother was making deals with a neighbor about our chickens. Mother threw in two chickens free of charge to take care of my and Marysia's cats. I think Mother was more concerned about the cats than we were. Soon the truck drove up to pick up our luggage. Afterwards, there was nothing else for us to do at the hut of mud with the thatched roof and a little porch where we had spent many happy days. We picked up our bags, looked at the hut and silently said "Goodbye" to it and walked away.

We walked down the main road with hand luggage and a basket of food for the journey. At the administrative buildings, the trucks were waiting for us. Everyone was there. Those who were staying behind came to bid us farewell. Janka was there too, crying. The Girl Scouts, dressed in their uniforms, came and, looking straight at me, because I was one of them, sang our farewell song.

Standing inside the trucks, we said goodbye to all who came to see us off. We waved our hands until the dust, stirred up by the wheels of trucks and buses, obscured our vision. A few friends ran after us to the gate that separated our camp from the native village. Looking at the disappearing camp, I was sad to leave Africa. I arrived there when I was 10 years old, and I left as a teenager. I thought of those left in the cemetery. For them, the journey had ended there, in Koja, Uganda, Africa.

Our destination was a small railway station in Mukono. A large crowd of natives gathered by the railroad. As we were going to the waiting train, we noticed an albino boy who was about six or seven years old. His features were Negroid, only his skin was sickly white, devoid of pigmentation. I was surprised to see a "white" Negro child. Marysia was awe-struck by the huge black steam engine noisily belching out clouds of steam. We boarded the train, made ourselves comfortable on the wooden benches, and waited anxiously for the train to pull out.

The train journey to Mombassa took four days and four nights. On the fifth day we arrived at our destination. There we stayed in a camp for a few days, waiting for more people, among them our sister Janka, to arrive. During those days, we walked along the beaches of the Indian Ocean, watching the tides come and go, along with a native man with beautiful shells who was making obscene sexual gestures to go with him behind the bushes. We were amazed how swiftly the native boys climbed the tall coconut palms, cut the fruit down, and then tried to sell it to us.

At last the trucks arrived. We boarded them and rode to the docks. Standing in line, we slowly boarded the passenger ship "Carnarvon Castle." We were already on board when we saw Janka waiting in line. We waved to her and shouted with delight that she was coming with us. Dr. Melzak kept his word, and we were grateful.

Our cabin was on the main deck. There were sixteen beds. We took the corner close to the door. I took the upper bunk, and Marysia took the lower one beneath me. Leaving my bags on the bed, I told Mother that I was going to check the area and that I would be on deck.

A few minutes later, my friend Stasia joined me. Leaning against the railing, we watched the last person come aboard. The ground crew was removing the steps, the sailors were weighing the anchor, and slowly our ship began to move away from the dock. All passengers came out to look for the last time at the strange and exciting continent. Some were smiling, and some had tears in their eyes as they waved goodbye. I was filled with mixed emotions. I was glad to be going somewhere, and at the same time, I was sad to leave now distant Koja in Uganda, the place of my adolescent years. As we were pulling farther away from Africa, almost all the passengers returned to their cabins to rest. Stasia and I remained. The two of us stood in silence, gazing at the vanishing continent. Then Stasia turned her face to me and said, "Do you think we will ever see Koja again?"

"No, I think not. But we will never forget it," I replied.

As the continent of Africa disappeared from the horizon in the glow of the setting sun, we turned to go to our cabins and found two young and handsome British officers in front of us. Very politely they said, "Hello," and introduced themselves.

*

The winds of change still keep on blowing, bringing changes to many others. Long ago, the winds wiped out our footprints in Poland, the USSR, Iran, India, and Africa, and not a trace remains of our ever having been there. Perhaps the graves and cemeteries are witnesses to our presence, but in a short while they too will disappear and be forgotten.

EPILOGUE

We arrived in England on March 8th, 1948. For a short time we lived in a former military camp, Daglingworth Hostel in Gloucestershire. Father and Antek came to see us after a long separation. It was an exciting reunion. Father took a step back and said, "When I went away, you were small children. Now you are all grown up, except Marysia." To me, Father no longer looked thin and gaunt. He had put on some weight, and he looked very handsome in his army uniform. Antek looked so grown up and good-looking with his blond, wavy hair. Olesia, Antek, and I reminisced about our childhood, and how the three of us roamed through the forest, exploring every nook and corner of Gajówka.

Soon after our arrival to Daglingworth, Janka married Roman Rawłuszkiewicz from Grodno. They had two sons, Ignacy and John. The rest of us moved to another former military hostel Keevil in Wiltshire. Olesia and I moved to London, Antek to Bristol, and Marysia to Stowell Park to continue her education. Later, Olesia married Teodor Lukaszyk and moved to Dursley, Glos. They had two daughters, Elzbieta and Barbara. Antek married Janina Biskup. They had two children, Edward and Helena. After the death of his first wife, Antek married Zofia. Their children are Barbara and John. In the hostel Keevil near Trowbridge, Wiltshire, England I met and married John Seluga (US Air Force), an American of Polish descent, and moved to the USA. We had two children, David and Susan. Marysia married Zdzisław Polkowski and for many years lived in London. They had two sons, Marek and Ryszard. Eventually, Mother and Father moved to Long Eaton near Nottingham. Antek also settled in Long Eaton. Then Janka came there, then Marysia.

As of this writing, Janka, Marysia and I are the only survivors. The three of us are widows. Janka and Marysia still live in Long Eaton. I live in Albuquerque, New Mexico.

Poselstwo R. P. w Teheranie
Légation de Pologne à Tehran

No. *079467*

RZECZPOSPOLITA POLSKA
REPUBLIQUE POLONAISE

PASZPORT   PASSEPORT

Obywatel polski
Citoyen polonais — *BOGDANIEC Katarzyna*

Zamieszkały
Domicilié à — *Teheran*

W towarzystwie żony
accompagné de sa femme
et ses enfants — *dwoje Zona*
dzieci — *Femme*

Fotografia

Rok urodzenia
Date de naissance — *1898 r.*

Miejsce urodzenia
Lieu de naissance — *Wólka pow. Luninie.*

Stan
État civil — *zamężna - mariée*

Zatrudnienie
Profession —

Wzrost
Taille — *średni — moyenne*

Twarz
Visage — *pociągła — allongé*

Włosy
Cheveux — *brunetka — noirs*

Oczy
Yeux — *niebieskie — bleus*

Znaki szczególne
Signes particuliers —

Podpis posiadacza
Signature du porteur

Dzieci - Enfants		
Imię - Nom	Wiek - Age	Płeć - Sexe
Aleksandra	*15*	*żeńsk. fem.*
Jadwiga	*11*	*" "*
Maria	*6*	*" "*

Termin ważności paszportu kończy się z dniem
Ce passeport expire le : *29 maja 1943*

Data
Date *20.1.42*

Pieczęć
Sceau

WIKTOR STANKOWSKI
WICEKONSUL R. P.

Keevil Hostel nr. Trowbridge
Wiltshire England
Janka, Olesia and Nadia

Union-Castle Line. R.M.M.V. "Carnarvon Castle. 20,122 Tons

Olesia 1980   Nadia   Janka   Antek   Marysia

Long Eaton 1985

Albuquerque 1994 - Marysia's birthday
Prof. Charles McLelland, Betty Hahn, Marysia and Nadia

Nottingham UK 1997 - Marysia's birthday

REUNION IN LEICESTER, ENGLAND

Marysia   Ryszard Kaczorowski   Nadia   Karolina Kaczorowska
President of Poland in exile   (nee Mariampolska)

Mother - Katarzyna Bogdaniec Mieljaniec
(Bohatyrewicz)
1898-1970
Painted by: Mrs. W.A. Land, London 1968

In Memory of Poles - Families who lived in Uganda
during 1942-1951
REPUBLIC OF POLAND

Plaque of Honour 1998

Cemetery in Koja - restored in 1998

SAW WORLD HARD WAY
By Jacq Woolsey

As a child in her native Poland, Mrs. John Seluga, 310 W. Ash, dreamed of seeing the world.

Her dream came true.

But it didn't happen overnight, and most of the time it was a nightmare, rather than a pleasant dream.

Mrs. Seluga went through a Russian labor camp and Iranian and African refugee camps before she became a displaced person in England and finally a naturalized American.

How did this "dream in reality" start for Mrs. Seluga, wife of a Schilling staff sergeant and mother of two children?

Mrs. Seluga, then Nadzieja Bogdaniec (Nadzieja was changed to Nadia when she was married) was only nine years old when the Russians marched through Lunin on Poland's eastern border in February, 1940.

It's an experience she can never forget.

With her parents, Mr. and Mrs. Josef Bogdaniec and her three sisters and brother, Nadzieja was routed out early in the morning by soldiers.

Forced Into Labor Camp

The Bogdaniecs, forced to leave all their belongings behind, were taken to a Russian labor camp at Arkhang[e]lsk near the White Sea.

Mrs. Seluga, unfolded her story in fluent English while seated in her comfortable living room with her cherished U.S. citizenship papers nearby – a far cry from the two hunger-filled years she spent in the labor camp from which there was no escape.

"I remember the hunger and misery but as far as I remember there was no physical cruelty", she said.

Men in the camp worked as lumberjacks in the forest and the women stripped bark from logs and worked in the fields while the children were required to attend school or they didn't eat.

"Forget Your Homeland"

According to the Salinan the children were told to forget about Poland because they would never get out of Russia and were told it was best to think the Russian way.

The temperature would drop to 40 below zero in winter and warm clothing was hard to come by.

However, Mrs. Seluga said that conditions weren't quite so hard in summer when they could gather food in the woods.

Public gatherings were forbidden in the all Polish camp. After Stalin granted amnesty to camp inmates the Bogdaniec family began a two-month trip by boxcar south to Uzbek, Iran [through Uzbekistan to a refugee camp in Iran].

Mrs. Seluga recalls little of her stay in Iran because most of her time there was spent in hospitals.

Suffers Illnesses

First she and her sister contracted typhus and later at the refugee camp she developed measles, dysentery and pneumonia.

They spent almost a year in Iran, where adequate food and clothing also were scarce.

Then they went for a time to Karachi, now in Pakistan.

Mrs. Seluga's next bout with disease, this time malaria, came during a five-year stay in African refugee camps.

"I don't remember how many times I had malaria", she relates.

The African camp for Poles, called Koja, was located in Kampala, Uganda.

The houses were constructed of mud and straw and the area was infested with snakes and "other wonders" of Africa.

During these years Mr. Bogdaniec and his son were away from the rest of the family.

The camp was restricted to Polish women and children and old and disabled men, while the able men were called to military service.

Bogdaniec served with the Polish and British armies in Italy and his son was sent to a British military school in Egypt.

After the war Bogdaniec was given a choice of going to England or returning to Poland. He chose England, where his family finally joined him in 1948.

Meets Husband In England

It was while living in Trowbridge, England, that Nadzieja met and married her Air Force husband, who then was stationed at Brize Norton AFB near Oxford.

Seluga, of Polish descent, now is the 36th Munitions Maintenance Squadron at Schilling.

He was transferred back to this country and his wife followed him in April, 1953, after months of red tape.

The Seluga children were born in this country.

"It was quite early in the morning when the boat arrived in New York and I was wondering what this strange land had in store for me", said Mrs. Seluga.

Never Been Sorry

"I've never been disappointed".

Since having come to the States Mrs. Seluga's parents bought a house and settled in Long Eaton, Nottingham, and her sisters and brother also have remained in England.

Mrs. Seluga's travelling didn't end when that ship docked stateside eight years ago.

She has accompanied her husband to bases in Illinois, North Carolina, Virginia and Washington State.

They first were stationed at Schilling in 1959 and returned this spring after a "few months" duty in Denver.

Salina, Kansas,
Sunday August 20, 1961
A TREASURED POSSESSION
Mrs. John Seluga proudly displays
U.S. Certificate of Naturalisation.
(Journal Photo)

To Marysia

Do you remember one Sunday in Autumn,
When leaves were gold and the day was warm?
When joy and peace poured from the sky
Over the ruins, the mountains, and us?

It was the day when we saw the ruins
As they slept under the azure sky,
Now abandoned and sad they dream of the past,
And only Aeolus whispers and sighs.

Can you recall while walking along
A breathtaking view which opened before us:
The Rio Grande with its lazy flow,
The majestic Sandias all-knowing and wise,
A few puffs of clouds…
That's to balance this picture for us!

Let this be a gift from Me to You –
It is wrapped in the sunshine and tied with a glow:
Open it now and see –
"The wonderful moment" of You and Me!

~ Nadia Seluga
New Mexico 1992

**Praise for the first edition of *Far From My Home, Never to
Return: A Polish Child's WWII Memoir*,
formerly titled *Winds of Change***

*How can one human being behave so cruelly, so callously to
another human being? But there were hundreds of them. Had they
no mother? No sister? No brother? No wife? No children? Your
suffering was horrendous.*

*I could not understand why it had been printed, not
published. It is extremely publishable. As I told Marysia on the
phone. She said that you could deal with it in America. Please,
please, Nadia, do make every effort to get it published. It should be
available for everyone to read, not just a mere eight-hundred.
Have you read 'THE LONG WALK' by Slavomir Rawic? His book
is still being sold and talked about. There has also been mention of
it being made into a film. Nadia, what you all went through should
be known. We have to learn from the past. We have to know the
nature of the enemy.*

~ Dolly Sewell, former teacher of writing

*I want to say how impressed and moved I am by Winds of
Change – written in such a direct and compelling style, revealing
clearly a little known piece of history, and telling the story of a
lively, loving, and totally admirable family and how they lived
through some of the tragic circumstances of World War II.*

*The author – uncomplaining, compassionate, plucky, and
humorous – sounds exactly like who she is: the daughter of the
courageous and devoted parents that she describes.*

~ Edith H. Jonas

It was well written and in a style that would appeal to a very wide audience of readers. ...I felt its appeal was similar to "Wild Swans" and an excellent way of telling the world of the fate of the people who lived in Eastern Poland. It was at times factual, sometimes funny and often sad and the contents undoubtedly supported by the general philosophy of existence in that 'If one has a "why" to live, one can cope with any how' (Nietzsche).

~ Jadwiga Bridges

This is not a story well-known outside the Polish community that lived through these terrible experiences. What makes her memoirs so compelling and touching is the pure child's view, so clearly reflecting the confusion, lack of information, and will to make some sort of normality out of a daily life that often defeated adults. The author's own subsequent training as a historian and understanding of the world events that conditioned her experiences as a child do not intrude much on the stream of memory. In this respect her book is an act of will and recalling, to remember how it felt and appeared as a child.

It is a book I would like even the spoiled, bored children of much of today's English-speaking world to read. These memoirs have a universal character transcending even the horrible historical experiences that shaped the childhood experiences they record in such vivid, unforgettable ways.

~ Charles E. McClelland,
Professor of History and Director of European Studies (Emeritus),
University of New Mexico (USA)

... I have read it and it is a most important document. My wife has read it and it had opened her eyes. It deserves to be read widely.

--Conrad Wood, Imperial War Museum

ABOUT THE AUTHOR

Nadia Bogdaniec-Seluga was born on January 1, 1931 in a small village in eastern Poland called Łunin. Łunin was in a beautiful part of Poland known as "Polesie." Unfortunately, Polesie is no longer a part of Poland, but is now within the boundaries of western Belarus.

Nadia and her family were deported in 1940 by the Soviets from their idyllic life in Polesie to work and starve in the soviet labor camps. They were lucky to finally manage to escape from the labor camps, but it was no easy journey. After leaving Siberia, they travelled through central Asia and Iran and eventually made it to the British Dominion of East Africa in Uganda, where they lived for a few years before finally moving back to the Western world sometime after the end of WWII. Sadly, however, they would never return to Poland. All the siblings, including Nadia, married and had children. They all now have grandchildren. Nadia, Marysia, and Janka are the only current surviving original members of the adversity detailed in Nadia's memoirs, *Far From My Home, Never to Return: A Polish Child's WWII Memoir.*

To learn more about Nadia and her memoir go to:

www.nadiaseluga-memoir.com

Readers may also connect via:

www.facebook.com/FarFromMyHomeNevertoReturnNadiaSeluga

Made in the USA
San Bernardino, CA
20 February 2017